SOUTHERNERS ALL

SOUTHERNERS ALL

BY

F. N. BONEY

Revised Edition

MERCER

The paper used in this publication meets
the minimum requirements of American National Standard
for Information Sciences—Permanence of Paper
for Printed Library Materials, ANSI Z39.48-1984.

Library of Congress Cataloging-in-Publication Data:

Boney, F. N.
 Southerners all / by F. N. Boney.—Rev. ed.
 ix + 231pp. 6 x 9'' (15 x 23cm)
 Includes bibliographical references.
 ISBN 0-86554-375-5 (alk. paper)
 1. Southern States—Civilization—1775-1865.   2. Social classes—
Southern States—History—19th century.   I.   Title.
F213.B64   1990   90-5619
975'.03—dc20   CIP

CONTENTS

PREFACE

This volume has evolved over many years of scholarly labor and, like every other book, it has been affected by the author's lifetime experiences. A mother from the tiny county seat of Boydton in Southside Virginia and a father from the much-larger town of Kinston in eastern North Carolina reminded me early that Southerners were diverse as well as similar. My hometown of Richmond, Virginia, introduced me to the urban-industrial New South and simultaneously reminded me of the power of the past. Eight years at Westhampton Public School followed by four years at St. Christopher's Preparatory School allowed me to get to know a wide variety of young Southern whites but, in the 1940s, no young blacks. A Negro maid and cook named Thelma Evans introduced me to the obscure black masses who lived in other sections of town, and a bright, imaginative older brother encouraged me to think for myself. A handful of teachers and coaches made the high school years a true "learning experience."

Four years at Hampden-Sydney College in Prince Edward County, Virginia, brought me back to the rural roots of the Southern people, and a few professors there began to lure me away from the sciences and toward the humanities. Four years in the "real world" of the small businessman accelerated this trend, which ultimately led to a Ph.D. in history from the University of Virginia in 1963. Near the Blue Ridge Mountains and in the shadow of Jefferson's Monticello, a wealthy rural chivalry (often rich Yankees) coexisted with the thriving little university city of Charlottesville. There, a struggling graduate student could live frugally with his wife and child on Copeley Hill in veterans' housing left over from the Second World War.

Unleashed with the magic degree, I began my teaching career at Murray State College (now University) in the western tip of Kentucky. I have gone on to spend many years at the University of Georgia at Athens, which is nestled among the low hills of the northern Piedmont where cotton fields years ago yielded to endless acres of commercial pine forests. Two significant interludes along the way helped teach me that Southerners were an integral part of a much larger tribe called Americans. Eighteen months in the middle 1950s at Frankfurt/Main, West Germany, with the United States Army and three years in the middle 1960s at Washington State University in the "Inland Empire" region of the Pacific Northwest certainly broadened my perspectives and deepened my interest in my native Southland and its people.

My research and publication activities first concentrated on Virginia—home by birth—and then shifted to Georgia—home by choice—before spreading out to include the rest of the South. Along the way many friends and associates influenced my work. Edward Younger directed my thesis and dissertation on John Letcher, Virginia's Civil War governor. General John S. Letcher (United States Marine Corps, retired) almost had to adopt me when I came to Lexington, Virginia, to study the personal papers of his grandfather. At Washington State Professors Raymond Muse and David Stratton and graduate students Arlen Fowler and Burton Smith exchanged ideas and impressions with me during the years that I spent in that far Northwestern region, which was not as different from the South and the rest of the nation as it thought it was, and recently I have worked with Richard L. Hume, my very able replacement there. I have also benefited from the perspective of another "outsider," my wife France from the country of the same name, which is really more a state of mind than a chunk of territory. I have tried, of course, to fathom the opinions and attitudes of my children, Bernard and Claire, part of a rising generation of Southerners and Americans.

For more than two decades now at the University of Georgia, I have profited from association with a number of able colleagues, especially Kenneth Coleman, Peter C. Hoffer, Lee Kennett, Lester D. Langley, Ronald R. Rader, Carl J. Vipperman, and Charles E. Wynes. I am also indebted to some of the graduate students, especially three who worked under my direction: John E. Simpson, Clarence L. Mohr, and James M. Gifford.

Directly and indirectly many other scholars and academics have helped me, and many patient professionals at courthouses, archives, and libraries have enabled me to probe the local records of the South. Their assistance has been invaluable, but the responsibility for this book and its interpretations rests solely with the author.

I am also indebted to Washington State University, the American Philosophical Society, and especially the University of Georgia for financial support over the long haul. Finally, recognition is due to scholarly journals that published my articles on the South and Southerners and granted me permission to use again excerpts and passages from these earlier pieces in this volume:

"The Redneck," *Georgia Review* 25:3 (Fall 1971)

"Southern Blacks," *Centennial Review* 16:4 (Fall 1972)

"Thomas Stevens, Antebellum Georgian," *South Atlantic Quarterly* 72:2 (Spring 1973). Copyright 1973 by Duke University Press.

"The South's Peculiar Intuition," *Louisiana Studies* (presently *Southern Studies: An Interdisciplinary Journal of the South*) 12:4 (Winter 1973)

"The Southern Aristocrat," *Midwest Quarterly* 15:3 (Spring 1974)

"Nathaniel Francis, Representative Antebellum Southerner," *Proceedings of the American Philosophical Society* 118:5 (15 October 1974)

"The American South," *Journal of Popular Culture* 10:2 (Fall 1976)

"La tradition militaire dans le Sud," chapter 3 of *Le système militaire des Etats-Unis: bilan et perspectives,* sous la direction de Lucien Mandeville (Toulouse, France, 1976)

"The American Middle Class," *The Callaway Journal,* 1977

"The Military Tradition in the South," *Midwest Quarterly* 21:2 (Winter 1980)

"Grassroots Reconstruction and Continuity in the South," *Southern Studies: An Interdisciplinary Journal of the South* 19:3 (Fall 1980) [This was originally read as a paper at a conference on "The First and Second Reconstructions" at the University of Missouri, St. Louis, on 16 February 1978.]

"Slaves as Guinea Pigs: Georgia and Alabama Episodes," *Alabama Review: A Quarterly Journal of Alabama History* 37:1 (January 1984)

INTRODUCTION

"The South! The poor South!" gasped the dying John C. Calhoun, greatest of all professional Southerners, and a little more than a decade later the South turned into the Confederacy and began a modern war for survival. By the spring of 1865 the Confederacy had crumbled into dust, leaving its people, white and black, battered and bewildered. Old man Calhoun's words had been all too prophetic.

Years passed before the defeated South regained its old place in the Union, and generations passed before other Americans started seriously considering the possibility that Southerners were full-fledged Americans again. Even today, more than a decade after a Georgian entered the White House, the South and its people still seem unique to many Americans. Scholars and experts of every stripe continue to examine and analyze—and almost dissect—past and present Southerners, and often they continue to describe a different Dixie, which never really fit into the national mainstream. Calhoun is still right; the South, the poor South, has had a long row to hoe even after the Civil War and Reconstruction, and on the scholarly front the end is not yet apparent. This volume is yet another contribution to the vast literature on the South, one more scholar's effort to "set the record straight" on the enigma of Dixie.

The late antebellum period—roughly from 1830 to 1860—represented the crucial period in Southern history, the time when the South really jelled as a culture and a civilization and Southerners really became a recognizable people who have changed little in fundamental ways in the last century. The roots of this permanent Southern culture run straight back to Jamestown, where a great nation and a great people began in 1607. Indeed, the Southern folk, white and then black, were the first modern

American immigrants. They came before the *Mayflower;* they blazed the trail for all the others who would follow. As Confederate General Nathan Bedford Forrest, another professional Southerner, would have put it: they got to America "first with the most"—or, for local color, "fustest with the mostest." Southerners created the original American mainstream in Tidewater Virginia, and they never really departed from that broadening current, not even in the heyday of slavery, not even during a Civil War that exterminated more than 600,000 Americans, Northerners as well as Southerners. They have been and remain one of the most representative of all the tribes and types that make up the diverse yet similar American people.

The South—the slave states that briefly became the fighting Confederacy—had largely matured when the Civil War erupted, and it was already indelibly, hopelessly American. In this sense it could not really leave the Union, even as it tried to fight its way out; this was the profoundest tragedy of that terrible war. Perhaps the problem of slavery could only have been solved with a bloody sword, but no war could permanently separate the American people. Northerners and Southerners had moved together too long in the American mainstream to part permanently.

Like other Americans, late antebellum Southerners were a mixed people, a confusing conglomeration of hardy individualists spread out over a varied countryside. They simply do not fit into neat, precise categories, but with much effort they can be squeezed into several broad, overlapping categories. A great many of the tiny minority of whites called "aristocrats" were not at all aristocratic in any traditional, European sense; they can best be understood as wealthy, successful businessmen—usually "agribusinessmen" owning many slaves—within the generally capitalistic system in antebellum America. The great majority of Southern whites were "rednecks," tough folk who cultivated their own land and occasionally did well enough to purchase slave laborers to help out. The general white population, including most "aristocrats" and most "rednecks," is better described by the term "bourgeoisie."

Like other antebellum Americans, most Southerners had a basically middle-class attitude: they believed in the work ethic whether or not they were Protestants in good standing, and many practiced as austere a brand of Calvinism as any Yankee followed. They worked hard at their jobs—or calling—which usually but not always was agriculture, and they wheeled and dealt like expectant capitalists in a credit-fueled, free-enterprise, profit-oriented economy. Some succeeded spectacularly, most did reasonably well, and not many slipped into "poor white" or "poor white trash" status. By world standards they (including some women) owned considerable land, and they recognized the sanctity of a contract and of private property (including black slaves). By international standards the literacy rate was extremely high among whites, and only a few regions in the advanced Western world did a better job of educating the mass of their citizenry. Each adult white male had one vote in a system that is sometimes labeled "*Herrenvolk* democracy" (for whites only). The mass of whites felt they were an integral part of a reasonably flexible and fair system that, as in the North, allowed white men to rise or fall on their own and acknowledged the principle that all white men are created equal. They showed the optimism and confidence of a chosen people on the make with a reasonable chance to succeed, to "get ahead" and lead a "respectable" life. Overall, the whites of the antebellum South, whether "aristocrats" or "rednecks," lived in a bourgeois world far removed from any kind of Old World seigneurialism or feudalism. Later hard times might make many white Southerners financially poor, but most retained the bourgeois spirit that had formed so powerfully in the late antebellum period.

This bourgeois spirit radiated out in all directions, even down into the ranks of the oppressed black slaves. Less and less African and more and more American and Southern with each passing generation, the slaves absorbed many middle-class ideas and ideals, and many demonstrated that they could function effectively within the whites' system when given half or even a quarter of a chance.

This view of the South as it reached maturity does not trickle down from theories, formulas, and patterns that evolved from broader studies of world history, but rather it builds up mainly from a close examination of local, grassroots records of the Old South, especially federal census data and the various official documents still housed in county courthouses all over the region. Antebellum newspapers and autobiographies and memoirs have also been used extensively in an inductive process of examining a host of isolated facts and figures as a prelude to fashioning general conclusions and interpretations. The emphasis has been on firsthand, on-the-scene testimony that bears clear witness, but the scholarship of recent decades has been consulted frequently too.

No study of the South and Southerners can claim to be entirely original, and this volume has certainly benefited from many previous publications, especially the following. Clement Eaton's *The Growth of Southern Civilization* and other works on the antebellum period provided general balance despite a mild infatuation with the elite. Daniel R. Hundley's *Social Relations in Our Southern States* presented a contemporary picture of the sprawling middle class on the eve of the Civil War. Frank L. Owsley's *Plain Folk of the Old South* exploited federal censuses and local courthouse records to reveal the same influential middle class. James Oakes's *The Ruling Race: A History of American Slaveholders* stressed the great diversity among Southern whites during the antebellum period. W. J. Cash's *The Mind of the South* stressed continuity in Southern history and effectively presented pen portraits of representative Southerners. Robert William Fogel and Stanley L. Engerman's *Time on the Cross* revealed the robust capitalism of the antebellum Southern economy. Robert S. Starobin's *Industrial Slavery in the Old South* demonstrated the flexibility and adaptability of slavery—and the slaves themselves. John W. Blassingame's *The Slave Community* and *Slave Testimony* showed how unique grassroots records and testimonials could be used to reveal more of the life of ordinary slaves, a subject often ignored in traditional scholarship. Many other works have been helpful; some have been cited in the text and others listed in the bibliography at the end of the volume.

Some recent studies by European and Europeanized scholars have been very useful for the outsider's perspective. Certainly the "Annales" school of French scholarship with its stress on grassroots records and descriptions of the "day-to-dayness" of life had at least an indirect influence. But other studies have been ignored or criticized in the text because they have attempted to take theories and formulas devised in the European context and transfer them whole across the broad Atlantic. Often this simply does not work. The New World is indeed new, especially the United States. Southerners and other Americans have long been very much alike; surface mannerisms vary, often misleading the most skillful foreign (and domestic) observers, but in the basics Americans are the same everywhere. They differ significantly, not from each other, but from the other peoples of the world, even their friends and allies in Western Europe. Broadly speaking, all the peoples of the wide world belong to the same family of man, but in a practical and real sense the people of the United States are and have long been—for better or worse—something special and unique and not just transplanted folk from older worlds across the sea.

In attempting to describe Southerners to the general reader as well as the scholar, this volume has omitted traditional academic footnotes. Instead, important sources, manuscript depositories as well as printed material, are mentioned in the text itself. This allows the amateur to pursue any general theme that arouses his interest and at the same time tells the expert where the author received his information. Thus this book, which deals with ordinary folks as well as elites, is directed at the general reader as well as the specialist. Perhaps both will learn more about Southerners; certainly both should try to do so, since the Southern people have long been at the core of the historical puzzle called America.

CHAPTER 1
The Aristocrats

O f all the antebellum Southerners, the aristocrat stands the tallest. His image towers over the black and white masses and at times over the land itself. Powerful in the old tidewater regions, strong in the newer agricultural areas sprawling all the way to east Texas, especially the vaunted cotton kingdom, the elite's image weakened only in the hill country and mountain areas beyond the Southern mainstream.

The passage of time has only magnified the aristocracy's prestige; the more homogenized and modernized America becomes, the more it idealizes the elite of the Old South. All over the nation American energy and ambition have always been partially motivated by snobbism. Americans have always wanted an equal opportunity to show themselves superior to their neighbors, so naturally they have always grudgingly admired their betters, the Northern and Southern aristocrats at the top of the heap.

Most contemporary images of the antebellum Southern aristocrat are relatively favorable, but still, he was "Ole Massa" in the slave regime and a leader of the enemy Confederacy, so a negative image also exists in the North and West. Sometimes the Southern aristocrat is seen as debauched and degenerate, a genetic disaster created by too much intermarriage between first cousins (or, in more fertile imaginations, too much interbreeding between brothers and sisters). Such a creature would obviously prey upon his defenseless slaves, committing the kind of unspeakable atrocities described in modern novels like *Mandingo* and *Falconhurst Fancy*. Brutal and lustful, tobacco-stained and whiskey-soaked, Southern gentlemen specialized in raping black women, torturing black men, and generally terrorizing the quarters. Their even more vicious ladies waited for the right moment to inflict more mayhem or, while still in their prime, to passionately seduce any available male regardless of race, creed, or color. These Southern aristocrats were a far cry from the stereotyped New England elite, a scrawny, tubercular merchant hunched over his dusty ledgers and his equally insipid wife whose sexuality resembled the early stages of rigor mortis. By 1861 the Southern power elite clearly could only be eliminated or reconstructed by a great military crusade to make the nation safe for democracy. Four years later the Union army triumphed, and the United States was reborn, cleansed in the life's blood of more than 600,000 men.

Most unfavorable images of Southern aristocrats are less grotesque and gothic. As demonstrated in William R. Taylor's *Cavalier and Yankee: The Old South and American National Character*, antebellum critics were usually content to picture them as inefficient and ineffectual—born losers. Awkwardly friendly, the "Colonel" or the "Judge" rocks away the lazy hours on a spacious veranda, blowing out great clouds of cigar smoke and steadily sipping bourbon. This "cavalier" is a nice enough fellow, honest and sincere, but he simply cannot solve any real problem. He is just not the kind of person you can leave in charge of the store. There he sits in a rumpled suit that bears a few traces of grits-and-gravy. Flabby of body as well as mind, this tireless conversationalist really has nothing to say.

His sweet, shallow wife flits around him incessantly, talking even more and saying even less. She too has run a little to pasty plumpness over the years, and she always seems a little uncertain and unsettled. Once she was pert or cute, if not quite beautiful, but an adolescence filled with superficial soirees and a young adulthood filled with pregnancies have taken their toll: now she just looks empty. She still tries to act lighthearted and still wears fancy clothes that are much too ornate, but these old habits accentuate rather than conceal her sense of frustration and failure. She absentmindedly adores her many children, the living and the dead, and she loves her husband after a fashion, ignoring his many faults, which include an occasionally rather pathetic dalliance down in the slave quarters. In emergencies she reacts by swooning or pleading some more exotic "female trouble," and in the final crisis of the antebellum period she could only wave gaily as her menfolk rode off to the slaughter.

These negative images have acquired all manner of variations over the years, but recently the tendency has been to see Southern aristocrats in a much more favorable light, even to glorify them. Americans have lost much of their traditional optimism, becoming increasingly skeptical of the old concept of progress and increasingly critical of the nation's unique brand of capitalism. They look back nostalgically at those antebellum Southerners who seem to stand so proudly above the national mainstream, a chivalry above the crassness, a feudal elite uncorrupted by greed and materialism. The vision of a graceful, refined planter family living with joy and dignity in a splendid Grecian mansion overlooking lush fields seems like a long-lost Garden of Eden to many contemporary Americans. Even the stain of slavery has been somewhat diluted (but not erased) by modern studies like Eugene D. Genovese's *Roll, Jordan, Roll,* which reemphasized the old concept of planter paternalism presented a half century earlier in Ulrich B. Phillips's *American Negro Slavery* and *Life and Labor in the Old South.*

Now the wealthy planter emerges again as a Great White Father to his slave children, a firm but benevolent master who presides over a subtle system of interlocking duties and responsibilities. He dominates but graciously allows blacks some room to live and develop too. The aristocrat towers over not only the blacks but also over the white masses who defer to his obvious superiority. The great planters establish their hegemony over all Dixie, which becomes a unique, seigneurial civilization different from the agrarian capitalism of the Old North and even more different from the new industrial capitalism emerging in areas like New England.

Yet paradoxically this genteel planter and gentle master is often also pictured as a very belligerent citizen. The antebellum violence so dramatically described in John Hope Franklin's *The Militant South* seems to be a hallmark of the hotblooded chivalry. The true aristocrat could hardly be expected to brawl in the streets with rednecks and poor white trash; but it was permissible in 1856 for Congressman Preston Brooks of South Carolina to redeem the honor of his family and his Southland by caning Senator Charles Sumner of Massachusetts within an inch of his life in the hallowed halls of Congress. Sumner had delivered an offensive speech, and besides, he was a Harvard man and thus worthy of the wrath of a berserk Southern gentleman like Brooks.

In cases like this it was difficult to draw the line on acceptable Southern upper-class violence, but assuredly aristocrats were expected to have at one another in formal duels. Like medieval knights, Southern gentlemen were supposed to battle again and again in affairs of honor. The scenario begins at misty dawn, preferably "under the oaks," but "down by the river" or just plain "out in the woods" would do too. Rapiers, the sissified weapons of the French, yield to manly pistols. Somber seconds, a stern referee, and the proud, fearless combatants each play a stereotyped role. The duelists exchange measured shots until one falls or honor is satisfied. The whole affair becomes a stylized rite, almost a delayed circumcision ceremony for adult, male aristocrats. Every middle-aged aristocrat was supposed to have gunned down several opponents and to have been "pinked" a few times in return. How any elite class could survive and reproduce amidst the general carnage is puzzling, but such carping hardly disturbs the image of the gallant chivalry of old Dixie.

These dramatic duels only previewed the greater challenge of war. The legendary Southern aristocrat was born for battle, and he quickly responded to every call to the colors—Washington in the Revolutionary War, Jefferson Davis in the Mexican War and, of course, Robert E. Lee and his officer corps in the Civil War. Like Roland and Bonnie Prince Charlie and other doomed heroes from a millennium of European history and legend, "Marse Robert" ultimately failed; he now sleeps in a quiet, dignified chapel tucked away in the Shenandoah Valley like a miniature Saint Denis or Westminster Abbey or other shelter of old-world grandeur. The recumbent marble statue on the top of his tomb seems ready to join the medieval chivalry in a special, exalted Valhalla reserved for true aristocrats.

The Southern aristocrat exchanged the medieval lance and armor for a light, curved saber and a pistol, but he remained a mounted warrior: the mechanical paraphernalia of the artillery and the dust and grime of the infantry were not his ideal milieu, but the navy might do in a pinch. Obviously those who led in peacetime could do no less in war, so the aristocrat had to be an officer, preferably at least a colonel and as far away from the enlisted ranks as possible.

In combat he fought gallantly and recklessly. Against foes like the red-coated British and the blue-bellied Yankees, he saved his best for an opponent of comparable social standing, the younger son of an English lord or a former classmate from West Point or Yale or Princeton, for example. He might take the time to ride down some common infantrymen too, but the best pistol shot or the surest saber slash had to be saved for a fellow gentleman. Winning or losing one of these latter-day jousts was no more important than performing grandly, and naturally in the dazzling imagery the Southern aristocrat always does, killing or being killed according to true chivalry.

Special problems arose in battles against Indians, Mexicans, rebelling slaves, and other lesser breeds without the aristocrat's law. Not all of these people were totally scorned. An aristocratic family could handle a Latin or Indian ancestor, especially a discreetly distant one. Indeed, the very elite of the Southern elite, the fabled First Families of Virginia, include a few clans that boast of their descent from the Princess Pocahontas. This sort of Indian connection was acceptable, especially after the frontier had passed far to the west, but close kinship to ordinary run-of-the-forest red-skins was not. Similarly a Spanish grandee back several generations was all right—perhaps the "blood of the caesars" had coursed through his veins—but Southern aristocrats viewed the mass of Latin Americans much like Theodore Roosevelt (the son of a Yankee aristocrat and a Southern lady), who was known to use terms like "jack rabbits" and "contemptible little creatures." Genetically blacks were considered the very bottom of the barrel; even the most paternal planter wanted no Negroes, even African princes, in his lineage. Although planters contributed generously to their slaves' gene pool over the generations, black was still ugly, the color no elite family would tolerate (or admit to) in its coat of arms.

Generally aristocrats fighting such red, brown, or black legions were content to direct the slaughter. Mounted erectly on prancing stallions, they watched their yeoman troops sweep the field, and only rarely would they cross swords with a bespangled Latin generalissimo or, like John C. Calhoun's rugged father, engage in single combat with an Indian chief. Even rarer was man-to-man combat with the leader of a slave insurrection. Tragic heroes like Gabriel Prosser, Denmark Vesey, and Nat Turner were beyond the pale and ultimately faced only redneck hangmen.

No matter how the vision of combat might vary, the warrior-planters are always strongly supported by their womenfolk, who also seem to undergo a magical metamorphosis in wartime. Sometimes these ladies are seen as sturdy helpmates who operate the plantation for the duration, but more often they are vaguely pictured as fascinating females who, along with their menfolk, became the first "beautiful people", in American culture. They run the gamut from precious little girls in crinoline to vivacious, lovely wives and sisters to fine, dignified mothers and grannies and, like the fabled Spartan women of old, they all demand victory and glory. Of course, aristocratic soldiers are spurred on to incredible deeds of valor by these assorted damsels and dames who, like the heroes' horses, can best be described as "spirited." Such ladies are the last, best facet of a complex image that, no matter how else it fluctuates, consistently pictures the Southern aristocracy as unique within American society.

All of this imagery is persuasive and, like all legends and stereotypes, it contains a touch of truth. Reinforced by traditional Southern toleration for eccentricity, the Dixie elite was diversified. A few planters were daydreaming boobs. Like other Americans, Southern aristocrats tolerated considerable violence. Some led troops in battle, and a very few became professional soldiers. A few fought formal duels (usually over politics or property), but even these spectacles became rare by the late antebellum period. Some Southern ladies were empty and frustrated, and some were "spirited." Splendid Greek-revival mansions graced a few isolated landscapes, and a few of their ruins still haunt the modern South. One group of battered Corinthian columns reaching into the sky hypnotized the urbane journalist Alistair Cooke, leading him to eulogize a long-time-gone "feudal" South in his *America* film series. The races did interbreed extensively and, like other Americans, Southern aristocrats were infected with racism; a very tiny minority may even have remotely approached the ideal of medieval chivalry. Paternalism flourished on a few plantations. But these are scattered bits and pieces wrenched out of historical context, the exception rather than the rule, and all this obscures the broad, basic truth about the antebellum Southern elite.

Stripped of all the laden-on imagery, the actual Southern aristocrat was essentially a rich white person. Manners and morals, family connections and education and massive self-assurance all helped, indeed might even allow a fading family to survive in the elite for another generation, but in the long run what really counted was wealth. Money and property could be inherited, but this was a rigid, sterile procedure that could not long endure in America's fluid economy without very skillful management. Every real, functioning aristocrat had to be a good businessman with enough talent, energy, and luck to stay way ahead of the pack in a competitive, expanding economic system.

The spectacular rise and fall and second rising of the famous Byrd family in Virginia illustrate this basic reality. Bourgeois immigrant William I wrestled wealth and prestige from the rough, new English colony in the seventeenth century; his haughty, talented son William II expanded and enjoyed this awesome wealth and power in the first half of the eighteenth century; and his grandson William III squandered it before killing himself at the beginning of the Revolutionary War. Though his widow, Mary Willing Byrd, salvaged some of the estate through prudent management, the Byrds soon vanished from the ranks of the elite. For more than a century they had to console themselves with labels like "respectable" and "good family." Only in the twentieth century did this early American family regain its old place in the upper levels of the aristocracy when young businessman Harry Flood Byrd generated his own wealth in the apple orchards of the Shenandoah Valley. Like his great-great-great-grandfather William I, industrious, ambitious young Harry clawed his own way up from the solid middle class to the elite; the aristocracy's admission requirements had not changed much in almost three centuries. His ability to parlay his great wealth into a distinguished career as governor and United States senator was in keeping with the traditions of the Byrd family in its rich phases, and many other wealthy aristocratic American families like the Rockefellers and the Kennedys have operated in the same manner. Harry's younger brother, Admiral Richard Evelyn Byrd, added more glory to the family name, but the real key to the resurgence of the Byrds was the older brother who got rich quickly.

Even in stuffy old Virginia where an especially illustrious name might be numbered like European royalty, a family could not long remain among the *crème de la crème* without solid, enduring financial assets. At best, the financially fading family could cling to the outer fringes of the elite long enough to marry back into big money. The distinguished family of gallant but erratic and unbusinesslike "Light-Horse" Harry Lee came upon hard times. His brilliant son Robert Edward obtained a subsidized higher education at West Point and then reestablished the family's finances by marrying into the wealthy Custis family. Thus the young career army officer became master of a splendid Potomac river estate named "Arlington" which, ironically, became the burial ground for the heroes of a nation he almost destroyed in battle.

Aspiring middle-class families might also use profitable marriages to make their initial penetrations into the ranks of the elite. Lawrence Washington and his half brother George both married great wealth. Talented Peter Jefferson married into the rich, prominent Randolph clan, and his son Thomas wedded a well-to-do widow. Ambitious Henry Clay married into the emerging Kentucky aristocracy. Calculating John C. Calhoun greatly enhanced his fortunes when he married into the Charleston aristocracy. Howell Cobb made a similar great leap forward by marrying the daughter of Zachariah Lamar, one of the richest planters in Georgia. Most of these marriages seem to have been affairs of the heart, but they also played a significant role in bringing new blood into the aristocracy.

Essentially this white elite was composed of very successful businessmen who knew how to make and keep money. From the very beginning the rich new lands running endlessly beyond the western horizon offered fabulous opportunities to refugees from crowded, stratified old Europe. This sudden access to the riches of a lightly defended and loosely administered new continent was more "revolutionary" than most of the jolts and spurts in the development of Western civilization that have been labeled with this most overused of scholarly words. Hordes of hustlers and opportunists rushed to exploit emerging America's bounty. Many failed, more achieved moderate success, and a chosen few gained enough wealth to become American aristocrats.

This was a new kind of aristocracy based on current wealth rather than past lineage. In old Europe the aristocracy was porous enough to admit a trickle of talent from the lower classes, but in the emerging American

South the aristocracy was more like a sponge, readily absorbing whites with exceptional talent and ambition. By traditional European standards it was not a real aristocracy at all.

The new Southern aristocrat was home-grown; very few had significant blood ties with European nobility. Theoretically even the humblest immigrant could claw his way to the top; the American dream of a poor boy making good was possible. W. J. Cash's *The Mind of the South* described just such an odyssey: an ambitious young Irishman and his sturdy wife plunge into the South Carolina backcountry around 1800 and through backbreaking labor and shrewd management accumulate enough wealth to have their family ensconced in the newer ranks of the elite; their daughter marries a Charleston aristocrat, and their son, a prominent lawyer, rises rapidly toward the governorship, only to fall in battle at the head of his Confederate regiment.

The unkempt Anglo-Saxon farmer, the lean, hard Scots-Irish frontiersman, the sturdy German laborer, all had this sort of long shot at the Southern or American aristocracy. In practice only a tiny handful ever achieved this much success, and they were usually bourgeois types with business experience who carried on the progress of at least one previous generation. Even exceptional families faced great odds and could usually rise no higher than the middle layers of a fluid, complex society. But this was a phenomenal achievement for folk who had been mired for centuries and generations in the sluggish, stratified societies of Mother Europe. The not-quite-nascent United States, North and South, was truly a land of opportunity, a once-in-a-millennium chance for a new folk called Americans, who responded with fierce energy and optimism.

The self-made aristocrats of the colonial South were often diversified, mobile entrepreneurs who functioned as merchants and land speculators as well as planters. Gradually plantation agriculture became more stable and profitable, especially after the massive importation of slave laborers began late in the seventeenth century. True to the capitalistic instincts of later captains of industry like Andrew Carnegie and Henry Ford, most Southern businessmen followed the path of least resistance and most profit. They therefore specialized in cultivating tobacco, wheat, rice, indigo, corn, cotton, or for that matter, sweet potatoes or pork or lumber or any other cash crop in demand through local, national, or international markets. A mystical love of the land did not motivate these successful planters; commercial considerations came first. They would have had no difficulty figuring out Willie Sutton's more recent explanation for his persistent habit of robbing banks—that's where the money was. Plantations grew larger, more efficient, and more profitable. They were not late-blooming European manors but rather modern capitalistic centers of production. The great planters were skilled managers, agribusinessmen who achieved outstanding success against vigorous competition.

As the new American nation emerged from the tumult of revolution and moved confidently into the nineteenth century, most Southern planters continued to concentrate on agriculture, though many encouraged diversification too. Furthermore, as industrialism swept through the advanced areas of the Western world, many planters quickly responded to new economic opportunities. They invested generously in the new railroads that began to snake across the nation as early as the 1830s. The nation's first significant railroad began at Baltimore, and briefly the Charleston and Hamburg Railroad, which ran 136 miles into the South Carolina interior, was the longest line in the world. By the time of the Civil War the South had one of the world's most effective rail networks. It was fragile by modern standards and unready for the terrible demands of total war; however, as Robert William Fogel and Stanley L. Engerman's *Time on the Cross* demonstrated, it was quite advanced and efficient for the late antebellum period.

Industries developed more slowly, but again, the South made significant progress before the Civil War. The "Old South," not the "New South," first championed and developed modern industry. Antebellum plantations had always employed some skilled workers and artisans and nurtured cottage industries, and by the 1840s it was the rich planters who led the move toward industrialization. Robert S. Starobin's *Industrial Slavery in the Old South* revealed that it was the planters, not the bankers or merchants, who provided most of the investment capital. Many of them also sent their slave laborers into the new textile mills, iron foundries, machine shops, lumber mills, and other factories, mines, and railroad complexes that were developing steadily. Planters did not feel threatened by industrialization; they welcomed it in general as a further refinement of their economy and in particular as another way to make money. They were, after all, not old-fashioned patroons but modern capitalists, eager to continue prospering in a rapidly changing national and international economy.

Railroads and industry developed rapidly enough to make the South an extremely dangerous opponent in the Civil War. Matched against one of the world's leading industrial powers, the Confederacy finally crumbled, but only after a long, bloody fight for survival. The Confederates made skillful use of the Southern rail system, and they greatly expanded their industrial production to meet the relentless demands of modern warfare. Recent works like Emory M. Thomas's *The Confederate Nation* and Raimondo Luraghi's *The Rise and Fall of the Plantation South* consider these achievements spectacular and revolutionary. Actually, though, while quite impressive, they were no more than wartime extensions of prewar developments. Industrialism came to the antebellum South; the technology and know-how, along with skilled laborers and experienced managers, existed before 1861. The Confederacy simply shifted the whole Southern economic machine into high gear as it fought for survival.

Suppose the Confederacy had been allowed to secede in peace and had waged its great war against Mexico or had unleashed an expedition to seize Cuba from the Spanish. Or imagine the Confederacy transported miraculously across the ocean to battle some African or Asian kingdom. Which side then would have been the irresistible juggernaut? Which side then would have exploited its technology to win? The Confederacy lost the Civil War not because slavery made it inefficient and uncompetitive in a fast-changing world, but because it was matched against one of the most advanced, powerful nations on earth. The antebellum elite emerged from defeat and Reconstruction relatively intact; down at the grassroots level no revolution occurred and most wealthy prewar businessmen remained at the top of the heap.

Antebellum planters welcomed industry, and they were even more enthusiastic about the expanding credit facilities that fueled worldwide capitalism. Incurable optimists, they played the game shrewdly, borrowing to expand their most profitable enterprises. Varied and complicated systems of credit developed over time to meet every need. Some bumblers got in over their heads (and disappeared from the elite), but efficient planters flourished. Even the most successful liked to grumble about being exploited by factors, commission merchants, shippers, insurers, bankers, and all manner of entrepreneurs in Natchez and New Orleans and Charleston, or Boston and New York, or London and Liverpool. Actually the fees and commissions and interest charged were usually reasonable, planters and their agents were often on very friendly terms, and Southern crops usually found lucrative markets in many parts of the world.

Besides, the same planters who complained so bitterly about greedy, parasitic middlemen often performed the same functions themselves in their own neighborhoods. Often rich planters loaned money at interest and established country stores where farmers could buy manufactured goods on credit and later market some of their crops for a service charge or two here and there. The successful, powerful planters' reflex bellyaching about "the system" was no more convincing than George McDuffie's "forty bales" theory of exploitation or John C. Calhoun's more sophisticated pontifications on Yankee economic imperialism. The planters knew what they were doing, and they were doing quite well. Yet as good old American hustlers, they were forever poor-mouthing and, indeed, they became the first group of Americans to master the technique of crying all the way to the bank.

By the last decades of the antebellum period these optimistic, mobile capitalists had spread lightly over much of Dixie. Probably the most representative of these diverse, individualistic planter-aristocrats emerged in the cotton kingdom of the Deep South, but even there the "average planter" is an elusive fellow, difficult to isolate and evaluate. Famous men like Calhoun of South Carolina, Robert Toombs of Georgia, Judah P. Benjamin of Louisiana, and Jefferson Davis of Mississippi used plantation profits to finance their political careers. Such official "great men" kept extensive records, many of which have been preserved by later generations of respectful Americans. Patient scholars have plowed through mountains of these materials and produced many illuminating biographies, but these scholarly volumes tell much more about "great statesmen" than "average planters."

Even in the small planter elite the representative or average man has been overlooked. Recent efforts to uncover grassroots reality have concentrated primarily on the lower classes and minority groups, so the ordinary planter remains obscure except when he is distorted by legend and myth. Since he was a successful businessman, he kept operating records adequate for the early, unsophisticated capitalism that had developed, and antebellum newspapers sometimes mentioned such rich entrepreneurs. Occasional published reminiscences of elite families tell a good bit too, but they must be used with special care: the moonlight shining through the magnolias has blinded many a good historian.

Most of these rather personalized records of the nonfamous elite have faded away with the passage of time, but enough have survived to begin recreating the real Southern aristocrat. Large amounts of more general and official records tell a great deal more about the entire wealthy class as well as individual planters. The original federal census reports are very useful, especially in 1850 and 1860 when the amount of statistical information increases greatly. Most informative of all are the surviving county records, which also become much more detailed and precise in the late antebellum period.

All of these records containing significant statistical data have attracted the attention of a new breed of historians, quantifiers armed with computers. In their controversial *Time on the Cross*, Fogel and Engerman fed very limited amounts of such records, especially census data, into computers to prove the big planters' profitable use of slave labor in capitalistic agriculture. A more traditional scholar using more traditional methods, Julia Floyd Smith analyzed similar data, especially county records, in a less controversial manner to make the same general point about planters in *Slavery and Plantation Growth in Antebellum Florida*. And James Oakes's more recent *The Ruling Race: A History of American Slaveholders* sees old-fashioned paternalism crumbling everywhere before the onslaught of liberal capitalism.

Still, the Southern upper class remains partially distorted, still hidden behind the misleading concept of aristocracy. The term "planter" is probably more accurate, but it too can be misleading and inaccurate. One way to see antebellum reality more clearly is to go right down to the rural grassroots and isolate and examine closely several "representative planters" who all at one time or another owned the same piece of valuable property, a slave named Fed.

Large, robust Sterling Finney moved from Northampton County in eastern North Carolina to Morgan County in north-central Georgia around 1817. The Creek and Cherokee Indians held on tenaciously in Georgia, and only in 1802 did whites gain control of this area. The following year the state surveyed this land into symmetrical 202 1/2 acre lots, which were then given away to the citizens of Georgia by lottery. This original planned pattern of medium-sized yeoman farms never completely vanished, but Morgan County lay in the midst of the emerging cotton kingdom of Piedmont Georgia, and some large plantations began to evolve as aggressive entrepreneurs like Finney moved in. Relentlessly acquisitive, he engaged in all sorts of business activities, buying and selling slaves as well as land in the fluid, expanding economy; yet like most astute businessmen in this fertile area, he concentrated on agriculture. Soon he accumulated fifty-seven slaves and 2,000 acres of land, which produced large crops of corn and cotton and pastured sizable numbers of sheep, hogs, and cattle. Though never quite as influential and powerful in Morgan County as the Saffold, Walton, and Johnston families, the Finneys had done very well indeed, and Sterling himself had joined the local elite. As a member of the county's political establishment, he served a year in the state legislature before he died in 1831.

Early in his career, when he was shifting his business operations farther south, Finney bought a young slave boy named Fed for $310 and then sold him in Georgia to Thomas Stevens for $350, a neat profit of almost thirteen percent. A native Georgian, Stevens began his own career as an ambitious, skillful businessman in nearby Baldwin County, only a few miles from the state capital at Milledgeville. Fair-skinned and dark-haired, Stevens had a quick laugh and an even quicker temper. With only a rudimentary education he started as a jackleg carpenter, a miller, and a distiller of corn whisky, but like Finney he was a rural hustler and soon shifted into the lucrative corn and cotton agriculture of Piedmont Georgia. He also rose rapidly in a land of white opportunity. He was never as successful as Finney, but he did eventually accumulate thirty-one slaves and hundreds of acres of good land. Mobile like Finney, Stevens in 1823 moved northwest about sixty miles into new DeKalb County (now part of metropolitan Atlanta). He continued farming, but he also speculated in real estate, invested in one of the area's first cemeteries, and joined four other entrepreneurs in incorporating the DeKalb Manufacturing Company in 1832. Like most planters, he was receptive to industry or almost anything else that promised a profit; he certainly did not see industrial development as an alien threat to his way of life. This particular textile mill was never constructed, but many others were as cotton factories began to spring up near the cotton fields long before the coming of the vaunted "New South."

Aging but still acquisitive, Stevens moved northwest again a few miles—into an area just evacuated by the Cherokees—before he died in 1839, and his three grown sons carried on in the same general manner as the Civil War approached. The slave boy Fed ("Fred" in Stevens's will) grew into a restless man while the Stevenses prospered, and finally he ran away. But it was a long, long way from Georgia to freedom, and after a series of misadventures, Fed found himself in Mississippi under a new master.

Theodorick J. James was the wealthiest of Fed's masters by far with ninety-five slaves and real estate valued at $80,000 in 1850. A native of South Carolina, he moved to Louisiana and then to the new, rich cotton lands in Washington County, Mississippi. Yeoman farmers originally settled this region, but soon it was dominated by great plantations, including James's estate on the Shirt-tail bend of the Mississippi River.

Aided by a wife as shrewd and grasping as himself and several industrious sons, James won out in the competitive, commercial struggle for wealth in the heart of the cotton belt. His children could someday flaunt the trappings of wealth if they wished to, but old "Jepsey" and his wife were too busy making money to bother. He and his family lived in a dirty log hut that looked good only in comparison to the pitiful slave cabins around it. Like so many other prosperous American business people, the Jameses were completely committed to their occupation and total prisoners of the fabled Protestant work ethic—or Southern success syndrome. "Jepsey" James became phenomenally successful, wealthier than all but a tiny fraction of the American people, North and South.

He and Stevens and Finney all succeeded in Southern agriculture, and all three profited from the labor of the slave Fed and many more like him. This proud, restless black man still yearned for freedom, and finally he made good his escape by following the Mississippi River northward. He continued on into Canada and finally reached England, where the British and Foreign Anti-Slavery Society published his memoirs in 1855 under the title *Slave Life in Georgia.* This little book, though occasionally polemical, is an authentic story that holds up well under scholarly analysis and evaluation. Fed, known in freedom as John Brown, was illiterate and provincial—the slave codes saw to that—but he was also intelligent and observant. He had no love for his old masters, but he remembered them well. All three emerge from his narrative as ambitious, energetic, rural capitalists. Each was, as Fed put it, "a man of business." The same image of the planter as an agribusinessman emerges from other slave narratives like Solomon Northup's *Twelve Years a Slave,* which has also been thoroughly edited and authenticated. Obviously this is only one special way to select at random typical planters for evaluation, but when the slaves' testimony is checked out in the grassroots records of the antebellum South, the case looks stronger and stronger.

Corroborating testimony comes from the other extreme of the Southern social spectrum. Mrs. Rebecca Latimer Felton was a well-to-do Southern lady and an outspoken reformer in postbellum Georgia; in 1922 at the age of eighty-seven she became the first woman to hold the office of United States senator (for one day). Three years earlier she published *Country Life in Georgia in the Days of My Youth* and candidly concluded that upper-class Southerners in the antebellum era defended slavery mainly because of "the profit in it." Slavery, one of the bases of the aristocracy's power, is best understood not in terms of paternalism but rather in terms of "the profit in it" for "a man of business." Translated into pompous Latin—*homo in negotiis, est in lucris*—such phrases could have emblazoned the do-it-yourself coats of arms of the South's instant aristocracy. These gentlemen-slaveholders had moved confidently into the modern world of international capitalism, but occasionally a few liked to imagine that they were living like grand seigneurs. They were fooling themselves, of course, but they have also fooled many later historians.

After all, who were these elite folk of the Old South? The simplest and most practical way to isolate the bulk of them statistically is to find the large slaveholders recorded in federal censuses. These figures for 1860 reveal the exclusiveness of the elite. The slave states had a total white population of just over 8,000,000, but only 2,292 people owned as many as a hundred slaves, only 10,658 had fifty or more, and only 46,274 claimed as many as twenty. The census defined any agrarian who owned twenty slaves as a "planter," and this small minority of whites forms a reasonable "upper class," but the exalted title of "aristocrat" should probably best be reserved for those with at least thirty or maybe even fifty slaves. Certainly the owners of fifty or more slaves were a chosen people in the antebellum economy, the equivalent of today's rich folks and in some cases every bit the equal of contemporary millionaires. The number of large slaveholders should be multiplied by four or five to include families and not just individuals among the elite. It would also be prudent to at least make note of occasional lopsided estates of large landholders who rented slave or free workers, and wealthy slave traders who owned no plantations, along with others who prospered in businesses and professions requiring no slaves. Any kind of numbers game that attempts to classify Southern whites too rigidly will have flaws, but clearly the large slaveholders were a special, privileged group, limited in numbers like any other aspiring aristocracy.

Most of these rich folks were only a generation or so removed from the dirt farmers all about them and often even closer than that to the raw frontier. Some were well educated and a handful made major contributions to literature, such as William Gilmore Simms of South Carolina (who married into the elite) or science, such as John and Joseph LeConte of Georgia (who were born into it). Many of the remainder were at heart rednecks on the make, as rough and ready as similar nouveau-riche types in the antebellum North. A few were Northern capitalists who had no difficulty at all becoming Southern capitalists, or recent European immigrants like Frederick Stanton, an Irishman who lived the American dream to its fullest in Mississippi.

Most of the elite were plain agrarian folk, polite but not refined, intelligent but not intellectual, since they were too busy for such "frills." A few were outspoken unbelievers, more were quiet skeptics, but most were regular churchgoers, and many were committed Christians. Most had no moral qualms about the slave foundation of their wealth; slavery seemed the only practical way to keep an inferior race harnessed to a profitable economy and, besides, the Bible and history seemed to condone this ancient institution. They resented abolitionists as outside agitators and hypocrites, and they feared that fanatics such as William Lloyd Garrison might stir up another bloody slave insurrection like Nat Turner's. The psychological basis of their hostility, however, was not the guilt complex William W. Freehling mistakenly diagnosed among the lowland planters in his *Prelude to Civil War: The Nullification Controversy in South Carolina.* The few who really suffered conscience pangs about slavery could not openly support the hated Yankee abolitionists, but they sometimes did move quietly in that direction by joining the American Colonization Society and sending their valuable slaves to freedom in Africa. Even this halfway measure ran counter to Southern sentiment, but before the Civil War erupted, more than 15,000 Southern blacks, mostly freed slaves, were actually returned to their ancestral homeland. Only a tiny fraction of the slaveholding elite liberated their valuable property in this way, an act usually motivated by religion. John Hartwell Cocke, a general reformer, won considerable attention by sending some of his Virginia and Alabama slaves across the sea to freedom; more quietly Emily Tubman, the widow of a wealthy Georgia merchant, sent forty-two of her slaves on the same journey and spent the rest of her life giving away the rest of her fortune to worthy causes, especially struggling churches.

Elite Southerners ran the religious gamut from Baptists and Methodists and Presbyterians through Catholics, especially in southern Louisiana, to even a few Jews. Like the American elite today, the antebellum Southern elite often found the formal ceremonies but relaxed discipline of the Episcopal church congenial; but the American Revolution ended forever any kind of established church in the South (and eventually even in Massachusetts), so a Southern aristocrat could easily pop up at the other extreme of the Protestant spectrum when he had been born again in a fundamentalist manner. Wealthy Southerners lived in a world of religious diversity, but the great majority, including those with no formal church affiliation, were powerfully influenced by an old-fashioned, work-ethic Protestantism that blurred denominational distinctions all over the nation.

Some of the elite took extended and expensive vacations in other parts of the nation as John Hope Franklin has described in *A Southern Odyssey: Travelers in the Antebellum North,* and others learned to love the luxuries of Europe, but as a group they lived no more extravagantly than the Northern elite, perhaps even less so. Most stayed close to home, minding their business affairs. Surviving plantation journals tell the prosaic story of these straitlaced, hard-working families who took their calling very seriously and helped blaze the way for modern American workaholics.

Most planters lived comfortably but not luxuriously in large, frame farmhouses; stately mansions and formal townhouses were more the exception than the rule. These plain, sturdy, two-story homes often radiated a simple but sincere hospitality, and they grew at approximately the same rate as the owner's family and bank account. Added on to in stages, mostly in the rear but sometimes on the sides as well, these homes were functional, not artistic. Most furnishings remained plain and utilitarian, but some refinements like fine china and silver dishes and expensive mahogany furniture began to appear, mostly at the instigation of the lady of the house. Only a few of the elite were willing or able to build a brand new mansion and stock it with expensive new baubles; many were too likely to move on to newer, more fertile land to sink in such plush and permanent roots. Most planters lived in a mixed environment: inside the home a beautiful piano or a solid silver tea service might symbolize opulence, but outside crops often grew up close to the house and farm implements and other accoutrements of agriculture might well overflow from sheds and barns right up into the front yard and even onto the front porch—if one existed.

Business and family life blended inextricably on Southern plantations; a planter's home was also his place of business. This put the Southern lady in a unique position among upper-class American women. In the North a wealthy businessman left home to go to his work, and his wife remained behind in a completely domestic environment. As one foreign observer said, she found herself put "on the shelf" and isolated from the hustle and bustle of the commercial world. Not so the Southern lady who, whether she liked it or not, lived right in the middle of her planter—husband's agribusiness. Still saddled with the traditional duties of wife of one and mother of many, she also had to help supervise the slave labor force, which was not just part of one big, happy family but rather a separate, professional work force. The Southern lady usually had less time for lavish entertainments and other social diversions than her Yankee sister. Far from being put "on the shelf," she was more likely to be put in an early grave by the endless responsibilities of personnel management on her plantation.

A few fragile flowers wilted, and a few plantation ladies went far beyond routine duty and achieved striking success. The most famous of all emerged in colonial South Carolina. Born and educated in England, Eliza Lucas found herself at seventeen running three plantations near Charleston for her father, a British official in the West Indies. She conducted many botanical experiments and in 1744 introduced the cultivation of indigo, which quickly became an important money crop in coastal Carolina. The same year, at age twenty-one, she married forty-two-year-old widower Charles Pinckney, a wealthy planter, and soon she bore him three children, including Charles Cotesworth and Thomas, the most famous scions of that distinguished South Carolina family. She continued her experiments and general work in agriculture, and when her husband died in 1758, she carried on, managing the family's sprawling plantations until her sons were old enough to take over. Overcoming the disadvantage of being a woman, she succeeded as usual. Petite and charming, she was very much the Southern lady—and also one of the great agricultural pioneers of her age.

A generation later, though Southern women had gained a few more rights (a very few), no late antebellum plantation lady could match her achievements. But most did their duty and performed vital services within their husbands' business operations. Some chafed and grumbled. A Virginia lady recalled: "Had slavery lasted a few years longer, it would have killed Julia, my headwoman, and me. Our burden of work and responsibility was simply staggering." Her daughter, Myrta Lockett Avary, elaborated further in *Dixie After the War*.

> In the ante-bellum life of the mistress of a Southern plantation there was no menial occupation, but administrative work was large and exacting. The giving out of rations, clothes, medicines, nursing of the sick, cutting out garments, sewing, spinning, knitting, had to be directed. The everlasting teaching and training, the watch-care of sometimes several hundred semi-civilized, semi-savage people of all ages, dispositions and tempers, were on the white woman's hands.

The kitchen was but one department of that big school of domestic science, the home on a Southern plantation . . . and the white mistress . . . was principal and director.

Similarly, Victoria V. Clayton of Alabama declared in *White and Black under the Old Regime:* "I often said to my husband that the freedom of the negroes was a freedom to me, a freedom from responsibility and care." And Caroline Merrick of Louisiana remembered in *Old Times in Dixie Land* being "subject at all times to the exactions and dictations of the black people who belonged to me, which now seems too extraordinary and incredible to relate."

Other less vocal plantation ladies assumed their responsibilities more readily. Eliza Carter, wife of one of the richest planters in Georgia, performed very efficiently and often ran the home plantation alone while her husband Farish traveled widely on other business. Widows simply had to perform competently or go under in the competitive economy. During the Civil War many other ladies had to run plantations on their own while their menfolk fought far away, and generally they did a pretty good job. Like wartime industrialization, this was only the acceleration of an antebellum trend. Most antebellum Southern belles had had little time to stand on pedestals as they faced an early type of "liberation" far ahead of their upper-class sisters in the North.

Southern ladies and gentlemen came in all sizes and shapes and many individualistic personalities. The Southern elite was a bewilderingly diverse conglomeration of rich white people who could not always agree on the time of day. Most practiced agriculture, but the rhythm and needs of their specialties varied considerably. The hemp growers of bluegrass Kentucky and the sugarcane growers of Louisiana needed tariff protection against foreign competitors. The tobacco growers of the upper South and the many cotton growers of the lower South did not; they vigorously opposed protective tariffs and some even denounced them as unconstitutional. Inland planters away from easy water routes championed canals and later railroads and other internal improvements. They then argued among themselves over whether to use private, state, or federal funds or perhaps some combination of them. Comfortable coastal planters often rejected all of these schemes as impractical or extravagant.

Then many planters began to invest in new industrial enterprises, and some of the upper class such as Joseph R. Anderson of the Tredegar Iron Works in Richmond and William Gregg of the Graniteville Textile Mill in South Carolina became full-blown industrialists with their own hodge-podge of varying special interests. A few of the elite were professional men, especially doctors and lawyers, and a very few like Robert E. Lee were professional soldiers, far from the commercial mainstream of the aristocracy.

Persistent imagery to the contrary notwithstanding, the Southern elite class was not especially attracted to the military as a career; indeed, over the long haul it has probably been less belligerent and militaristic than the Northern upper class. Still, antebellum aristocrats generally supported their country when it went to war, and some who had been peacetime leaders also led in war—but only for the duration. When peace was declared, all of the citizen-soldiers, officers and enlisted men, immediately went home, leaving the tiny antebellum American army to do the best it could along the restless frontier.

Even during the great war that raged from 1861 to 1865, the Southern elite did not particularly distinguish itself. Not every aristocrat rushed into the fray, and the Confederacy's controversial "twenty nigger law" exempting white men who supervised gangs of slave laborers was a convenient loophole for wealthy men dodging the new draft. Bell Irvin Wiley in *The Road to Appomattox* concluded that the elite wavered before the common people as the Confederacy fought to survive, though he was properly cautious in generalizing about such a diversified upper class.

The antebellum aristocrats' political affiliations varied as much as their professions and policies. On the local level the rich competed with one another and others for patronage, and on the state level they belonged to every conceivable faction and movement in the region's lively and highly personalized politics. By the late 1830s national political affiliations were jelling, and Whigs and Democrats began to attract large numbers of elite supporters. And when the great political crisis came and the South decided to secede, the upper class remained divided and uncertain. The upper South moved very cautiously, but even in the more disaffected lower South the elite could not really close ranks on the brink of the Civil War.

They came closest in South Carolina and Mississippi where Unionist sentiment was brushed aside quickly; but as William L. Barney demonstrated in *The Secessionist Impulse*, much more of a struggle occurred in Alabama, with young, on-the-make planters tending to be much more radical than older, more established, more Whiggish planters. Michael P. Johnson's *Toward a Patriarchal Republic* showed that the struggle was even fiercer in Georgia before the secessionists finally triumphed. All over the South individual gland structure, temperament, and character seem to have been at least as important as class standing when the elite deliberated and argued and then marched off to war, out of step with one another as usual.

Such a disjointed and divided upper class might sporadically lead, but it could not really dominate the democratic white masses of the antebellum South; or, to put it in more contemporary jargon, the antebellum Southern aristocracy did not exercise real hegemony, except possibly in the Carolinas. It could not even find an effective spokesman for its own restricted membership. John C. Calhoun had a considerable following in reactionary South Carolina, but he bored more of the Southern elite than he converted. After his death in the spring of 1850, intellectuals like Edmund Ruffin, George Frederick Holmes, and Nathaniel Beverley Tucker of Virginia and James Henry Hammond and William Gilmore Simms of South Carolina—analyzed in Drew Gilpin Faust's *A Sacred Circle*—and George Fitzhugh—analyzed in Eugene D. Genovese's *The World the Slaveholders Made*—functioned like most American intellectuals; they spoke only for themselves. Far from the mainstream of the divided, pragmatic upper class, they whistled in the wind as the storms of war blew toward their homeland.

Yet many recent scholars insist on describing the Southern upper class as a tight-knit, homogeneous, dominant, landed aristocracy similar to such groups in traditional Europe. The prestigious Yale University Press joined this growing trend in 1974 by laboring mightily, publicizing widely, and finally bringing forth into the scholarly world a five-pound, two-ounce tome entitled *The Children of Pride: A True Story of Georgia and the Civil War*. Meticulously edited by Robert Manson Myers, it contains a generous sampling of the massive antebellum and wartime correspondence of the elite family of Charles Colcock Jones, a rich cotton planter and Presbyterian minister. The Reverend Jones was a weary, debilitated intellectual who briefly flirted with the abolition heresy in his youth but quickly retreated to his inherited plantation wealth and began a lifelong crusade to bring the Christian gospel to the slave masses. His wife and first cousin Mary was a tougher specimen, and much more of a hawk as war approached. Their two dutiful sons studied at Princeton and Harvard, favorite schools of the Southern elite, and prepared for distinguished careers in the professions of law and medicine. Their daughter stayed even more on the straight and narrow by marrying another prominent Presbyterian minister.

The whole Jones family was self-consciously prominent, securely ensconced on several lush plantations along the coast a little south of Savannah. Over the years almost a hundred blacks slaved away their lives in this environment, which was much more paternal and seigneurial than most large plantations. The old coastal estates, ancient by American standards, had largely been superseded by the newer plantations, which stretched all the way to east Texas. Some of the old Eastern grandees like the Manigaults of South Carolina and Georgia kept pace with the nouveaux riches of the interior; as detailed by James M. Clifton in *Life and Labor on Argyle Island,* their management of complex rice plantations illustrated just how skillful Southern agriculture could be. But others had lost some of the old agrarian drive or carried it inland into the heart of the cotton kingdom.

None of the Joneses retained a primary commitment to agriculture; much of this responsibility was relinquished to obscure white overseers and black drivers and other underlings seldom mentioned in the massive correspondence. The Joneses did exercise some supervision and, like the newer elite, they also readily invested funds in railroads and factories, but their three plantations started deteriorating a little as their home became more of a backwash in the 1850s. Yet even in this relatively relaxed, old-fashioned setting, paternalism was very limited. The Joneses did not really know their slaves at all; and when Sherman's troops brought freedom, the overwhelming majority of their blacks simply departed, leaving their old mistress to rage at their perverseness and infidelity.

In one respect the Joneses did remain well within the mainstream of the Southern elite. The old man and his wife preached and the children, especially the ambitious boys, practiced the stern Protestant work ethic. They selected their callings, worked hard and then harder and harder and finally prospered as part of the elect or the elite. Old John Calvin was alive and well in the Jones family, and in less sectarian garb he flourished in many other elite homes all across the South.

Still, the Joneses were not much more representative of the Old Southern upper class than great philosopher-statesmen such as Jefferson and Calhoun or a warrior chieftain such as Lee, who spent all but the last five years of his adult life in military uniform. All differed noticeably from the typical Southern aristocrat, a hard-nosed, thick-skinned businessman who usually made most of his money in agriculture.

Basically, wealthy Southerners ran their plantations and other businesses as wealthy Northerners ran theirs—for "the profit in it." Southern planters were not significantly more paternal than Northern industrialists; scholars have overestimated paternalism in the South and underestimated it in the North. The Northern and Southern elites spoke the same capitalistic language, and both pursued the fast buck wherever it might lead. The irrepressible Gazaway Bugg Lamar wheeled and dealed as successfully in New York City as in Savannah, and many other able Southerners operated effectively in the North just as able Northerners did well in the South. The business of antebellum America was business, and the Mason-Dixon line had no commercial significance.

Practical and opportunistic, optimistic and aggressive, very similar to contemporary American "fat cats," the great majority of antebellum upper-class Southerners swam swiftly in the economic mainstream of American life. In the traditional European sense of the word, they were not aristocrats at all but simply very successful American businessmen. Highly individualistic, they did not clump together in a homogenized body or rigid class. Generally they shared the life-style of most of their less wealthy friends and neighbors and associates. They did not awe or dominate the masses of proud whites and, though influential far beyond their limited numbers, they were not the most significant group of late antebellum whites. Even more important were the great masses of Southern whites, the rednecks.

CHAPTER 2
The Rednecks

The redneck best represents the antebellum South. The word itself did not come into common usage until the 1930s, but the people it literarily describes were the great mass of Southern whites before the Civil War. These hardy agrarians overwhelmingly outnumbered the tiny elite, yet they remain in the shadows, ignored by posterity. In a sense this is benign because America has little use for the contemporary Southern redneck; he has an image problem. Every culture needs villains as well as heroes, and the redneck has served admirably as one of the nation's leading bad guys, especially since the civil rights crusade of recent decades.

Every good American needs a mudsill to look down on, but it is no longer fashionable to degrade blacks, Catholics, Jews, "Japs," and other traditional ethnic and religious minorities. New, authorized villains have emerged to suit every taste—syndicate mobsters, Watergate or Chappaquiddick conspirators, environmental polluters, gas guzzlers, imperialists, Commies, junkies, Moonies, and groupies, to mention only a few—but most American opinion-makers who specialize in moral judgments agree that the infamous redneck belongs high on any list of leading despicable types.

In modern America the redneck can be generally described as any white Southerner in the lower or working class, and his image looms large when the media focus in on the South in transition. He stalks through the land

harassing blacks, Yankees, pointy-headed intellectuals, Federal authorities, United Nations representatives, and all the other good guys. His beefy,
thuggish image grinds deeply into the American mind, and even his
scrawny, snarling women and sallow, sullen children have found a place
in the contemporary American nightmare.

In an age of unrestrained profanity and slander, when old fighting
phrases like "son of a bitch" sound almost friendly, when Oedipus seems
to live again in every man, even the thickest white skin can be penetrated
by the terrible taunt, "redneck!" This white equivalent of "nigger" really
stings, not only shattering the immediate recipient but also degrading his
ancestors and damning his descendants. It reaches to the very genes, and
stands as a modern curse of Cain.

Fascinated by turmoil in the land of the redneck, hosts of specialists
and experts and observers have swarmed through modern Dixie, which was
officially proclaimed a "problem" as early as the New Deal. Some came
armed with cameras and tape recorders and computers and all manner of
other sophisticated hardware; others traveled fast and light with luggage
bearing a strong resemblance to the old carpetbag. Almost all brought along
an overwhelming sense of moral superiority as they probed into every dark
corner of Southern life. The main conclusions reached could have been
written before the investigation started: the South is a mess and the redneck is no damned good.

Reinforcing testimony came from some native Southerners. Blacks had
many legitimate grievances that they spelled out in detail, but some of the
most devastating analyses of rednecks came from other Southern whites.
The heralded Southern literary renaissance of the twentieth century was
spearheaded by writers who had little sympathy for the lower orders of white
society. Some of the most grotesque of the "Southern Gothic" writings
zeroed in on inarticulate rednecks and struck hard. From the corncob lover
of Faulkner's *Sanctuary* through the pitiful, depraved farmers of Erskine
Caldwell's *Tobacco Road* up to the mountain freaks of James Dickey's *De-
liverance* and the bizarre yokels of Flannery O'Connor's stories, the American reading public got what it wanted in the way of literary exposures of
the Southern redneck way of life. A few exceptions like Marjorie Kinnan
Rawlings's *The Yearling* and Caroline Miller's *Lamb in His Bosom,* both Pulitzer-prize winners, could not stem the heavy assault on the redneck.

Many recent intellectual liberals from the South have told the same familiar story as they moved north toward new homes or settled into universities, foundations, or other hospitable Southern enclaves away from the redneck masses. Some of these bright, talented people come from the comfortable middle class, but almost all are kith and kin of the rednecks, sometimes not even a generation removed from the pale rabble. Rednecks hang all over their family trees and redneck culture permeated their youthful environment. This seems to bother them a great deal, and many are compelled to write autobiographically of their stirring ascent up from knavery. Inevitably the redneck fares badly in such works, but the writers do very well indeed. They are spiritually cleansed by this kind of written confession to the world, and their writings usually sell well, especially if they describe enough rednecks and other weird Southerners. And finally, if this kind of autobiography is done with enough flair and ferocity, it can lead to quick acceptance into the official American intelligentsia, a real but nebulous group concentrated mainly in the Northeast. With such fabulous rewards within reach, it is no wonder that some Southern intellectuals repudiate the redneck with a fervor seldom matched by the most patrician figures on the Southern literary scene.

All these various critics, whether Southerners or outsiders, gang up on the redneck and mercilessly dissect him. He is undereducated; he talks funny in a bewildering variety of Southern accents, which feature double negatives, jumbled verb tenses, slurred and obsolete words, and all manner of other crimes against standard, television English. He is too physical in his approach to life; he sets too high a premium on athletic prowess and he gets into too many fights. He comes on too strong with women, and he may even scratch when he itches, wherever he or it might be. He eats too much coarse, greasy food like cornbread, grits, fried chicken, chicken-fried steak, and all manner of pork, everything from chops to a wide variety of barbecue. He even likes vegetables such as collard greens and turnip greens and string beans cooked in his beloved pork and, worst of all, he seems to infringe on the black monopoly in "soul food." He tends to drink too much whisky, and he spends too much time in tacky beer halls that play only country music and always on "high." He is noisy but inarticulate. He doesn't ski and has never seen a psychiatrist. He sometimes

smells bad, especially after an eight-hour shift or a hunting trip. He occasionally still repairs his car in the front yard, and he might even leave
the engine hanging from a branch of a china-berry tree for a while. His
presence may well depress the local real estate market. He is reactionary
but sometimes radical and thus politically unreliable. His women (not ladies) reflect many of the same traits, and besides, they chew gum vora-
ciously and wear plastic hair curlers in public. And his children act as if
they think they are just as good as anybody else.

Rednecks are known to have peculiar names. Males of the species go
by such designations as "Bubba," "Slick," "Ace," "Rusty," Melvin, Leroy,
Alvin, T.J., and L.W.; and sometimes grown men, even people in positions of great authority, run around calling themselves Bobby or Billy or
Jimmy and insisting that everyone else do the same. Females answer to
such names as Billy Jean, Lou Ann, Loretta, Ginny, Sue Ellen, Lawanda
Kay, Peggy Joe, LaBelle, Mavis, Flo, Rose, and sometimes in the welter
of Jodies, Bobbies, and Johnnies it is hard to tell whether the names are
masculine or feminine. But whatever the name or sex, you can be sure of
one thing: the redneck is, above all else, an incorrigible racist.

This modern critique of the redneck emphasizes style more than substance, but it has some validity. The redneck is a rather plain, direct fellow, and he certainly will fight, especially when pushed. This fighting spirit
often embarrasses the nation in normal times, but in wartime it is welcomed, and rednecks are among the first to enlist. One needs only to visit
the neat, quiet American military cemeteries that now dot the globe to
appreciate the depth of their commitment to a nation that so often scorns
them.

And the last, major charge against the redneck is certainly true; he is
and always has been a racist at heart. But who isn't and who wasn't? From
the first settlers in Virginia and Massachusetts to the founding fathers, from
every colony right on up through the modern America of affirmative action, the whole nation, North and South, black and white, remains powerfully influenced by concepts of race and tribe. This is an ancient story
in human history, perhaps mankind's original sin. Certainly ethnic hos-
tilities seethe and bubble more vigorously now in other areas of the world
like southeast Asia and the Indian subcontinent and Africa than in the

United States. Even Latin America, which was so often touted as an example to benighted North Americans, has upon closer examination been shown to have its own deep cleavages. And who can forget modern Germany's final solution of the race problem, or Indonesia's treatment of its Chinese minority, or China and Japan's longstanding attitude toward "foreign devils," or the endless Arab-Israeli struggle in the Middle East, or the persistent ethnic tensions within Great Britain and the Soviet Union? From the beginning of recorded history the family of man has warred upon itself with ethnic distinctions being the most convenient excuse for mayhem. Only in the most isolated, sanitized eddies of human development have these terrible furies lain dormant.

The Southern redneck fits into the general harsh history of mankind, but given the extreme ethnic mix of his historical environment, he has earned no special distinction as a racist. His record is about par for the rugged course. The redneck's main problem is that he has always been open and candid in his conviction that blacks were inferior to whites. Yet at the same time over the centuries he has blended his culture and his blood with blacks, and in many day-to-day, practical ways he understands blacks far better than his white detractors do. In a rough, earthy kind of way he may be less of a racist than those whites who denounce him so harshly.

The redneck's privileged, well-to-do critics preach truth and beauty, brotherhood and integration, but often they lead a very different private life. The scenario is all too familiar. The classic liberal male—the kind of guy who jogs all the way to his vasectomy—and his equally trendy wife surge out into the rotten world at dawn. They emerge from a luxury, high-rise apartment that stands in the heart of a great city but is totally removed from the real life of the urban masses, or more likely they drive into the inner city from a comfortable, sheltered suburb. On the way to work they drop off their precious children at a properly sanitized private or parochial school—not lily white, of course, but ivory white with only a few token middle-class black students. Then they speed on downtown past several rundown public schools swarming with the great unwashed black and white and brown masses. These committed crusaders hardly notice; they have a busy day ahead, including afternoon conferences with reform groups dedicated to eradicating America's many ills, especially racism. Then finally

the workday ends and they quickly return to their ivory-tower apartment
or, more likely, to their safe suburb, which is just about as meaningfully
integrated as their children's school.

The redneck and black masses, the spearhead of the great crusade for
integration, can only stand and watch this spectacle, wonder at the moral
and verbal contortions of their betters, and then return to their thankless
task of making America actually function. The ordinary black may get a
little recognition for his efforts; however, the redneck gets nothing but
more criticism. Both are shunned until the nation gets into a war and needs
sturdy manpower to hurl into the slaughter, but the redneck alone has assumed the title of national scapegoat.

Yet in recent years a few voices have sounded in his defense. The shrill,
abrasive challenge of George C. Wallace of Alabama stirred strong working-class support far beyond the borders of Dixie. In nearby Georgia obscure Jimmy Carter even proclaimed himself a redneck, but only long
enough to get elected governor, the first step in his drive to the presidency. A few books such as Paul Hemphill's *The Good Ole Boys* and William Price Fox's *Southern Fried Plus Six* presented the redneck in
sympathetic terms and sold only moderately well, but Hemphill's later
work, an autobiographical novel entitled *Long Gone,* has been more warmly
received.

Even the grand moguls of television and the movies have eased up a
bit on the redneck recently, as Jack Temple Kirby demonstrated in *Media-
Made Dixie.* Stock-car racers like Richard Petty of North Carolina have
roared out of the dirt roads of the rural South right into national television
hookups, and country and western music has made a similar great leap forward from the Grand Ole Opry to prime time. Fiery redneck baseball players like Dizzy Dean of Arkansas and Ty Cobb of Georgia and Enos
"Country" Slaughter of North Carolina were popular long before television, and more restrained contemporaries still stand out. Popular redneck
wrestlers such as Virgil Reynolds (known professionally as "Dusty Rhodes,
The American Dream") draw large, heavily integrated audiences and score
high on television ratings as well. The national ritual of Sunday afternoon
and Monday evening professional football games has been dominated by
rednecks and blacks for years. Paul "Bear" Bryant, who acquired his nick-

name back in rural Arkansas in his tender teens when he wrestled a car-
nival bear, emerged as the dean of the Saturday afternoon fraternity of
college football coaches. Television producers were only too happy to allow the nation to watch his powerful, well-integrated Alabama Crimson
Tide roll forward in its annual pilgrimage for the national title (God, Notre
Dame, and Southern Cal willing, but not necessarily in that order). And
now his clones coach football at every level in every section of the nation.

A few television and movie dramas have been downright friendly to
the redneck, following in the tradition of Jean Renior's *The Southerner.*
The Walton family on television won a large national following picturing
the sturdy, almost noble hill-country yeomanry in Virginia during the
Depression. Even the redneck sheriff emerged a hero in two popular *Walking Tall* films about Tennessee lawman Buford Pusser. Even more popular
and profitable were a series of fast-paced, humorous adventure films set in
the Deep South and featuring Burt Reynolds, a West Palm Beach jock out
of Florida State University. He plays a special kind of redneck, the "Good
Ole Boy." Rough around the edges and wild in general, much addicted to
the traditional temptations of cigarettes and whiskey and wild, wild
women, he is nevertheless a true friend and at heart a decent and even
heroic fellow. In each film Reynolds plays this basically good guy who raises
all kinds of hell but finally frustrates the forces of evil, hollering and
laughing all the way to final victory.

These kinds of lively, glandular testimonials for the redneck make
American intellectuals very uncomfortable, especially in the staid Northeastern establishment. But even in that hostile territory, one voice speaks
out forcefully and realistically for the beleaguered redneck and other disadvantaged or despised Americans. Psychiatrist Robert Coles examines
such men, women, and children closely and even writes sympathetically
of *The Middle Americans.* Somehow he survives in the elitist academic atmosphere of Harvard, possibly by staying on the road most of the time.

But all of these sympathetic voices are only a whisper in the traditional
chorus of criticism and ridicule directed at the redneck. The hostile tide
has slowed a bit, but it has not turned. Most Americans, especially the
highly educated minority, still regard the redneck as a national embarrassment, the lyncher and the Klansman, the rural ruffian and the blue-

collar bully, the ham-handed cop, the general American *Untermensch*—all of whom are made in Dixie.

In truth the redneck is a representative American whose main faults hardly remove him from the national mainstream. Howard Zinn's *The Southern Mystique* took this essentially negative approach, contending that the modern South is only a slight magnification of the whole nation, which is racist, violent, hypocritical, xenophobic, conservative, and generally in need of reform from the romantic Left. More conservative citizens who have not yet soured on the traditional American way of life can take a more positive approach and still find the redneck in the national mainstream. In terms of bedrock fundamentals the average redneck acts very like the average American. He works hard at a regular job, supports a nuclear family, belongs to a church and a few other accredited organizations like a local P.T.A. or Moose Lodge, pays his taxes when he has to, obeys most laws most of the time, votes fairly regularly, and serves in the armed forces when necessary. Overall he is a pretty decent fellow as Americans go, with more virtues and fewer vices than advertised.

But the American people are not quite ready for this last hard truth: the redneck is not only a representative Southerner but also a representative American. The term *redneck* grows increasingly awkward and unacceptable as scholars, bureaucrats, and assorted other experts cram all Americans into rigid, antiseptic classifications like middle class or lower-middle class. Underneath all this sterile verbiage the good ole redneck stands tall and firm, too deeply rooted in the fertile Southern past to be ever completely eradicated.

Back in the formative, late antebellum period, long before the word came into general usage, the real redneck was much more visible. He made up the vast majority of the white population, not just as a class or as a state of mind but as an actual state of being. This silent, almost invisible majority won the title "redneck" by hard labor. Rednecks toiled in the fields year after year and acquired calloused hands, hard muscles, and endurance. Where exposed to the blazing sun, the skin became tanned and leathery; where protected by clothing, it remained pale. The back of the neck was especially exposed, and it soon reddened and chapped under the assault of the elements. This red neck became a symbol or badge for the ordinary dirt farmer who was the backbone of Southern society.

At the top of the agricultural scale, a few agrarians held sufficient land, slaves, and other resources to become "aristocrats." This privileged handful retreated from the fields to managerial responsibilities. Their hands got smoother and their muscles softened and their exposed skin got paler. A larger group achieved more moderate success with hundreds of acres of land and some slaves—perhaps as many as twenty or thirty or even more—but most of these well-to-do planters remained close to the soil that nourished them, and they retained the ruddy, hardy appearance of the great masses of Southern farmers.

The yeoman farmer was the average man, and the family farm was the most common social, cultural, and economic setting in the Old South. These redneck farmers owned their own land and cultivated their own crops with only the aid of their families and perhaps an occasional hired hand during the busy seasons. A few increased their land and other assets enough to justify the acquisition of slaves. This usually meant that the white farm family owned a rather similar black family; but occasionally the redneck acquired up to fifteen or twenty slaves.

At the other end of the redneck spectrum, a few fell into "poor white" and "poor white trash" categories. These two groups were far from the same; indeed, the unwary observer could get into real trouble by not knowing the difference between these tough, sensitive people at the bottom of the white heap. Sympathetically described in J. Wayne Flynt's *Dixie's Forgotten People,* poor whites simply lacked economic resources, but they lived in a land of great white mobility and might surge ahead at any time. On the other hand, poor white trash lacked more than just money; this small minority was the exception that proved the cardinal rules of Southern society: white equality and black inferiority. Though probably more the victims of strong germs than weak genes, poor white trash were looked down upon by blacks and whites alike and considered hopelessly deficient in character as well as resources. Many ridiculed and denounced them, but seldom to their faces, for their pride distilled into meanness and they could be very dangerous people to cross. Even when combined, the poor and the trashy were relatively few in number, but they bore a bewilderingly large number of nicknames like "tackey," "peckerwood," "sandhiller," and "cracker" among fellow whites and "buckra" among the blacks.

This sort of partly playful and partly serious slang has always confused visitors to the South, but in the antebellum period the various types of lower-class whites lay only on the periphery of the huge redneck majority. The great mass of rednecks were proud, independent, landowning farmers, the basic folk of the land. They began at the very beginning in 1607 as a handful of Englishmen who struggled to survive along the coast of Virginia. They almost faded away like Raleigh's Carolina settlement a few years earlier and like the much-earlier Viking probes of the newfound land called Vinland. But these first redneck Englishmen hung on tenaciously. Like their Celtic and Anglo-Saxon and Danish and Norman ancestors who over the centuries came to England for precious land, now they came to America for land. They were mostly poor agrarians, often dispossessed farmers, and before them lay rich soil that seemed to stretch on forever beyond the western horizon. There lay the promise of a bright future for themselves and for their posterity, so they moved inland slowly but relentlessly.

Before the birth of Christ their distant ancestors had roamed the Eurasian heartland as a jumble of tribes of farmers and herdsmen warring for the best land. Gradually they had gathered their strength as the mighty Roman Empire slowly crumbled, and finally early in the Christian era they had flooded into Western Europe to sink roots deep into the fertile soil. The same thing happened along the coast of Virginia and the Carolinas and later Georgia; the rednecks gradually gathered their strength and drove westward against the increasingly vulnerable Indians. This was a great people's struggle for supremacy and not really a matter of laws and treaties and abstract morality. The stoical Indians understood this much better than many modern historians, and they fought back ferociously and gallantly— and hopelessly. Western Europe had surged ahead of the rest of the world as the modern age dawned, and her people were politically, technologically, and militarily superior to the natives of the lands and continents they invaded. The redneck, Europe's cutting edge in the emerging colonial South, finally prevailed over the red man, but only after many pitched battles and even more skirmishes and individual clashes all along the fluid frontier. Casualties were staggering with diseases carrying off far more people than hostile Indians, but the redneck kept coming, reinforced by wave after wave of hopeful new immigrants.

These people were fired with the promise of a new and better life in a new and better land, and nothing could dampen their optimism. Never before in human history had ordinary people had such opportunities, and they surged forward to seize them. The basic English stock continued to predominate in the redneck masses, but important new tribes added their blood to the mainstream. A trickle of French Calvinists came, and by the 1700s a much larger wave of stern Calvinists flooded in. The Presbyterian Scots-Irish originated in lowland Scotland where they struggled against fierce highlanders to the north and expansionistic Englishmen to the south. Then they moved to the Protestant enclave in Northern Ireland where they warred against the Irish Catholics along the border in a seemingly endless struggle. Then, again seeking a better life, they migrated massively to America. Some moved inland from the Northern ports where they first landed, but many filtered southward through the Shenandoah Valley into Virginia and the Carolinas. Almost instinctively they sought new land along the frontier and warred against the Indians. Tough and tenacious, they cut a bloody swath through the redman's country and left an indelible mark on the new nation they helped build.

Though not as numerous, many German immigrants also came into the South in the 1700s, and they blended quickly into the general redneck population. County officials in the rural courthouses of the colonial South showed the same impatience with clumsy "foreign" names that immigration officials later demonstrated at Ellis Island; many had trouble enough properly recording good English names in the county archives, and they had no intention of wrestling with a bunch of outlandish new names. The German newcomers were plain, practical people who had come to stay in the new land, so they usually allowed their names to be quickly Anglicized. Only where they settled together in large numbers did the old ways and old language survive for long.

By the end of the colonial period a rich new genetic mix had evolved in the South. The basic English stock had been supplemented by French, Scots-Irish, German, and other European immigrants and by some other Americans with Indian or African ancestors in their mixed heritage. Peoples who had lived in virtual isolation for centuries, especially in remote villages and districts in Europe, and had interbred generation after generation among the same limited population, were suddenly transported across the sea and sprinkled in among large numbers of "outsiders" or "foreigners." The resultant interbreeding over several generations created a new people with a complex new gene pool drawn from three continents. Perhaps this new genetic mix reached a critical stage and unleashed powerful new folk energies. Certainly this new hybrid redneck became an integral part of the general American population in the new nation. Grady McWhiney's *Cracker Culture: Celtic Ways in the Old South* described these Southerners as predominantly "Celtic" and hence separate from the antebellum American mainstream, but this nebulous concept, not entirely new, is no more useful than describing Germans in the 1930s as principally "Nordic" or "Aryan." In reality Southerners were part of the American "old stock." In the broadest possible context, they were the WASPs or "Anglo-Saxons" and very much part of the confident mass movement of Americans westward to conquer a continent.

The great continent yielded only grudgingly, but by the end of the colonial era redneck pioneers like Daniel Boone had pierced the Appalachian Mountains and moved into dark and bloody and fertile lands such as Kentucky. The vast interior was only beginning to be penetrated by whites, but the Indians were already whipped; and the next century became a relentless mopping-up operation over the rest of the continent. The redneck spearheaded the westward surge in the South, though he was almost as obscure as his Indian enemies. He had come to the New World unheralded, often "in steerage" as a poor indentured servant obligated to serve another for years. Then he and his descendants had made their own way along the shadowy frontier and laid the foundations for a new, emerging nation. The same heroic story of ordinary people triumphing unfolded in the colonial North with the same basic set of characters. Puritan myths can be as persistent in the North as aristocratic myths in the South, but in reality the pioneer and frontier saga of colonial America unfolded similarly from New England to Georgia.

Slavery developed in all of the colonies, but only in the staple crop South did it really boom. This did not make the Southern redneck fundamentally different from the Northern farmer, for most rednecks owned no slaves at all. Rednecks believed strongly that blacks were inferior and properly belonged in a subordinate position. They were no more awed by the great slaveholders than Northerners were cowed by their own elites, but they preferred that planters own and control the black labor force to having to compete with and mix with a large, free black population—but only as long as the system gave the common white man a reasonable chance to rise to the limits of his ability.

North and south the system remained flexible; the white masses in colonial America had left forever the rigid, highly stratified societies of old Europe, and traditions of deferring to one's betters weakened steadily in the New World. Men who stood on their own two feet and cultivated their own land and felt in control of their own destiny lost the old habit of bowing and scraping and groveling. They might well still exhibit a rough kind of politeness or courtesy, especially in some of the more isolated areas of the South and West, but this was a far cry from traditional European deference. The colonial American farmer was no longer a European peasant; he was something new in the world, not someone to trifle with at all.

This proud, independent spirit permeated all of the colonies and led to the violent break with England. And of course the redneck fought as he always had, this time not for his land but for his country. No famous statue symbolizes the sturdy rednecks who fought under Southerners like Washington and Northerners like Nathaniel Greene and foreigners like LaFayette through the long Revolutionary War. The most appropriate statue available would be the sturdy, defiant Minute Man standing in Massachusetts where the shooting started. In blood and spirit he was almost the redneck's twin, and together they made a revolution that still shakes the world.

The new United States won its independence on the battlefield but found no permanent peace. In 1812 it clashed again with the British, successfully reasserted its freedom by fighting the world's most powerful nation to a draw, crushed Britain's Indian allies in the process, and capped off the whole affair with an almost unbelievable victory at New Orleans. The unceasing *drang nach Westen* accelerated rapidly, and in the 1840s Mexico was decisively defeated and partially dismembered. The old Northeast was somewhat disaffected in both of these wars, but many ordinary Yankees, the sons and grandsons of the Minute Men, fought side

by side with rednecks who naturally flocked to the colors when the shooting started.

But the redneck's finest hour as a fighting man came during the great
crusade for Southern independence, the most famous of many American
lost causes. Neither the Northern nor Southern masses wanted war, but
when the cannons roared at Fort Sumter, both rushed to enlist. Huge new
armies of blue and gray formed overnight, and the slaughter soon began.
In the early stages of the war German General Helmuth von Moltke, a
visiting expert who would soon lead his army to victory over France, may
not have been too far off the mark when he described the opposing armies
as "two armed mobs chasing each other around the country, from which
nothing could be learned." But both sides learned quickly, producing a
whole generation of lethal American military experts. Soon these amateur armies became the world's most efficient killing machines as modern,
total war came to America.

The new Confederacy labored under many severe handicaps. Its railroad and industrial development, though considerable, could not compete over time with the massive Northern industrial complex. Southern
whites were outnumbered better than three to one by Northern whites from
the start, and then the slave masses grew increasingly restive as the war
continued. Slavery itself frustrated the kind of foreign alliance that had
saved the American Revolution. The rebels had no real navy or merchant
marine when the war started, and Confederate political leadership lacked
the skill and flair needed to win against long odds. Yet the Confederacy
hung on for four years, shielded by powerful Confederate armies. A few
brilliant generals evened the odds a little, but the power of the rebel armed
forces was based primarily on the flesh and blood and spirit of the redneck
masses—not just the soldiers themselves, but also their women back home.

These plain white women on the home front lived all over the rural
countryside, and they held on determinedly while their men fought far
away. Burdened with the entire responsibility of the farm as well as the
family, fearful of slave unrest, dreading each new casualty list from the
front, they grimly supported the rebel war effort. The problems and complaints of upper-class Southern women have been rather well preserved in
letters, diaries, and reminiscences, but the majority of redneck women

carried their burdens silently. Most could write a crude, phonetic English, but not much of their correspondence survives, only the letters that soldiers managed to save in the field and some written complaints to public officials. Bell I. Wiley's *The Plain People of the Confederacy* demonstrated just how desperate the situation could become at home. Some women begged their men to come back to help with the harvest or sick and hungry children or other sudden crises, and such pleas caused many redneck soldiers to go home to their families, then in many cases to return to the front when the home emergency had passed. The desertion and A.W.O.L. rate in the Confederate army climbed rapidly as the war continued; in U. S. military history it was surpassed only by the Union army during the same war.

But most letters to soldiers from their women at home were much more positive and encouraging. They discussed weather and crops and bills and other business matters without emphasizing problems and analyzed family affairs and local gossip in great detail, often with considerable humor. Though seldom articulated eloquently, concepts like duty and honor and country still shine through the faded pages; the redneck often understood patriotism better than the elite. Eventually the enemy's relentless war of attrition destroyed the Confederacy, and many redneck women who had borne up under privation for so long then had to live out unnatural lives as widows and spinsters. They became the embittered old-maid aunts stuck away in back rooms and the pale, bone-weary mothers struggling to raise four or five children alone. Often haunted by a fading old photograph of a proud Johnny Reb in his best uniform, they remembered the war in a special way, with a bleak fury, and it was usually they who taught younger generations of Southerners to say "Yankee" with a snarl.

Thousands and thousands of their menfolk at the front paid an even greater price. More died of dysentery, common communicable diseases, gangrene, and infection than actually fell in battle, but by the end of the war 260,000 of them were gone forever. The Yankee enemy suffered similar staggering losses, which constituted a larger number of men but a much smaller percentage of the total white population. As Charles P. Roland's *The Confederacy* concluded, the redneck masses suffered stupendous casualties, and finally they paid the highest price of all: they lost.

But the redneck fought well and occasionally during this dismal war, especially in the mighty Lee's Army of Northern Virginia, the Confederate G.I. was touched with a special fire. The cavalry usually had an edge on the enemy in the early stages of the war, and Jeb Stuart's boys—mostly rednecks, not aristocrats—occasionally pulled off dramatic coups like riding completely around the huge Union army in the Peninsula campaign of 1862. The artillery was usually outgunned by the enemy, but it too on occasion performed brilliantly, rushing mobile batteries forward to blast a hole in strong defenses or digging in and mowing down wave after wave of attacking Yankees.

But the main body—and heart and soul—of Lee's lethal army was his redneck infantry. Not as well fed or clothed or equipped as the enemy and always outnumbered, it fought ferociously, and sometimes, when the confusion of battle sorted out properly and luck ran with the gray, Lee's rednecks won stunning victories with their favorite tactic—a head-on infantry assault. American soldiers have always fought best on the offensive, and the Confederates were no exception; they were, after all, as American as their opponents. Densely packed ranks of attacking rebel infantrymen had to absorb heavy rifle and cannon fire from the defenders and, as Grady McWhiney and Perry D. Jamieson stressed in *Attack and Die: Civil War Military Tactics and the Southern Heritage,* even the most successful of these assaults often incurred heavy losses. But the physical and psychological impact of such an attack often devastated the defenders; when done right, one of these vicious surges could break the spirit of a whole army and gain a spectacular victory.

The headlong élan of the redneck infantry peaked during the battle of Chancellorsville in the spring of 1863. A huge Union army of 130,000 seasoned troops moved south from Washington and was intercepted by Lee's army near Fredericksburg, only fifty miles from the rebel capital at Richmond. Only 60,000 Confederate troops barred the way, but Lee, the dignified, aristocratic Virginian with the instincts of a riverboat gambler, unleashed a daring attack. Holding off the blue behemoth with only a thin redneck line in the center, he dispatched "Stonewall" Jackson and 30,000 infantrymen to slash at the exposed Union right flank.

This daring attack had to be executed properly, and Jackson was the man for the job. The son of ordinary yeoman stock from the mountains of far western Virginia, a graduate of West Point, and a veteran of the Mexican War, Jackson was teaching at the Virginia Military Institute when the war started. The eccentric professor, called "Tom Fool" by students, immediately joined the rebel army and rose fast, becoming Lee's right arm in a series of bloody battles. Jackson drove his men relentlessly, and his area of any battlefield quickly became the main killing ground. This dour Presbyterian wielded the terrible, swift sword of the Lord; since the martyrdom of John Brown the North had no match for this grim, awful Southern Puritan, a throwback to Cromwell and his Roundheads. Jackson got the best from his rednecks, many of whom were touched by the same Calvinistic determination to win or die as God willed it. They marched and fought hard and fell in droves for this committed Christian soldier of the South.

Jackson did not expect to survive the war, but as he moved his troops into position for the climactic assault at Chancellorsville, he could not have known that this would be his last battle, that he would fall at the moment of his greatest triumph. His men were finally ready late in the afternoon on 2 May. Then suddenly they surged out of the woods in headlong attack, preceded by the blood-curdling rebel yell.

This shrill, prolonged cry came with every Confederate attack. The elite Virginia historian Douglas Southall Freeman, author of *R. E. Lee* and *Lee's Lieutenants,* speculated that it was derived from the yell of upper-class fox hunters riding down upon their prey. More likely, it came from the redneck masses, a down-home hog call or coon- or possum-hunting cry or a frontier battle cry answering the Indians' high-pitched challenge or a good ole boy's scream of joy during a tavern brawl.

Whatever its origin, the rebel yell flashed ahead of the gray waves of redneck infantry at Chancellorsville as they rolled out of the woods and crashed into the Union right flank like a tidal wave. Many of the Union defenders were sturdy Germans fighting for their new country, but they had no chance this day: the redneck infantry shattered General Leopold Von Gilda's brigade, plowed into the rest of General Charles Devens's division, and then rolled up the divisions of General Carl Schurz and General Adolph Von Steinwehr, leaving the whole Eleventh Corps a shambles. The grandsons and great-grandsons of these Johnny Rebs would shatter many another German division in distant lands across the sea, but Chan-cellorsville was the redneck soldier's finest hour. His headlong attack crumbled the whole Union right flank, and after several more days of fighting the Union army reeled away, beaten again by Lee's outnumbered veterans who could not surround and annihilate such a huge force.

After consulting with President Davis, Lee launched an invasion of the North, determined to "conquer a peace" in the enemy's heartland. His reinforced army of 75,000 men presented a singular appearance as it trekked northward. Uniforms and equipment varied widely, and clothing was often tattered and sometimes more civilian than military. But a closer look re-vealed more: lean, hard bodies and clean, well-oiled weapons and a fight-ing spirit that blazed like a torch.

Never have American soldiers marched into battle more confidently, and never were the stakes higher for the whole American people. Un-opposed, the rebel troops moved in good order through the Pennsylvania countryside, though many Northern hogs and cattle were killed in self-defense (and then eaten). These Johnny Rebs were not the "peasant sol-diers" so dear to the heart of every European leader seeking solid cannon fodder for his next military adventure. Rather, they were Southern red-necks, independent farmers with every bit as much at stake in their new nation as the enemy had in the old Union. Many of these rebel agrarians commented expertly on the rich Pennsylvania countryside, but one un-gallantly evaluated the Pennsylvania "Dutch" women as the ugliest he had ever seen.

Then, suddenly, the gray Army of Northern Virginia and the blue Army of the Potomac collided at Gettysburg; the holiday was over and the killing began again. This time the confusion of battle did not sort out properly for the rebels and luck ran with the blue. At the same time that the rebel bastion on the Mississippi at Vicksburg fell, Lee had a bad few days in Pennsylvania, and the Union army he had so often beaten finally began to find its head and its heart. Lee attacked, of course, but without Jackson he could not score a decisive breakthrough. Two days of heavy fighting left the battlefield strewn with blue and gray dead, and Lee was stymied. Rejecting more cautious advice, he once again decided upon a daring maneuver. Once again he called on his redneck shock troops for the kind of audacious headlong attack that had won so dramatically at earlier battles like Chancellorsville.

He marshaled Pickett's fresh division of Virginians, reinforced it with North Carolina, Mississippi, and Tennessee units, and then hurled the entire 15,000-man force straight into the center of the Union entrenchments. First massed rebel artillery pounded the Union defenses on Cemetery Ridge for over an hour, and then the redneck infantry swept forward, as cocky as ever. Michael Shaara's novel, *The Killer Angels,* best captured the human drama of this historic moment when the future of a continent hung in the balance as the gray waves rolled slowly over almost a mile of open ground. Union artillery opened up almost at once, tearing great holes in the rebel lines. The rednecks closed their ranks and kept coming. Then they came within range of the waiting lines of blue riflemen who poured in devastating volleys. And finally the Union artillery began to fire canister point-blank, like huge shotguns.

The rebel lines were torn to shreds, but a handful of survivors bunched for one last surge and, following the order of General Lewis Armistead, "Virginians, With me! With me!," they raised their battle cry and crashed into the Union defense. No more than a hundred made it, and they were quickly shot down by the defenders. Armistead died in the arms of a young Union officer, asking to see his old friend from the prewar army, General Winfield Scott Hancock, the commander of the Union defenders.

Pickett's charge was the beginning of the end for the Confederacy, but the war dragged on for almost two more years. Lee's defeated army retreated safely back into Virginia, but never again did it roll forward in a major offensive. Forced into an unwelcomed and almost un-American defensive strategy, the redneck infantry dug in and fought tooth and nail, inflicting huge casualties on the attacking Yankees. But the tide had clearly turned, and it was only a matter of time.

Battlefield attrition steadily thinned the gray ranks, which could not be replenished, while the Army of the Potomac grew steadily stronger, easily replacing its heavy losses. Now commanded by the able Grant, it ground ahead steadily but not flawlessly. During the spring offensive of 1864 he rashly hurled a full-scale infantry assault at powerful Confederate defenses at Cold Harbor. It was Pickett's charge all over again—another headlong American attack—but this time wave after wave of blue troops were torn to shreds in brave but hopeless attempts to penetrate rebel defenses. In less than an hour almost 7,000 Union soldiers fell as the assault disintegrated. But it no longer mattered; the Confederacy was crumbling, the home front ravaged by inflation and shortages and the army bled white in battle. Yet the redneck soldiers fought on and on, still confident they could somehow win.

Strangely the North that was winning seemed no more confident than the South that was losing; both sides were infected with innate American optimism. Only the rashest scholar would attempt to analyze the complex mind of the North; but it may well be, as Michael C. C. Adams proposed in *Our Masters the Rebels: A Speculation on Union Military Failure in the East,* that many Northerners, especially generals like Hooker at Chancellorsville, were overawed by the legend of Southern martial superiority; that Northeasterners especially had an inferiority complex about waging war against the South and its vaunted military tradition; and that this negative attitude hampered Union military operations. Adams and his former professor, Marcus Cunliffe, in *Soldiers and Civilians: The Martial Spirit in America* were certainly correct to reject the whole legend of the unique martial prowess of the antebellum South. Bell I. Wiley's *The Life of Billy Yank* and *The Life of Johnny Reb* showed just how similar the opposing troops were in the Civil War. They were all Americans, occasionally close friends like Armistead and Hancock, and most of their differences were no more profound than the color of their uniforms. Even "the Negro question" did not divide them as much as many thought. Northerners and Southerners fought equally well, especially on the offensive. Both had moments of great triumph, like Chancellorsville for the rebels and Vicksburg and Gettysburg for the Yankees, and both suffered stunning defeats and reversals. They spoke the same language and worshiped the same God. Both came from democratic, freedom-loving societies and had great difficulty adjusting to military discipline, though David Donald in *Why the North Won the Civil War* concluded that it was such a problem in the rebel army and nation that the Confederacy actually "Died of Democracy." Basically the Rebs and Yanks shared the same pragmatic worldview and the same free life-style. In comparison with most other great wars of modern times, the bloody struggle in America in the 1860s was truly a *civil war,* the nation's greatest tragedy. And when the tumult finally ceased, the weary combatants emerged from the chaos of battle with one significant difference: the Northerners had won and the Southerners had lost.

Despite the clear verdict of the battlefield, the legend of the uniquely martial South and the uniquely belligerent redneck persisted. This latter image had been strengthened by antebellum Southern humorists like Augustus Baldwin Longstreet, whose *Georgia Scenes* in 1835 sketched his rustic neighbors in all kinds of wild and woolly escapades. Joseph G. Baldwin (author of *Flush Times of Alabama and Mississippi*), William Tappan Thompson, who moved from Ohio to Georgia, Johnson Jones Hooper of North Carolina and Alabama, and others followed. Yet one of the most dramatic pen portraits appeared in Daniel R. Hundley's *Social Relations in Our Southern States,* which tried on the eve of the Civil War to explain the South to a puzzled North.

Hundley was born into the planter elite in Alabama, and he quickly developed into an authentic snob, a special subcategory within the Southern aristocracy. Study at the University of Virginia and Harvard refined his snobbism, and marriage into a wealthy family gave him plenty of leisure time to write about lesser breeds of antebellum Southerners while he lived in, of all places, Chicago! A straitlaced, teetotaling gentleman, he disdainfully described a special kind of rough-and-ready Southerner:

> There is in most of the Southern states a species of Bully—a swearing, tobacco-chewing, brandy drinking Bully whose chief delight is to hang about the doors of village groggeries and tavern taprooms, to fight chicken cocks, to play Old Sledge, or pitch-and-toss, chuck-a-luck, and the like, as well as to encourage dog-fights, and occasionally to get up a little rawhead-and-bloody-bones affair on his own account. This is the Southern Bully *par excellence,* for in all the world else his exact counterpart is no where to be found. Ay and a valiant Southerner is he too! . . . The Southern Bully at all times feel[s] able and prepared—cocked and primed, in his own vernacular—to flog the entire North; with his tongue, that is, and very conveniently while the poor North has her back turned. Thunder and bludgeons! how he'd like to get at 'em, the crazy old mild-sops! Split the Union? By all means, let her rip, the cussed old concern! Yankees fight! Blamnation, man, we'd lam'em afore they could say Jack Rob-

inson—we'd put 'em through a course of sprouts in short order, so we would! . . .

And, *imprimis*, he is not necessarily always poor. Sometimes he boasts of extensive estates, though not often, and then chiefly when he is young; for as he grows old, his wealth seems to take wings and fly away, so rapidly is it squandered. But as a general thing he is poor. . . .

The poor Southern Bully, in nine cases out of ten, is a loafing ex-overseer, whose drunken dissolute habits have lost him his situation, as well as the character that would enable him to produce another. When not an ex-overseer, he is either a disgraced dry-goods clerk, a bankrupt groggery-keeper who has poured all his liquors down his own throat, or else the quondam rich Bully in the era of his decline. The poor Bully's dress is usually loose-fitting, dirty, tobacco-stained, liquor-stained, and grease-stained. His hat is woolen, with a limp, flapping brim, battered crown, dirty and fuzzy, and on the whole might be called a shocking bad hat. His hair is habitually matted and unkempt, being in most instances of the Saxon peculiarity, that is, either red, or flaxen, or carroty-colored, or sandy. His beard is coarse and unkempt like his hair, and grows in great luxuriance all over his face, or else in ragged patches here and there, intended to represent imperials, mustaches, "literary dabs," and the like precious ornaments of the civilized man. His breath is foul with all diabolical scents—rum, filth, tobacco—just such a breath as you can inhale any day in any police-court the world over, and which once inhaled, you will ever more pray that it shall not come betwixt you and the wind again. But his speech is fouler than his breath. He can out-swear a special policeman; can out-lie a Toombs lawyer; can use more obscene language than the vilest pimp who ever laid snares to entrap lecherous countrymen. . . . It is wonderful, indeed, what a gift of gab the fellow possesses; what a multitude of strange and agglomerated oaths he can interlard his discourse with, and how he manages to survive the constant damnings he is ever heaping upon every hair upon his head, and every bone in his body. . . . Oh! to see him at a chicken-fight—where there are gamecocks in the pit, and the bets range from one to five dollars . . . the swearing and profanity he can give utterance to—perfectly sublime, so wholly is it beyond the conception of less depraved and more scrupulous minds! But if to see him at a cock-fight is glorious, to see him looking on at a dog-fight—bull-dogs, with cropped ears, stump tails, bow legs, and most villainous chops—is more glorious still, while most glorious of all, grandest of all, most inspiring of all, is, to witness the conduct of the Southern Bully, as he stands outside the imaginary ring in which is being waged a bloody *man-fight!* O thou soul-stirring spectacle! Hip, hip, hurrah! See, with what a gentlemanly grace Jones bungs up Smith's peepers! See, with what a sweet smile Smith plucks away half of Jones's yellow beard! How comfortable must have been the "left" which Jones let fly into Smith's breadbasket! How refreshing to the sight the claret fountain so unceremoniously started from Jones' mug by the noble Smith! Hurrah for Jones! Hurrah for Smith! Go in Boys! Let 'er rip! Never say die! Hit 'im agin! Dam—! Y-a-a-a-a-ou! Ugh-h-h! O-o-o-o-oh! And the glorious work is done!

This sort of boozy brawler did exist in the Old South, but as even the supercilious Hundley conceded, he was only a tiny fraction of the redneck population, more visible than representative. In New England the Boston Brahman, a special subcategory within the Northern aristocracy who bore a strong resemblance to the Southern snob, spoke similarly of a creature who inhabited his region: a fellow of the Celtic rather than the Saxon peculiarity; a stereotyped loud, drunken, brawling Irish Catholic who already threatened the Yankees' traditional domination. Moreover, well-bred Easterners who moved west made similar complaints about some of the crude transients who raised so much hell along the frontier.

In truth, the whole nation harbored a highly visible minority of marginal men with a taste for violence. John Hope Franklin's *The Militant South* isolated and examined some of these wild Americans, and a similar work on the antebellum North, using the same carefully selected evidence, would prove the same point. Actually the whole nation was a new land, free and undisciplined, where all white men were created equal and titles of nobility were unconstitutional. Diverse immigrants poured in as the raw frontier moved rapidly west. Such a fluid, restless society inevitably generated tremendous energy, including violence, which was part of the price Americans paid for their experiment in modern living.

Rednecks were very much a part of this American experiment. From day to day they lived much like most Americans; they were full-fledged citizens. They worked their own farms in a rural environment where land was still relatively plentiful and cheap. They paid a very low annual property tax on land, and some also paid a similar tax on a few slaves. They voted, served on juries, and occasionally became involved in court litigation, which usually involved disputes over property or debts. Sometimes they transacted business important enough to record in a formal deed—almost always the purchase of land or other property.

County officials duly recorded these activities, so rednecks left a faint but true trail during their lifetimes. And when they died, they left one final testament for posterity. Most wrote wills in which they tended to first look after their wives and eventually to divide everything equally among their children, the boys and girls (or their husbands) sharing equally. Whether they left wills or not, their estates at the time of death were thoroughly inventoried by county officials; every bit of personal property was listed and evaluated, providing posterity with a detailed outline of the deceased's way of life. Finally, from 1790 on the federal government every tenth year duly recorded census information, which by 1850 had become rather detailed. But generally the federal and even the state government seldom directly intruded into the life of the ordinary redneck—until 1861!

The first extensive use of these various county and federal records came in 1949 with Frank L. Owsley's *Plain Folk of the Old South.* Some of his students continued to work on these grassroots records, and a few computer-armed historians have shown interest in the real redneck recently. On the whole, however, these plain folk have not attracted much attention even though more of their letters, diaries, and journals are also beginning to surface, and surviving antebellum newspapers contain much information on them too. Yet these people were the very flesh and blood of the Old South and one of the major elements in the conglomerate population of antebellum America; their story contains the essence of America's past.

These ordinary rednecks worked hard in the traditional rhythm of the farmer. The blazing heat of the summer did not stop them; they could not retreat before the sun's assault if they wanted to bring in a good crop. Apparently unaware of the conventional wisdom (and defense of slavery), which declared that only blacks could work efficiently in the hot Southern climate, they labored away in the fields. Even the minority of rednecks who acquired a few slaves remained in the fields where their muscle was still needed. Side by side they worked, master and slave, Saxon and Ibo, "redneck 'n nigger," and over the generations, from the Atlantic to the Rio Grande, they learned the same lessons of the soil.

Most rednecks had only themselves and their families as a work force. Their crops fluctuated with soil and climate, but they always raised most of their own food. Analyzed in detail in Sam Bowers Hilliard's *Hog Meat and Hoecake: Food Supply in the Old South*, the redneck diet lacked balance by modern standards, and vitamin deficiencies sometimes caused problems like pellagra, but by the standards of the mid-nineteenth century most Southerners ate very well. They consumed large amounts of sweet potatoes, turnips (roots and tops), and field or cow peas. Easy to prepare and preserve, highly nutritious and usually called simply "potato," the sweet potato served field workers well. Turnips and peas and other vegetables like collards and cabbage were boiled for hours in a pot with bacon, and the highly nutritious "pot-likker" at the bottom was soaked up in corn bread and consumed too.

In one form or another, corn was the main staple of the Southern diet. Almost everyone, rich and poor, relished corn bread or one of its variations like corn dodgers, hoecake, corn muffins, and egg bread. It was also boiled on the cob and cut off the cob and creamed and roasted in the shuck. Many soaked the corn grains to remove the husk and then boiled them to make hominy or went further and ground up the dried hominy and then boiled the meal to make grits. Borrowed from the Indians, corn grew almost everywhere in the South and was a very efficient foodstuff, good "roughage" with plenty of energy for working men but by itself low in protein and vitamins. Combined with pork, it was the basic subsistence for generations of ordinary Southerners.

Americans generally consumed large amounts of meat, often startling Europeans, but Southerners and Westerners concentrated on hogs. Hardy animals that could fend for themselves in the Southern environment, hogs could also be penned and fed corn, peanuts, or sweet potatoes (vine and root). Southerners consumed pork in many different ways. Even chitterlings (the small intestines) were eaten and often considered a delicacy, and spicy barbecues were popular too. Pork was a high-energy food and a good protein source when not too fat, but it was not easy to digest and made up too much of the diet of too many people. Rednecks raised and ate much less beef and mutton but did consume a lot of poultry, especially in the form of traditional fried chicken. They also consumed much wild game, especially turkeys, ducks, squirrels, rabbits, and opossums (roasted with sweet potatoes) and seafood, especially oysters from salt water and from every river catfish (rolled in corn meal and fried). Often supplemented with eggs, milk, and other dairy products along with fruits and other vegetables in season, the rednecks' diet, though not nutritionally ideal, fueled a thriving, rapidly increasing population. Most planters ate basically the same food with only a few noticeable luxuries. Indeed, the difference between what the masses and the elite ate was probably less apparent in the South than in the North. By the standards of the time, the redneck ate quite well.

Most rednecks raised more than just subsistence crops, and the more ambitious put considerable effort into money crops, especially cotton. They set aside some of their best land for this market crop, and in bad years they could fall back on their subsistence crops and wait out hard times. The redneck's family farm was flexible and resilient, and it often rode out recessions and wars better than the well-organized but delicately tuned plantation. Far from always being pushed off good land by expanding plantations, the redneck rooted in deeply and sometimes picked up some of the pieces when a large plantation disintegrated.

Efficient rednecks often gradually expanded their agricultural operations, buying new land to put into cotton and then taking the profits from the harvests to buy more land. This kind of jerky, onward-and-upward process of gradually increasing land and then slaveholdings allowed a steady trickle of rednecks to move on up into the exalted ranks of the planters. The line between prosperous redneck and small planter was so blurred and was crossed so often that upward mobility by the fittest rednecks was taken for granted by contemporaries but often overlooked by historians.

Rednecks and planters and American farmers in general rapidly depleted their land in an age only beginning to appreciate scientific farming, so they often moved on to fresh, fertile soil. The redneck was quite mobile, driven mainly by the reality of a huge land just waiting for the plow but perhaps also faintly by an innate wanderlust that had been stifled for centuries in crowded old Europe. Certainly county records document the mobility of rednecks who were appropriate ancestors for today's Americans on wheels.

Sometimes as a single family and sometimes in a larger group of kinsmen, coreligionists, or friends, rednecks shifted across the land, often in a westward drift but sometimes erratically like waterbugs on the surface of a pond. Samuel Davis moved from Georgia to Kentucky, where his son Jefferson was born, and then swung back south into Mississippi. Thomas Lincoln moved from Virginia into Kentucky, where his son Abraham was born (within a hundred miles and eight months of Jeff Davis), and then drifted north into Indiana and Illinois. All around them other rednecks moved across the land, restlessly and optimistically seeking a better life beyond the horizon.

Wherever he settled, the redneck farmed with his family in one close-knit group. The children learned to do chores early, but the wife carried far greater responsibilities. Like the planter's lady, she was closely bound up with her husband's business, which operated at home, not in a remote office or factory. She cooked and sewed and washed and cleaned and bore and raised a large flock of children, around five on the average and often ten or twelve or more. She usually had to help bury some of them too in an age of primitive medical science and hit-or-miss folk remedies.

She also played a major role in the family's social and intellectual life, which often (but not always) centered in a local church. Rednecks belonged to almost every conceivable Protestant church, but the Baptists and Methodists probably best represented those independent, individualistic rednecks who had been born again in Christ and thus became God's chosen people. This profound emotional experience did not always take permanently, but as long as it lasted it generated a self-confidence and self-esteem that made the haughtiest aristocrats look like shrinking violets. Most rednecks were not so sweepingly saved and elevated, but they remained steady, respectable churchgoers with no inclination to defer to anyone. They found their own God in their own Bible, and if they came to disagree with their current congregation of friends and neighbors, they could always depart and find or found a more congenial congregation.

Rednecks read their own Bibles though their education was usually quite limited—perhaps a few months a year for a few years in their youth. No real public school systems functioned on a statewide basis, but rednecks understood the need for literacy in the fluid, competitive environment; so when given half a chance, they mastered the basics though not the refinements of "reading, 'riting, 'n' 'rithmetic" at an "old field

school" or "academy" somewhere in the neighborhood. The family Bible
and an accompanying commentary volume might be about the only
books in many homes, but newspapers of the proper political persua-
sion were also popular as were almanacs and practical how-to-do-it
manuals and farm journals.

The exact literacy rate remains obscure, but the U.S. census estimate
in 1850 of eighty percent literacy among the adult white population was
a little optimistic; seventy percent would be a better guess. Certainly the
literacy rate fell considerably in backwoods and frontier regions where some
rednecks still lived on the eve of the Civil War. Newer areas of the American West had the same problem, but the more settled, urban Northeast
had almost eliminated illiteracy. Southern county records include some
wills and deeds signed with the illiterate's traditional "X" (his mark) and
others initialed rather than fully signed. These latter documents can be
misleading because some literate Southerners, like modern executives,
initialed rather than signed important papers on occasion. The grassroots
picture remains statistically imprecise, but clearly on the broader world
scene the redneck's educational level soared. The great mass of mid-nine-
teenth-century mankind remained mired in illiteracy and ignorance, even
in many areas of Europe, and "advanced" nations such as Britain and
France still tolerated systems that kept from a third to almost a half of their
citizens illiterate and disadvantaged.

Rednecks also lived far more comfortably than the overwhelming majority of mankind, even in Europe, and just as well as their fellow citizens
in the North and West. Along the raw frontier a crude hut or even a simple lean-to might be home for a while, but the great majority of rednecks
lived in sturdy homes. Some were expanded log cabins, strong from the
beginning and finally comfortable and sometimes even a little fancy. A
favorite kind of dwelling was two well-built cabins sharing the same roof
with an open "dog trot" between for ventilation in the summertime, and
some rather fine antebellum homes still standing today can be "peeled
back" to a small original log cabin built to last with virgin pine. Most antebellum homes were sturdy but plain frame houses, usually one story with
a considerable attic but sometimes a full two stories with a lower attic.
Often altered and expanded and seldom painted, they were quite func-

tional for fast-growing families but not valuable or permanent enough to keep an ambitious man from moving on to better opportunities elsewhere.

Rednecks centered their lives around family and community. A provincial folk, they could not afford to travel widely on vacations, so they found relaxation and recreation near home. Social visits included lengthy conversations and elaborate story and joke telling, which entertained young and old alike. Quilting bees and corn huskings mixed work and play, and much harder tasks such as clearing fields and building barns were sometimes community projects too. Music and dancing were popular, though "hardshell" churches frowned on such frivolity. The young folks spent considerable time in casual or serious courting, though the straitlaced environment restrained these activities somewhat, at least in broad daylight. Births and deaths and marriages brought kinship groups together to share food and fellowship as well as joy or sorrow. Court days at the county seat attracted large crowds to witness legal proceedings that decided old property disputes and sometimes generated juicy gossip too. Market days were not just business as whole families often came to town along with the money crops. Similarly, camp meetings and revivals added a further dimension to religious life.

Even the hardest-working rednecks found some time for sports. Horseback riding was not a monopoly of the elite, and hunting and fishing appealed to every class and color. Contests of strength and speed and skill attracted crowds, especially if local champions competed. Marksmanship with firearms, especially rifles, won much acclaim. Wrestling and fighting matches were also popular. They occasionally did get out of hand and degenerate into the kind of crude brawls the fastidious Hundley described with such repugnance, but more often they ended with victor and vanquished shaking hands and going off friends again. These matches and horseraces and dog fights and cockfights encouraged intense gambling, which was also an integral part of many popular card games.

A favorite diversion was the game of politics, which had been thoroughly democratized by the late antebellum period. As in the North, the professional politician might wheel and deal and pull off occasional coups, and the wealthy might exercise disproportionate influence, but in the long run even the most complex political formulas broke down into one simple equation: one white adult male equals one vote. Ralph A. Wooster's two studies of Southern officeholders in the 1850s, *The People in Power* and *Politicians, Planters and Plain Folk,* concluded that in the final analysis the voting power of the redneck masses was decisive. Furthermore, Fletcher M. Green's *Constitutional Development in the South Atlantic States* demonstrated that even in the more conservative states such as the Carolinas democracy had triumphed. Any politician who ignored this basic reality soon faded away. If anything approaching real hegemony could possibly exist in the whirl and tumult of Southern politics, the rednecks, not the elite, ultimately held the reins of power.

As in the North, ordinary folks held a good number of elective offices, especially on the local level, but they also held many seats in the state legislatures. The most important elective office was the state governorship; this election brought out more voters than any other. Significantly, on the eve of the Civil War half of the state governors—Joseph E. Brown of Georgia, J. J. Pettus of Mississippi, Beriah Magoffin of Kentucky, Isham G. Harris of Tennessee, John Letcher of Virginia, and old Sam Houston of Texas—were basically middle-class types, sprung from the masses, not the elite, and several others were barely planters and far from the real elite.

Most rednecks never held political office, but they followed politics closely and voted massively. Though usually literate, rednecks were a highly verbal people; they appreciated conversation and rhetoric. They greatly enjoyed the pageantry and ritual of antebellum politics: all-day barbecues and rallies, candidates who so expertly "pressed the flesh" and backslapped and chatted with their friends and neighbors, and especially lengthy speeches and debates accompanied by the whooping and hollering of partisan audiences.

The voters were mainly pragmatic, not ideological, more wedded to a candidate or perhaps a party than a platform. They had seen enough politics to know that great leaders (politicians who kept getting elected) swam with the current, changing policies to suit shifting public moods. Campaign rhetoric might passionately present "we versus them" themes and denounce another class or region or religion in the fiercest terms, but the South was a land of constant electioneering and the voters had heard it all before. They understood that politicians had the same license as poets and that after all the dust had settled, elected officials remained well within the mainstream of a broad political consensus. Politicians who clashed bitterly in elections remained the best of private friends; parties shifted principles overnight, remaining consistently devoted only to victory. It was all great fun and games for a hard-working people who needed recreation—until 1860!

Individualistic rednecks did not clump together in one disciplined, class-conscious party; Southern society was too fluid and flexible for that. Local needs and aspirations often dominated, splitting the redneck masses in a dozen different ways. The "hillbilly" farmers of northern Georgia, eastern Tennessee, the western Carolinas, and western Virginia had different concerns from the Piedmont farmers, scattered all through the huge cotton belt, who in turn differed from the farmer-fishermen of the Tidewater regions. Livestock herders and drovers, drifters along the western frontier, landless rural day laborers, urban workers who were sometimes Irish-Catholic immigrants, the rising class of "linthead" industrial workers, and other smaller groups of rednecks had even more varying perspectives. Rednecks were a diverse mass of people who could not be herded along or taken for granted by any politician.

Sometimes great issues arose that captured the attention of the masses for a while, and candidates did spin elaborate defenses of slavery, state sovereignty, Southern rights, and other eternal truths accepted by all major political factions, but antebellum voters seldom paid as much attention to such weighty matters as recent scholars have. Often voters simply tried to elect the best man. This led to all kinds of whoopla and demagoguery, but it also led to the rise to power of some very good men.

Even in the final antebellum crisis when the voters of the South sent delegates to state conventions to decide whether to secede from the Union or not, few candidates were unqualified secessionists or Unionists. Most stood somewhere between these extremes, not totally committed to any simple action in the mad rush of events. The voters accepted this flexibility or expedience and often elected the man they considered best qualified to handle such a terrible responsibility. Under differing circumstances and by varying margins these democratically elected delegates voted to carry almost all of the Southern states out of the Union. However, not even the most sophisticated computer techniques can work back to the initial elections and construct a neat ideological or political portrait of the diverse redneck masses who both participated in and enjoyed Southern politics.

Overall the rednecks had a pretty good life. Most led a decent, middle-class existence with a living standard that soared above the world average, but visitors with preconceptions about the slave South often refused to recognize the obvious. New England agriculturalist Frederick Law Olmsted traveled through the South early in the 1850s, published his impressions in a series of letters in the *New York Times* in 1853, 1854, and 1857, and in the late 1850s reworked his material into *A Journey in the Seaboard Slave States* and two other books. These books pictured the South as lazy and debased, and many scholars have cited them as gospel ever since. Only recently, with the publication of the second volume of the Olmsted Papers in 1981 by the Johns Hopkins University Press, has the unreliableness of these three books been revealed. *The Cotton Kingdom,* a fourth work compiled in 1861 with the obvious intent of discrediting the Confederacy, has never been taken very seriously by sophisticated scholars, but now Olmsted's earlier three gospels have been challenged too. The Kansas-Nebraska controversy of 1854 turned Olmsted passionately against the South, and his subsequent books reflected this prejudice by the omission of some material favorable to the South and the addition of some strong criticism not found in the earlier published letters. Unfortunately his original pre-1854 notebooks have disappeared, so his most open-minded observations will never be known, but in his books he simply refused to recognize the great mass of well-off rednecks in the middle between the elite and poor white minorities.

Rednecks lived as well as the Northern masses, but life had a darker side too. Medical science was still in its infancy, so the planter's wealth gave him no real advantage as diseases cut a wide swath through the whole population. Infants and children died frequently, and parents could usually do no more than watch them waste away. Childbirth threatened mother as well as infant. Nobody understood contraception, and the babies just kept coming, often one every second year. Mothers loved their children, but each pregnancy was like a new game of Russian roulette; and as Anne F. Scott's *The Southern Lady* illustrated, some women came to dread new pregnancies. Overall the odds were favorable, but even minor complications could be fatal.

Even when childhood diseases did not kill, they sometimes left survivors scarred or crippled. Epidemics of cholera and typhoid fever hit urban areas the hardest, and the warm Southern climate made yellow fever and malaria dangerous everywhere. The rural masses were more likely to be weakened by hookworm or killed by milk sickness, caused by drinking milk from cows that had eaten the white snakeroot. Common colds, pneumonia, tuberculosis, dysentery, and various undiagnosed diseases swept through the land, and venereal diseases also appeared. Some of the poor whites who seemed so lazy were more likely the victims of one or more of these debilitating sicknesses.

Even the healthiest rednecks might sometimes find rural life a little monotonous and dreary, and some developed psychological problems. Alcoholism claimed many victims, and nervous disorders surfaced too. Though probably more mentally stable than modern Americans—or perhaps simply less conscious of their "hang-ups"—rednecks could get quite "uptight." Violence flared sporadically all across the land. In the home wife beating occurred sometimes, but as with child and slave beating, it was a recognized right of the master of the house and would have to become openly excessive to draw community reaction. Divorces rarely occurred because they were frowned upon by society and also expensive and difficult to obtain. Still, simple separations and desertions occurred fairly often, and it is at least conceivable that some of the volunteers who trooped off eagerly to fight the Yankees in 1861 were partially motivated by a desire to escape from a nagging wife and half a dozen bawling brats.

Rednecks faced all of the personal problems that have always gone along with being human. Some in the slaveholding areas were also occasionally distracted by rumors of slave insurrections, but this occurred infrequently, much less frequently than many historians estimate. Even in the extremely rare cases when an insurrection did erupt, it was quickly crushed. The most remarkable thing of all was how quickly the turbulence subsided and the rednecks returned to their normal lives. The rhythm of life on the land could soothe as well as bore the redneck masses.

Overall, rednecks were ordinary Americans with ordinary concerns. The first American immigrants, they remained one of the nation's largest population pools, one of the taproots of antebellum America, and significantly, they were the seedbed from which sprang two of the nation's greatest leaders, Andrew Jackson and Abraham Lincoln.

Jackson was the son of a Scots-Irish immigrant family that settled in a frontier area of the Carolinas so obscure that the two states still haggle over his birthplace. His father died at age twenty-nine, and his two soldier brothers and patriot mother were just three more obscure rebel casualties in the Revolutionary War. Barely a teenager, Jackson served the rebels as a messenger in the bloody backcountry and received an ugly sword slash on his head when he refused to clean a British officer's boots—a score he would more than settle in the next war with the hated redcoats. Tall, slender, sandy-haired and tempestuous, Jackson was alone in the world at age fourteen. He had received only the most haphazard kind of schooling, and he never fully mastered the arts of spelling and grammar. He was extremely bright, though, so he went to Charleston and Salisbury, North Carolina, where he read a little law and raised a lot of hell. Fortunately the age of elaborate ratings and evaluations had not dawned, and young Jackson was able to satisfy two examining judges and officially become a lawyer in 1787. Then he moved west to new Tennessee, married well, and became a successful lawyer, land speculator, merchant, and planter—an instant frontier aristocrat with much land and more than a hundred slaves. He also killed a man in a duel and almost got killed in a brawl in a Nashville hotel. Most important, he rose rapidly in Tennessee's rough-and-tumble politics.

When the War of 1812 erupted, he held one of the juiciest political plums in the state as commanding general of the Tennessee militia. Officially the American state militias were ready for combat, but actually in 1812 (and again in 1861) they were paper tigers, woefully unprepared to campaign in the field. Yet, following orders from Washington, Jackson marched his Southern militiamen and volunteers deep into the Alabama wilderness and broke forever the power of the Creek Indians. Not yet recovered from injuries received in the brawl at the hotel, Jackson was still as tough as "Old Hickory," and somehow, by sheer force of character and charisma, he kept his hard-fighting but poorly disciplined rednecks going in a long, grueling campaign. Some, like good-old-boy Davy Crockett, drifted away, but Jackson kept a combat force in the field, and finally he received reinforcements that swelled his command to 2,000 men as the Creeks dug in at the Horseshoe Bend of the Tallapoosa River for a last stand. Jackson's men, including a wild young buck named Sam Houston, attacked and utterly defeated the smaller Creek force. Houston was one of the first to break through the Indian lines; he received a severe wound for his trouble, but like so many others who served under Jackson, he continued to idolize his commander through the rest of his own spectacular career in Texas.

A grateful American government, which had all too few victories to celebrate, commissioned Jackson a major general in the regular army and quickly gave him an even more difficult assignment. Barely recuperated from the lengthy Creek campaign, Jackson rushed southward to defend New Orleans against a massive British invasion. He arrived just ahead of the British armada, "tall, gaunt . . . very erect . . . sallow and unhealthy . . . thin and emaciated . . . [with a] bright and hawk-like eye" as one Louisiana lady described him. With him he had militia and volunteers from Tennessee, Kentucky, and the Mississippi Territory, and a few regular army units. Quickly he mobilized local reinforcements. Many Frenchmen rallied to take another crack at the old English foe, and plenty of local Anglo-Saxons joined them. A unit of free black militia volunteered, and Jackson also recruited Jean Lafitte's notorious pirates. He even had a band of Choctaw Indians among his troops. Hastily he organized his 5,000-man "army" and dug in south of New Orleans.

Never had a more "All-American" force taken the field and never had the chances of victory seemed slimmer as a British fleet and 10,000 troops, mostly veterans of the Napoleonic Wars, appeared under the command of the experienced General Sir Edward Pakenham, brother-in-law of the Duke of Wellington. After the Americans failed to wipe out the British beachhead and the British failed to blow the Americans out of their entrenchments with a heavy artillery barrage, the showdown came on 8 January 1815, two weeks after negotiators had tentatively agreed on peace at Ghent in Belgium.

At dawn the British unleashed a massive infantry assault. Wave after wave of redcoats rolled out of the mist, moving relentlessly toward the American entrenchments. Held firm by Jackson's iron will, the American defenders poured in withering artillery fire and then massed rifle and musket fire. Not even the most professional infantry could stand such punishment, and the British fell back with heavy losses. More than two thousand redcoats died and only thirteen Americans, mostly free blacks who left the entrenchments in their eagerness to close with the enemy. A motley but cocky force of rednecks and other ordinary Americans had whipped more than twice their own number of British regulars, supposedly the best soldiers in the world. The mystic drama of the Revolutionary War was reenacted. Once again a Southern planter, like Cincinnatus of old, left the land long enough to lead his people to victory; once again Americans put aside the plow long enough to smash elite enemy armies; once again the legendary American riflemen—Kentucky and Tennessee frontiersmen this time—played havoc with their deadly marksmanship. This time the story ended with a special flourish: General Pakenham's riddled corpse went back to England preserved in a hogshead of rum, and the victorious General Jackson headed for the White House.

One of the few truly great presidents, Andrew Jackson forged the Democratic party, the most powerful and persistent organization in the history of modern politics. Truly a man of the masses and for the masses, he firmly and permanently established the tradition of democracy (with a little "d"). He greatly enlarged the power and prestige of the office of the president, preparing the way for later presidents who had to act forcefully in time of emergency. A staunch nationalist, he preserved the Union from South Carolina's challenge in the 1830s, controlling his supposedly fiery temper and skillfully weaning his fellow Southerners away from the temptations of nullification and secession. When he retired in 1837, he left the nation far stronger and more confident; when he died in 1845, the whole nation mourned the passing of the man who became a symbol for a whole age in American history. He had blazed the trail for another son of the redneck masses who would hold the Union together in its hour of greatest peril.

Abraham Lincoln emerged from an even more humble, obscure Southern frontier environment than Jackson. Born a generation after "Old

Hickory," within a few months of Jefferson Davis, and on exactly the same day as Charles Darwin, Lincoln was truly a child of the raw redneck masses. Both his parents were Virginians by birth and independent, fatalistic Baptists by choice. Both were poor whites in a profound, melancholy sense. Probably illegitimate, Nancy Hanks could neither read nor write, and her ancestry faded quickly back into the obscure Southern past. Thomas Lincoln came from sturdier yeoman stock; the first Lincoln landed in Massachusetts in 1637, but within a century the family had drifted south into Virginia. The Lincolns were respectable farmers who seldom stayed put for long. Thomas drifted along the frontier most of his life and remained a ne'er-do-well, an indifferent carpenter and farmer who could barely scrawl his own name.

His son Abraham seemed destined for the same marginal existence. Off and on he accumulated perhaps a grand total of one year of formal education. When he was seven the Lincolns headed north into Indiana where, during the first winter, they lived in a crude three-sided hut that was really little more than a lean-to. His mother died of milk sickness when he was only nine, and though his father soon remarried, the Lincolns continued to live in backwoods poverty. Thomas Lincoln soon drifted into a rural area of central Illinois with many other Southern pioneers. Abraham grew into a tall, lean, rawboned, very bright young man not unlike young Andrew Jackson, but young Lincoln possessed extraordinarily great physical strength. Of all the American presidents in their prime, the only real competitor would have been George Washington, another tall, rawboned son of the South. Like his father, young Abraham drifted through an assortment of odd jobs, but then, like Jackson, he read law a while, passed a bar examination, and started practicing law and politics in earnest.

Lincoln's only military service involved noncombat duty in the Illinois militia during the brief Black Hawk War against nearby Indians. Lincoln later joked that he survived bloody struggles with mosquitoes and attacks on wild onion patches, a far cry from Jackson's deadly serious campaign against the Creeks in Alabama. With no martial glory as a boost, the relentlessly ambitious Lincoln had to be content with very slow political advancement.

At the age of thirty-three he married the vivacious, witty daughter of a prominent banker and slaveholder from his home state of Kentucky.

Working hard, he prospered as a lawyer and moved into the secure upper middle class of emerging Illinois. Progress came more slowly in politics, but he tirelessly worked his way up in the Whig and then the Republican party in the Midwest. A darkhorse candidate for the nomination of his party in 1860, he suddenly found himself being sworn in as president early in 1861 as the nation tore itself asunder.

Initially he overestimated Southern Unionism. He was not far off in judging his native Kentucky, which wavered uncertainly and even briefly declared itself neutral before splitting just like the Union. This left prominent men like Senator John J. Crittenden, the successor of Southern nationalist Henry Clay, with one son a general in gray and the other a general in blue. Lincoln underestimated the depth of disaffection in the Deep South, which had already seceded when he took office. Yet on a broader, deeper level he spoke the truth in his inaugural when he told his Southern "dissatisfied fellow-countrymen . . . who really love the Union" that "physically speaking, we can not separate. . . . We are not enemies, but friends. . . . The mystic chords of memory, stretching from every battlefield and patriot grave to every living heart and hearthstone all over this broad land, will yet swell the chorus of the Union, when again touched, as surely they will be, by the better angels of our nature."

In the short run he was wrong, for the Civil War erupted at Fort Sumter less than six weeks later, but ultimately he was right. Southerners could not really depart from the Union of their fathers: "mystic chords" actually did bind them to other Americans; try as they might, they could not even fight their way out. The Confederate experiment was predestined to fail, not in any scientific or rational sense, but in a mystical way that a fatalist like Lincoln instinctively understood and Southerners later came to understand and accept as they once again acknowledged the Americanness that had been bred into their very bone and marrow.

Lincoln preserved the Union from its greatest threat and tore slavery forever out of the fabric of American life with a peculiar combination of brute force and human understanding that perhaps could come only from a man who emerged from the redneck masses. Perhaps only a man from a stock that often seemed so hostile to blacks but in fact had become irretrievably entangled with blacks over the generations could be flexible and realistic enough to alter his own and others' misconceptions and prejudices in the heat of war. Lincoln grew in office as no other president, even Andrew Jackson, ever did, and in the process he expanded the power and prestige of the presidency even more than Jackson had.

How ironic that this scion of generations of Southerners should lead the crusade to crush the Confederacy and destroy its "peculiar institution." How strange that the wife of the president of the United States should lose three half brothers in the Confederate army and that her sister, the widow of a fallen rebel general, should find shelter in the circle of the Lincoln family at the White House in Washington. The polished and sophisticated European dignitaries who watched the great American struggle could probably appreciate such twists of fate; their own ancient cultures were full of tangled tragedies and ironies. But they could not really understand how the destiny of a great nation could rest in the hard, gnarled hands of a man like Lincoln. They simply could not comprehend how frontier rednecks could emerge as leaders of a nation they saw as little more than an extension of Mother Europe. Most simply could not see beneath the plain, rugged plebeian surface of an American like Lincoln. They also misunderstood and underestimated Andrew Jackson, another lanky, rough-hewn son of rednecks; but with Lincoln their condescension and contempt reached new lows as he was frequently and openly referred to as "the Baboon." A century later a North Carolina Israelite named Harry Golden explained the phenomenon of self-made Americans like Jackson and Lincoln quite succinctly in just the title of his book, *Only in America*, but the message still escapes many intellectuals, American as well as European.

Antebellum Southern boys could rise to great heights whether they stayed in the South like Jackson or moved North like Lincoln. All antebellum America was a land of great opportunity where white men could rise or fall rapidly through the porous layers of a flexible, fluid society. Southern rednecks were as free to seek their destiny as any other citizens of the new nation. They were the original American immigrants, the first founders of a new culture, which originated in old Europe but swiftly evolved into something quite new and even revolutionary. Over the generations rednecks remained in the American mainstream. They sent wave after wave of pioneer reinforcements to the bloody frontier as it moved west toward the Pacific Ocean, and they flocked to the colors when the new nation fought to be recognized in a hostile world and to be reborn in the cauldron of civil war. Yet through the tumult and violence of building a new nation in a new land, they remained basically farmers, an enduring folk who cultivated the land over a lifetime of hard labor and then slept forever in that fertile soil as their children carried on the old rhythm of life on the land. Mobile and optimistic, proud and freedom-loving, pragmatic and innovative, religious but materialistic, literate but provincial, democratic but racist, they were a diverse and individualistic people; above all, they were typically American. Perhaps, like Howard Zinn's modern Southerners, they were 110 percent Americans, and perhaps, ironically, this excess of old Americanism helped drive them into a war against their fellow citizens in the North who were evolving a little more rapidly. Certainly rednecks composed the largest single group in the antebellum South. They were not only the overwhelming majority of the white population but also the solid core of the great, broad bourgeoisie that dominated the antebellum Southern way of life.

ILLUSTRATIONS

Abraham Lincoln

The earliest-known likeness of Lincoln, taken in 1847 while he was serving a single congressional term in Washington.

The Reverend David Edward Butler
and his wife Jennie Walton Butler

A middle-class Baptist couple from Madison, Georgia, who visited New York City in the early 1850s and had a fine daguerreotype taken in the studio of Samuel Root on Broadway.

Private Edwin Francis Jennison

A Confederate soldier killed in action at the battle of Malvern Hill.

Sergeant Thomas Jefferson Rushin

*A Confederate soldier who was officially listed as missing in action after the battle An-
tietam.*

Taking the Oath and Drawing Rations

*John Rogers's statuette (1865), which dramatized the plight of many Southern women
after the Civil War.*

Confederate Prisoners of War

Winslow Homer's Prisoners from the Front, 1866.

John Letcher

Governor of Virginia from 1 January 1860 through 31 December 1863 and a representative member of the Southern middle class.

Cotton Mill Workers

Six employees of the John P. King Manufacturing Company who posed for photographer Lewis W. Hine at their home in Augusta, Georgia, in 1909.

Eagle Textile Mill in Columbus, 1851

One of the many modern, efficient industrial operations that developed in the South before the Civil War.

Lavinia and Nathaniel Francis

Part of the Southampton County bourgeoisie about a decade after Nat Turner's rebellion.

Lavinia Francis

One of the survivors of Nat Turner's rebellion who lived on in Southampton County until 1885.

Captain Nathaniel Thomas "Tinker" Francis

The second son of Nathaniel and Lavinia Francis, born only two years after Nat Turner's rebellion, was captured in one of the last battles in Virginia in 1865, and died in 1872, another middle-class Southern farmer.

The Nathaniel Francis House in 1978

The remains of the old Southampton County home, which at the time of Nat Turner's rebellion consisted of only the smaller section to the right (the larger addition to the left was added in 1837).

The Kappa Alpha Spring Party

The sons and daughters of the middle class at the University of Georgia around 1910.

Frederick Douglass

A portrait of the fugitive slave from Maryland done around 1845 when he first published his autobiography describing life in bondage.

John Brown

A slave in Virginia, North Carolina, Georgia, Louisiana, and Mississippi who became a free man in England and told his story in Slave Life in Georgia *(1855).*

A Slave Family in the Fields

A cotton field near Savannah photographed by Pierre Havens in the late 1850s or early 1860s.

A Slave Family in the Quarters

Five generations of one black family on a South Carolina plantation.

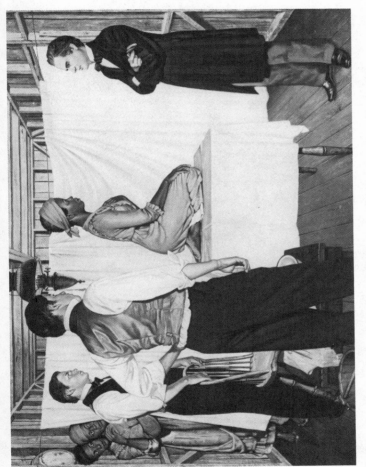

Doctor J. Marion Sims

The Alabama surgeon in 1845 preparing to begin a series of experimental operations on slave women.

Martin Luther King, Jr.

A son of the Southern black bourgeoisie at his birthplace on Auburn Avenue in Atlanta.

Inventory and Appraisement of an Estate in 1795

The property of Matthew Charles (deceased) of Southampton County, Virginia, with the valuations still calculated in pounds, shillings, and pence.

A Southampton County, Virginia, Indenture in 1800

A deed recorded at the courthouse describing the sale of approximately sixty acres of land for $475, a typical business transaction of the antebellum era.

ILLUSTRATIONS

Page 75: Courtesy of the Library of Congress.

Page 76: Courtesy of the Hargrett Rare Book and Manuscript Library, University of Georgia Libraries.

Page 77: Courtesy of the Library of Congress.

Page 78: Courtesy of the Georgia Department of Archives and History.

Page 79: Courtesy of the New-York Historical Society.

Page 80: Courtesy of the Metropolitan Museum of Art; gift of Mrs. Frank B. Porter, 1922. All rights reserved.

Page 81: Courtesy of the University of Alabama Press.

Page 82: Courtesy of the Hargrett Rare Book and Manuscript Library, University of Georgia Libraries.

Page 83: Courtesy of Reeves Brothers, Inc., Eagle and Phenix Division.

Page 84: Courtesy of Everette S. Francis, Richmond, Virginia.

Page 85: Photograph from William Sidney Drewry's *The Southampton Insurrection* (1900).

Page 86: Original image on glass restored in 1973 by Rem Studio, Athens, Georgia.

Page 87: Photograph by J. Dudley Woodard III, Courtland, Virginia.

Page 88: Courtesy of the Historic Costume and Textiles Collection, College of Home Economics, University of Georgia.

Page 89: Courtesy of the Picture Collection, The Branch Libraries, The New York Public Library.

Page 90: From the frontispiece of John Brown's *Slave Life in Georgia* (1855).

Page 91: Courtesy of the New-York Historical Society.

Page 92: Courtesy of the Library of Congress.

Page 93: Courtesy of Parke-Davis Division of Warner Lambert Company, © 1961.

Page 94: From Kenneth Coleman, *A History of Georgia* (Athens: University of Georgia Press, 1977; reprinted 1982) 373.

Page 95: Courtesy of the Virginia State Library, Richmond, Virginia.

Page 96: Courtesy of the Virginia State Library, Richmond, Virginia.

CHAPTER 3
THE BOURGEOISIE

The French have a word for it; indeed, given half a chance, they will provide a flood of eloquence to describe anything imaginable. But their word *bourgeoisie* has rooted deeply into the international vocabulary of educated people. For at least a century it has been pronounced with a sneer, especially in France itself, and that attitude has spread to the American intelligentsia. Many of America's cultural elite lead very bourgeois private lives—comfortable, centrally heated and cooled homes complete with all the trimmings, including hefty mortgages, carefully planned families, steady incomes, rational investment and retirement portfolios, and every allowable tax deduction—but publicly they heap abuse on the middle class, the great majority of Americans. Sometimes this is just a programmed Marxian response, but usually it is intellectual window dressing, the "thing to do" for those who have risen above the crude, materialistic masses and want to be sure everyone knows it.

Privately living a bourgeois life-style while publicly condemning it is at best a tad schizophrenic. Ordinary middle-class Americans might even consider it hypocritical, but what do they know? They have not logged in half a decade or more in a prestigious graduate school, stifled in dusty libraries and numbed in endless seminars. They ended their formal educations short of total fulfillment and quickly went to work for a living, and somewhere along the way they may even have bolstered the bourgeois-capitalistic system by serving in the nation's armed forces.

The controversial middle class has been the bedrock of American society for a long time, but its roots go back much further in the history of mankind. An active middle class emerged in the ancient Roman world. This great empire with its dynamic cities, sophisticated culture, legions of slaves, and marvels of organization and engineering finally decayed and fell before the barbarian invasions of the third and fourth centuries. A long period of adjustment followed, the so-called Dark Ages, with only bits and pieces of the classical age surviving in the feudal world to flourish again at the dawn of modern times.

By the twelfth century town life began to revive all over Western Europe, and in these scattered urban pockets the modern bourgeoisie steadily developed. The French word is clear enough; they were townsmen, merchants, and artisans concentrated in centers of renewed economic activity. They were indeed in the middle between the peasant masses on the land and the tiny feudal hierarchy. Full of confidence, they increased rapidly in numbers and influence, playing a significant role in Western Europe during the dynamic period of the Renaissance and the Reformation.

Europe surged out into the rest of the world, conquering and colonizing. The citizens of powerful new European nation-states carried their vigorous cultures with them when they ventured overseas, especially the English who came to North America not just to trade and explore but to settle in great numbers and to multiply rapidly. Most English settlers came from the lower classes, but sturdy middle-class folk joined the great migration, not just to New England but also to the South. More important, the emerging middle-class system, which was transported from England, developed into something unique in America, a land of opportunity literally made to order for bourgeois democracy. Poor colonists seized every chance to better themselves, almost overnight acquiring a restless, confident kind of New World ambition.

Women as well as men found more opportunities in the dynamic English colonies. Traditional old-world restrictions on their activities relaxed a little, and that was enough to propel some women into the business world, which was developing rapidly in the Southern as well as the Northern colonies. As Julia Cherry Spruill's *Women's Life and Work in the Southern Colonies* demonstrated, some Southern women operated farms and plantations and shops and stores and even a few newspapers, and others served as teachers and nurses. In most cases they carried on businesses begun by husbands or kinsmen, but occasionally they launched their own careers.

Even an Indian woman could rise in the fluid Southern economy, but she had to be an exceptional person like Coosaponakeesa, whose dramatic story is overdramatized in Dee Brown's novel *Creek Mary's Blood*. Born to a white trader and a Creek woman around 1700 in Indian country west of Charleston, she grew up knowing both red and white ways. In 1716 she became known as Mary Musgrove when she married a white trader from South Carolina named John Musgrove. Together they established a trading post on the Savannah River near the sea, and they prospered as middle persons in the flourishing trade between whites and Indians. When James Oglethorpe planted the colony of Georgia there in 1733 by establishing the town of Savannah, Mary Musgrove served the colonists first as an interpreter and then over the years as a diplomat who helped maintain friendly relations with the Indians.

After the death of her first husband, she married another white trader, Jacob Matthews, and they too prospered. By the 1740s they were pressing Georgia officials for proper compensation for her many years of service to the colony. Matthews died before this long dispute was settled, and in 1744 Mary married Thomas Bosomworth, an Anglican minister on the make. They operated a profitable trading post in the interior of growing Georgia and pushed her compensation claim vigorously. Finally in 1760 they received considerable cash and the entire coastal island of St. Catherine's, later a playground for millionaires. Here Mary Musgrove Matthews Bosomworth lived her last years, comfortably entrenched in the evolving middle class of early Georgia.

Able white male colonists had an easier time getting ahead in America. The original town orientation of the bourgeoisie continued as shopkeepers and craftsmen of all kinds populated growing towns and cities, especially in the North, but soon the burgeoning American middle class became predominantly rural, especially in the South. The colonial farmer did not remain a peasant in the European tradition. Even in England the yeoman farmer was encumbered by many traditional obligations and restrictions, but in America with its huge reservoir of "dirt cheap" land the farmer became his own man, securely ensconced in the middle echelons of society. A hardworking, poor man—even the humblest indentured servant—could eventually accumulate hundreds of acres of productive land and perhaps a few slaves too. He would feel little real pressure from the remote colonial government or the lax county authorities. Such a fellow could not be suppressed in the wide open spaces of British North America.

Not that it wasn't tried, especially in Maryland and the sprawling Carolina country. The haughty lords who owned proprietary Carolina commissioned the noted political scientist John Locke to draw up a constitution establishing a good, old-fashioned feudal system in the New World, but his plan was an immediate flop. No such scheme to turn back the clock could work in dynamic America, so far from its old-world roots. British control withered down at the grassroots level where the average colonial labored on the land; and when the home government tried to tighten up imperial administration in the 1763-1775 period, colonial opposition flared quickly and culminated in the Revolutionary War. Independence accelerated America's forward surge, and by the time of Andrew Jackson's presidency the United States was clearly the world's most exuberant bourgeois democracy.

This was as true in the South as in the North, though emphases and nuances varied a little between the sections. Even as late as the 1850s both sections remained mainly agricultural, but urbanization was progressing much more rapidly in the North, especially the Northeast. Still, a few significant cities flourished in the South, especially along its border with the North and along the seacoasts. Urban centers like Baltimore, Richmond, Charleston, Savannah, Mobile, New Orleans, Louisville, and St. Louis profitably mixed commercial and industrial activities with all manner of other capitalistic enterprises.

But Southern bourgeois life showed even more clearly in the smaller cities sprinkled across the agrarian South, mostly in the interior areas served by the rapidly expanding railroads. David R. Goldfield's *Urban Growth in the Age of Sectionalism* examined five such developing cities in Virginia—

Norfolk, Alexandria, Lynchburg, Petersburg, and Wheeling—as well as mighty Richmond and concluded that the Old South generally and many planters in particular supported this kind of urban-industrial expansion. All over the nation, North and South, cities expanded and slipped more and more into a national economy dominated by New York City; if there was an antebellum commercial culprit, a middle man who wrung disproportionate profits from the real producers, it was New York City, which increasingly dominated not just the Southern but the entire national economy. According to Goldfield, by the 1850s the six Virginia cities that were a part of this national network of cities had developed "an economic superstructure, an active civic elite, extensive urban and commercial services and an identity as a modern city."

The same thing happened in Georgia where old Savannah and Augusta faced rising competition from the thriving new cities of Macon, Columbus, and Atlanta. On a lesser scale the same thing happened in more thoroughly rural areas where small cities like Memphis, Nashville, Wilmington, Galveston, and Lexington (Kentucky) stimulated the general economy. And down even closer to the grassroots level where local records can best be interpreted, the same kind of bourgeois capitalism flourished in hundreds of towns on the make, places like Jacksonville in north Florida, Thomasville in south Georgia, Selma in central Alabama, Charlotte in Piedmont North Carolina, Knoxville in eastern Tennessee, Paducah in western Kentucky, Vicksburg on the Mississippi River, and Little Rock in the middle of Arkansas. Even smaller county seats and tiny rural trading centers showed traces of the same enthusiastic urban spirit that had emerged clearly by the 1850s, long before the vaunted "New South" of the post–Civil War era.

These widely varying urban pockets in the rural South harbored significant numbers of traditional bourgeois types. Shopkeepers, merchants, and proprietors, including some women, specialized in all manner of goods like jewelry, clothing, hardware, and groceries and services like livery stables, saloons, and hotels. Factors and commission merchants bought and sold for planters and other clients. Bankers operated aggressively while most doctors and lawyers projected a slightly more restrained image. Some artisans and craftsmen ran one-man operations while others directed the labors of other skilled workers, and some ambitious men became full-fledged industrialists. Brokers, shippers, insurers, wholesalers, warehousemen, building contractors, and other businessmen reinforced every urban environment.

Newspaper editors often ran rather small, personalized operations, and they could be found in virtually every town of any importance. Often they directed the selling of advertising space and subscriptions and then later supervised collecting the amounts due on these credit transactions. Whether large or small, their journals reflected the lively commercial atmosphere of the times by running on the front page many advertisements trumpeting good deals, everything from new shipments of choice goods to marvelous patent medicines. With a little "audio-visual" adjustment, these commercial messages would fit right into prime-time television; perhaps Tylenol, Geritol, and some of the other miracles of modern medicine are not so distant from "Linch's Anti-Rheumatic Powders" and even "Helmbold's Genuine Preparation of Highly Concentrated Compound Fluid Extract Buchu. . . . For Diseases of the Bladder, Kidneys, Gravel, Dropsy, Weaknesses, Obstructions, Secret Diseases, Female Complaints, and all Diseases of the Sexual Organs. . . . Joy to the Afflicted!!! . . . Infallible Remedy."

Finally, a colorful entrepreneurial type emerged in the rural as well as the urban South, a kind of jack-of-all-trades wheeler-dealer with a finger in every available economic pie. These small-time capitalists operated off and on, here and there, wherever the main chance beckoned and, although they publicly lamented that their generosity was driving them to the brink of bankruptcy, in private conversations with "good buddies" they would often allow as how they were doing "jes fine." They could move north or west and compete on equal terms with the wiliest Yankee trader, and they could hunker down and survive the hardest of times at home. Like their modern descendants, they often concealed sharp practices beneath easy-going, good-ole-boy mannerisms as they bought, sold, bartered, or rented (and occasionally borrowed without permission) everything from houses and land to horses and even black people.

Slavery did not really inhibit bourgeois capitalism in the South. After all, slaves were essentially private property, commercial items routinely figured into calculations of profit and loss. Of course, blacks were people too, but in the final analysis, on the bottom line of every ledger, they were primarily property. Even refined slaveholders had an "out of sight, out of mind" attitude and gave little thought to the personal lives of the masses of black workers in the fields. As long as the slaves behaved and produced, they seemed almost invisible and at the same time clearly inferior. Even trusted house servants seemed to fade into the woodwork at times. A perfunctory "howdy to the servants" in a letter often represented the extent of a master's personal commitment to his "people." Conscious brutality was not the central theme of Southern slavery, but neither was paternalism; profit was the key to the Southern system, free and slave.

Southern law struggled with the concept of blacks as both property and people. Most of the time the courts simply treated slaves as property, but occasionally, in extreme circumstances, slaves briefly became human beings, and the law punished whites for mistreating blacks. Boynton Merrill, Jr.'s *Jefferson's Nephews: A Frontier Tragedy* examined local records in Kentucky to recreate the vicious murder of a slave that led to the indictment of two wellborn whites (one committed suicide and the other escaped to end the affair). However, generally the law stressed the chattel nature of slaves, and only in rare, even bizarre circumstances were whites punished for abusing their slave property.

This negative attitude toward slaves was inevitable in a white society totally committed to the concept of black inferiority. Racism permeated antebellum society all over America. Studies such as Leon F. Litwack's *North of Slavery: The Negro in the Free States* have shown clearly that even in the North and West where few blacks lived and where antislavery sentiment evolved, whites shared what James A. Rawley in *Race and Politics: Bleeding Kansas and the Coming of the Civil War* called a "Caucasian consensus" on black inferiority. The academic community, analyzed in William Stanton's *The Leopard's Spots: Scientific Attitudes toward Race in America, 1815-1859*, reinforced popular prejudice. Even the new Republican party, which mushroomed in the North in the late 1850s with its tough antislavery message, still conceded that blacks should remain subordinate to whites. As Winthrop Jordan's *White over Black* demonstrated, racism was embedded deep in the white psyche, and no political party dared challenge this part of the American creed.

Southerners shared this prejudice with other white Americans; in fact, in a section where blacks were numerous and sometimes more than half of the population, white racism even intensified—at least in some ways. Southerners went to the extreme of defending slavery, an institution Northerners increasingly rejected. As Carl N. Degler's *The Other South* has shown, a handful of whites, usually committed Christians, did attack slavery in one way or another, but the overwhelming masses of whites, Christians and unbelievers, poor and rich, were willing to use force to defend their "peculiar institution."

Yet at the same time Southern whites blithely lived in close proximity to blacks—cheek by jowl and sometimes belly to belly. Visitors to the slave South always commented on these phenomena: the numerous mulattoes, a black mammy suckling a white infant (and occasionally a white woman suckling a black baby), public places like markets and train stations literally crawling with hordes of blacks and whites all jumbled together, everyone talking rapidly and seeming to head off in all directions at the same time, a virtual bedlam of temporary mixing. This massive integration at the grassroots level startled many visitors and put off some, especially austere reformers who loved mankind in the abstract but had little use for people in the flesh; but Southerners of every hue took for granted these practices, which had gone on ever since the slave system evolved two centuries earlier.

This system, based on the all-American values of race and profit, kept blacks down relentlessly, but it did not destroy white democracy in the South. If anything, it even intensified what George M. Fredrickson in his *The Black Image in the White Mind* described as "Herrenvolk democracy." Few places on earth offered adult white men more freedom and equality than the American South. Edmund S. Morgan's *American Freedom–American Slavery* may be partially correct in its complex description of the concurrent development of white freedom and black slavery in colonial Virginia, since clearly by the late antebellum period a middle-class democracy of whites rested firmly on a mudsill of black slaves all over the South. The great Jefferson fixed the intellectual keystone when he proclaimed "that all men are created equal," but, of course, he meant whites only as he grudgingly conceded in 1785 in his only book, *Notes on the State of Virginia.* Generations later the planners of his magnificent memorial building in the nation's capital reached into his *Notes* and other writings to mold a composite quotation worthy to be emblazoned on one wall of the structure:

> God who gave us life gave us liberty. Can the liberties of a nation be secure when we have removed a conviction that these liberties are the gift of God? Indeed I tremble for my country when I reflect that God is just, that his justice cannot sleep forever. Commerce between master and slave is despotism. Nothing is more certainly written in the book of fate than that these people are to be free. . . .

But, alas, in tidying up Mister Jefferson for the twentieth century, the planners left off the last part of the sentence in which he continued: "nor is it less certain that the two races, equally free, cannot live in the same government."

A generation later the great Lincoln said essentially the same thing when cornered during one of his famous debates with Senator Stephen A. Douglas in 1858:

> I will say then that I am not, nor ever have been, in favor of bringing about in any way the social and political equality of the white and black races—that I am not nor ever have been in favor of making voters or jurors of negroes, nor of qualifying them to hold office, nor to intermarry with white people; and I will say in addition to this that there is a physical difference between the white and black races which I believe will for ever forbid the two races living together on terms of social and political equality. And inasmuch as they cannot so live, while they do remain together there must be the position of superior and inferior, and I as much as any other man am in favor of having the superior position assigned to the white race.

Back in the 1830s the French visitor Alexis de Tocqueville commented on the same attitude in his famous *Democracy in America.* Many of his observations, especially about the South, were naive and superficial ("there are no families so poor as not to have slaves"), but some of his comments struck home. He observed that the "Anglo-Americans" argued over specifics and procedures in government but were "unanimous upon the general principles which ought to rule human society" and added more specifically that "the prejudice of race appears to be stronger in the states which have abolished slavery, than in those where it still exists." A generation later, on the eve of the Civil War, middle-class "Herrenvolk democracy" still flourished all over America, even among the antislavery Republicans in the North.

The international antislavery movement increased its activities in the 1830s, and the South grew less tolerant of outside attacks and internal dissent. Clement Eaton's *The Freedom-of-Thought Struggle in the Old South* documented this conservative trend, but the North was also capable of reacting harshly against radicals and "outside agitators" such as the Mormon Joseph Smith and abolitionists Elijah Lovejoy and William Lloyd Garrison. In neither section did middle-class white democracy crumble, and it is even possible that the South, which leaned so hard on its black slaves, may have been less prejudiced against some other minorities like Jews and Catholics and immigrants—as long as they did not challenge the slave system. Many Irish-Catholic immigrants found a home in the South by the 1850s, and they seem to have fought as hard for the Confederacy as their more numerous Celtic kinsmen in the North fought for the Union.

In both sections of antebellum America an economic elite exercised considerable influence but not hegemony. If Edward Pessen's *Riches, Class and Power Before the Civil War* accurately described the urban Northeast, then wealthy businessmen in the North may well have been more dominant than wealthy businessmen in the South. In both sections political power diffused broadly, and all major political parties cultivated the massive middle class where the votes were concentrated, but special attention should be paid to two influential groups of operators in the towns and cities, the lawyers and the newspaper editors. They were the shock troops in every political party. Editors poured out a steady dose of partisan propaganda on their lively editorial pages, and lawyers traveled widely on the court circuit, molding coalitions and alliances for the next election. These political operators (called "wire-pullers" then) abounded all over the nation. Lincoln is a classic example, but the South produced many of the same kind of professional politician.

Typical was John Letcher, who worked his way up the political ladder and just happened to begin his four-year term as governor of Virginia on the eve of the Civil War. His prewar career followed a familiar American pattern. His father was born and raised a redneck, but as a young man he moved into the busy little town of Lexington, nestled in the heart of the Shenandoah Valley. Unrefined but literate and ambitious, William Letcher worked his way up into the secure middle class as a merchant and diversified businessman. His son John had every advantage his father had lacked, but he frittered away his chance for an advanced education at local Washington College and flunked out in his freshman year. His disgusted father put him to work as a manual laborer. This shock treatment worked, and almost overnight young John embraced the work ethic of his middle-class parents (though not their stern Methodism) and settled down to a lifetime of hard labor as a lawyer and Democratic politician. For a while he also edited the party's local newspaper, the *Valley Star,* which waged an endless war of words against the *Lexington Gazette,* the organ of the local Whigs. The two journals argued over internal improvements, tariffs, banking, and other issues of the day, generally taking the standard position of their national party, and occasionally they clashed over which party could best defend slavery from the rising abolition movement. This kind of highly personalized journalism almost led to a couple of fist fights, but Letcher, a reasonable and gregarious fellow, always held back from such foolishness, and he never even considered duels or other "affairs of honor." He was a typical bourgeois man, practical and devoted to his wife and growing brood of children and to his callings, politics and law (in that order).

By 1847 he had already acquired a family of slaves (a father and mother and children) to serve his growing family (a father and mother and children) when he got involved in a hot debate at the local literary society and ended up championing gradual emancipation. He quickly cooled down and recanted this heresy; and then he rendered fine service at the Virginia Constitutional Convention of 1850-1851, which eliminated the last minor property qualifications for voting, prepared the way for reapportioning the legislature on the basis of white population, expanded the number of elective offices, including the governorship, and generally put the finishing touches on the evolution of middle-class democracy in Virginia.

Letcher used his new popularity to win a seat in Congress, where he served for four consecutive terms. Fundamentally a moderate, he defended the South against increasing attacks from the North but at the same time championed compromise, condemning secessionists as well as abolitionists. A convivial fellow, he especially enjoyed the company of other middle-class types, Northerners as well as Southerners, and like many of them he favored a frugal kind of federal government. Proud of his nickname, "Honest John Letcher, Watchdog of the Treasury," he performed competently but not spectacularly for eight years. He showed increasing concern over the surging "Black Republicans," but he never seemed the least impressed by the vaunted Southern elite. Finally in 1858 he made his long-planned bid for the governorship. He won the Democratic nomination at a raucous convention—a spectacle that would have been vigorously denounced during Reconstruction. Then a grueling campaign followed and finally in May 1859 he won the election as Virginia, so long the home of aristocratic imagery, once again selected middle-class leadership.

Energetic and optimistic, Letcher took office on 1 January 1860, and he remained a moderate and a Unionist as he privately condemned "madmen who are seeking to overthrow the peace of the country." Then the shooting started at Fort Sumter, and every American had to pick sides. Letcher dutifully followed his state out of the Union and into the Confederacy. For the next two years and eight months he served as the wartime governor of Virginia, and his leadership, minutely examined in F. N. Boney's *John Letcher of Virginia,* is a classic example of bourgeois pragmatism. He realized that a herculean effort would be necessary and that unity would be absolutely essential. He worked tirelessly to marshal all of his state's resources, and he tried hard to overcome his states' rights heritage and cooperate fully with the new Confederate government that had settled in Richmond. He made mistakes as he led nineteenth-century Virginia in the nation's first modern war, but stimulated by the constant presence of enemy armies, he generally performed well in a lost cause. The war made him a rebel and a pragmatic Confederate patriot, but when peace finally returned, he became again what he had always been at heart, a middle-class American who never sought the war that altered his life.

The war magnified and accelerated Letcher's career, but he accurately represented the professional Southern politician. Some of these lawyer-politicians such as Andrew Jackson and his rival Henry Clay also became wealthy planters, but they never really left the huge Southern bourgeoisie, and in the massive political movements they led, they never forgot that the middle class was the only practical foundation for success.

In the antebellum South this bourgeois life-style showed most clearly in the towns and cities, but it was also deeply rooted in the rural countryside: the land of the redneck yeomen where the great majority of people lived and worked. From the ideological perspective of studies such as C. Vann Woodward's *American Counterpoint: Slavery and Racism in the North-South Dialogue* and Eric Foner's *Free Soil, Free Labor, Free Men: The Ideology of the Republican Party Before the Civil War*, the rural South seemed distant and alien—in a sense un-American. But even a perfunctory examination of grassroots county records reveals the same open, mobile, materialistic society that operated (however imperfectly) in the North. The Midwestern farmers who founded the Republican party and the Southern farmers who met them in combat a few years later both lived in the broad American middle class. The passionate rhetoric of a "blundering generation" of politicians and the hazy pontifications of a handful of intellectuals in the years leading up to the Civil War shout out sectional differences; the quiet voice of dusty local records whispers basic similarities.

Antebellum Southern courthouse records varied a little by time and place, but almost always they describe a vital bourgeoisie. Land books and sometimes plats (maps) detailed the kind of property that anchored the free-enterprise system. Deed books demonstrated that speculation and credit transactions were ways of life. Entrepreneurs—sometimes lawyers and other town types but often plain farmers—bought land cheap and sold it dear. Some also speculated in slave property, sometimes fairly regularly, though they were never listed as professional slave traders. Private property of all kinds changed hands rapidly in the fluid economy, and many transactions involved so much money down and the rest payable over time with penalties for delinquency. Some farmers simply loaned money at interest with land as collateral, acting much like bankers, probably as eager to gain the land by default as to collect interest with repayment. Wills and inventories listed credits and debts as part of the deceased's estate. Many rural Southerners moved nimbly through an active economic milieu, practicing not "peasant cunning" but standard operating procedures for middle-class men (and occasionally women).

Inevitably all of this aggressive economic activity led to legal disputes. The largest crowds turned out for court proceedings dealing with dramatic events such as assault, murder or, rarest of all, divorce, but most cases involved prosaic property disputes. Occasionally a case mixed both elements as in 1841 when Wiley Carter, a hardworking farmer in eastern Georgia, shot and killed a neighbor named Usry after a bitter argument over a piece of property (a slave). He beat the rap with a plea of self-defense, which seemed to be supported by the evidence, and soon moved on to richer land in Sumter County in southwestern Georgia.

His branch of the Carter clan had long lived in the Southern middle class. His distant English ancestor landed in Virginia in 1637, and the family soon entrenched itself in the rich soil. In the 1780s Kindred Carter moved south to Georgia and operated a diversified, 300-acre farm near Augusta. His son Jesse started with a similar operation and then around 1830 moved west to Talbot County near the Alabama line where he soon became a prosperous cotton planter with sixty-nine slaves. Jesse's brother James settled in Talbot County too, and though he never matched his brother's wealth, when he died in 1859 he left a respectable estate of 303 acres (valued at $1,200) and six slaves (valued at $5,692). Impressed with Uncle Jesse's success, Wiley Carter, the first of James's nine children, moved west in 1851 and settled about fifty miles further south in Sumter County, near a little village called Plain of Dura (named for the place where Shadrach, Meshach, and Abednego were cast into the fiery furnace for refusing to worship Nebuchadnezzar's golden idol).

Putting the Usry episode behind him, Wiley gained considerable success, and by 1860, four years before his death, he worked 600 acres of farmland with a few slaves and produced 147 bales of cotton. He also owned an additional 1,600 acres of unimproved land plus 165 hogs and other livestock. A staunch Baptist like the rest of the family, he also sired twelve children, eleven by his first wife Ann and one by his second wife Sarah. Soon after the Civil War started, three of his sons joined the Sumter Flying

Artillery and fought through the rest of the war. Littlebury Walker Carter and his brothers survived the holocaust and returned to begin again the old cycle of hard work and gradual advancement. Over the last century the feisty Carter family remained in the middle class, constantly struggling to "get ahead" and finally sending one chosen son to Annapolis, the nation's nuclear submarine fleet, the Governor's Mansion in Atlanta, and ultimately the White House in Washington.

Thousands of ordinary Southern whites like the Carters can be followed closely over the years through the most useful local record of all, the annual county tax digest. Here every head of household declared his (and occasionally her) possessions in land of various grades, slaves, and sometimes other property such as livestock, carriages, wagons, homes and other buildings, jewelry, clocks, pianos and similar luxuries, and even stocks and bonds. These tax digests varied over time and by state and by the competence of county officials, but generally by the 1850s they were detailed and precise. Consistently, year by year, all over the South they recorded ownership of land and slaves, two accurate measures of wealth. Like other antebellum records, many tax digests have been lost or destroyed, but many survive and can be fed into computers to reveal more of the grassroots reality of Southern life. Or, to attain a narrower but more exact focus, these digests and other surviving courthouse records can be combined with other primary materials to reveal in detail one representative member of the bourgeoisie. Occasionally a unique, dramatic event generated even more original information about an ordinary Southerner.

Such a man was Nathaniel Francis who, at twenty-six years of age, just happened to be living in Southampton County, Virginia, in 1831 when it erupted like a volcano as Nat Turner led the bloodiest slave revolt in American history. This upheaval has been described by Stephen B. Oates in *The Fires of Jubilee: Nat Turner's Fierce Rebellion* and documented by Henry Irving Tragle in *The Southampton Slave Revolt of 1831: A Compilation of Source Material*. The central characters are Nat Turner and his black rebels, but white farmers who fought back—such as Nat Francis— also briefly emerge from the shadows. White Nat was only a few years younger than black Nat. They had known each other for years and had probably even played together as children, for they grew up in the same neighborhood of Saint Luke's Parish in rural Southampton County where a complete collection of antebellum records describes in detail a bourgeois man such as Nat Francis.

His father, Samuel Francis, worked hard cultivating large crops of cotton and corn, raising many hogs and some sheep and cattle, and making hundreds of gallons of brandy from the apples of his orchards. He belonged to the first generation of an old Virginia yeoman family that acquired true literacy, and when he died in 1815 he left his wife and ten children an estate that included sixteen slaves, more than a thousand acres of land, and a good number of promissory notes from neighbors and business associates. More significantly, he also passed on his bourgeois spirit to young Nat and his other children.

Reinforced by a small inheritance from this oft-divided estate, Nat was already a busy young agribusinessman helping his mother operate the old family farm of 363 acres (which he would inherit when she died) and cultivating his own 137 acres when the federal census of 1830 froze him in time as "Nathl. Francis." He was designated the head of a household that included his seventeen-year-old wife Lavinia, his aging mother Sally, a young overseer-assistant named Henry Doyle who was helping him learn his calling, two orphaned children of his dead sister Polly, fifteen slaves (six under ten years of age), and finally a family of six free blacks who lived on the property. County records indicate that this same year he purchased an adjoining lot of 430 acres for $800 and also bought a small carriage, a symbol of bourgeois respectability.

Nat Francis seemed comfortably settled into the middle class of his fathers when Nat Turner and his men struck before dawn on 22 August 1831. The revolt swirled throughout the southwestern part of the county, leaving sixty whites dead, mostly people who just happened to get in the way. Many victims were women and children, for Turner's only hope of success lay in total surprise, which could only be achieved by killing all whites. At first the whites, barely forty percent of the local population, reeled back in confusion as the alarm was spread by whites and blacks. Receiving reinforcements from nearby areas and hurriedly organizing, the whites launched a ruthless counterattack that killed several hundred blacks, some of them innocent bystanders who just happened to get in the way.

One of the first whites to hear of "trouble" was Nat Francis. Thinking at first that the hated British might be raiding along the coast again, he went to investigate and soon learned that his brother Salathiel and his sister Sally and her husband Joseph Travis (the master of Nat Turner) and their infant child had been hacked to death by slaves. In the meantime one band of Turner's men had overrun his farm, killing his two nephews and the overseer Doyle and recruiting four of his slaves. Lavinia, eight months pregnant, was hidden in the small attic by "Red" Nelson, a mulatto slave who had first spread the alarm. Turner's rebels swept on, and Lavinia emerged from the attic only to be threatened with a knife by her slave Charlotte and then shielded by another slave, Easter. Frightened but clearheaded, she joined other whites who survived by taking refuge in the swamps.

Her husband Nat had joined growing numbers of white farmers who had rallied and begun to fight back. Soon he heard what had happened at his home, and then he discovered Easter and Charlotte among a group of blacks detained for questioning. Easter he embraced and Charlotte he seized in anger and tied to a tree. Then he fired the first shot as a group of whites riddled her body with bullets.

By this time the revolt had reached a bloody climax. Neither Nat Turner and his blacks nor Nat Francis and his whites gave any quarter, and inevitably, after only two days superior white forces overwhelmed the black rebels. Nat Turner escaped and hid out in the woods for more than two months before he was captured and then quickly tried, convicted, and executed by hanging. Nat Francis survived the fighting too, and the blind rage that had driven him to lynch Charlotte passed quickly. Calmly he received back two more of his rebellious slaves, Sam, a leader, and Dred, a wounded follower. He simply turned them over to county authorities for trial and inevitable execution. Normally he had no taste for blood, and so he acted as a rational bourgeois man again. Doubtlessly he knew that according to Virginia law slaves killed in insurrections were simply lost property, whereas criminal slaves properly tried and executed by the state were confiscated property for which the owner received compensation. His slaves Charlotte, whom he killed, and Will, a tough rebel leader who fell in battle, simply vanished from his estate; but the hanged Sam and Dred brought $800 in compensation, and youngsters Nathan, Tom, and Davy, who were transported out of the state rather than hanged, brought another $900 in compensation.

These technicalities in Virginia law helped moderate the white repression as Southampton County slaveholders acted to protect their investments: not only was lynching ugly and likely to kill the innocent as well as the guilty, but it was also terribly wasteful of valuable property. The thrifty, practical whites of Southampton County, where there were few large planters but many slaveholders, abhorred unnecessary business losses even during a slave insurrection, and they were particularly determined to prevent trigger-happy, whiskeyed-up galoots from roaring in from nearby areas for a "turkey shoot" at their expense.

This mixture of practicality and decency diluted white rage and kept the black death toll to approximately 200 in a situation that could have led to genocidal retaliation. As the world goes, middle-class farmers such as Nat Francis seem to have been reasonably decent fellows, even within the Southern slave system. However, William Styron, a native of Tidewater Virginia, arbitrarily picked him to be one of the "bad guys" in his acclaimed novel *The Confessions of Nat Turner*. Styron had one slave refer to Francis as "dat mean sonabitch" and later had Nat Turner describe him in detail:

> I think it may have been seen by now how greatly various were the moral attributes of white men who possessed slaves, how different each owner might be by way of severity or benevolence. They ranged down from the saintly . . . to the all right . . . to the barely tolerable . . . to a few who were unconditionally monstrous. Of these monsters none in his monsterhood was to my knowledge so bloodthirsty as Nathaniel Francis . . . for he was . . . predisposed to cruelty. . . . A gross hairless man with a swinish squint to his eyes . . . on middling land of about seventy acres he eked out a sparse living with the help of six field slaves . . . and he did have a wife, Lavinia—a slab-faced brute of a person with a huge goiter and, through the baggy men's work clothes she customarily wore, the barely discernible outlines of a woman. A winning couple. Perhaps in reaction to the wife or (it seems more persuasive to believe) goaded by her after or before or during whatever unimaginable scenes took place upon their sagging bedstead, Francis achieved pleasure by getting drunk at more or less regular intervals and beating his Negroes ruthlessly with a flexible wooden

cane wrapped in alligator hide. . . . Such abuse had caused both of them [his slaves Will and Sam] to run away more often than either of them could remember, and Francis's alligator-hide whip had left knobs like walnuts on their shoulders, backs, and arms. Francis might have been a moderately prosperous landowner had not his roaring need to inflict misery on his Negroes smothered that logic which must have tried to tell him that halfway decent treatment would keep the pair, however reluctantly, home and busy. . . . [And he tormented the brainless slave Dred] with unspeakable tricks like causing him once (according to Sam, whom I had no reason to doubt) to copulate with a bitch dog before an assembly of local white trash.[1]

Styron, a Pulitzer-prize winner with this book but no scholar, could not be more wrong about Nat Francis. Surviving pictures of Lavinia taken after the insurrection show a respectable woman with no signs of a "huge goiter," a typical wife and mother who was rather attractive in her youth and certainly never "slab-faced." Surviving records give no evidence of the "monsterhood" of her young husband, who was doing more than just eking out a "sparse living" on "middling land" at the time of the insurrection. It is true that his slaves Sam and Will helped plot the revolt and that several others joined it, but this did not necessarily mean harsh treatment; often it meant the exact opposite, and Nat Turner himself readily acknowledged that Joseph Travis (Nat Francis's brother-in-law) had been a decent master. More significantly, the rebel Nat consistently referred to the white Nat without the customary "Mister" prefix. That this was familiarity, and even friendship, rather than contempt is seen clearly in the period after the collapse of the revolt when black Nat remained hidden in the woods. Once he became despondent and decided to give himself up, and he walked right up to the door of white Nat's home before changing his mind and retreating back to the woods. He would hardly have considered surrendering to one of the community's more violent, racist whites. Finally, the six free blacks who chose to live on the Francis farm would hardly have established such a dependency with a "mean sonabitch."

Young Nat Francis emerges from the shadows as a better-than-average white man from the slaves' viewpoint, and a rather typical middle-class

---

[1]William Styron, *The Confessions of Nat Turner* (New York: Random House, 1966) 299-301.

farmer on the make from the whites' viewpoint. After the insurrection he returned to the familiar rhythm of life on the land. The whole county soon returned to normal: blacks and whites drifted back into the powerful, conservative mainstream of Southern and American life with surprising rapidity; the blood vanished into the enduring earth and the scars began to fade, but memories lingered over the years. The slave majority in Southampton County was not significantly disrupted, nor did unusual numbers of whites depart. Even more surprisingly, the unusually large free black population lived on unmolested; it totaled 1,745 in 1830 and ten years later it had crept up to 1,799, still a significant percentage of the continuing black majority in the area. In the immediate aftermath of the revolt, a new record book appeared in the county courthouse containing the names of all free blacks and their white sponsors, but soon this volume was put aside and forgotten, left to gather dust in a corner.

For Nat Francis a return to normalcy meant striving to get ahead again. Detailed county records and a few surviving family documents tell the whole story. Briefly he retrenched, selling for a small profit the 430-acre tract he had purchased just before the uprising, but within a year he was moving ahead confidently once again, aided by a windfall of 300 acres of nearby land and a few slaves that he inherited from his murdered brother Salathiel. In 1833 he bought another 250 acres adjoining his land for $900 (perhaps the compensation money from the state for Nathan, Tom, and Davy), and two years later when his mother died he inherited another 411 acres, which included the original family home where his wife had almost been killed during the insurrection. In 1837 he tripled his living space with an $850 addition to his small house. The rectangular, two-story addition dwarfed the one-story original. The new whole was plain and awkward but solid and functional, and it served his growing family well over the years.

Lavinia had delivered her first child, a healthy boy, only a month after the revolt, and she continued to bear a healthy new Virginian about every other year for the rest of her married life, until her husband died in 1849. All but one of her nine children grew to adulthood; if she had been black she would have been known as a "good breeder"; but "Miss Venie" (as the blacks called her) was a middle-class white woman, a good wife and mother as devoted to her traditional calling as her husband was to his. Routinely she had taken a hand in the farm operations going on all around her, and after her husband's death she managed her business affairs (including twenty-one slaves in 1860) quite capably until her death in 1885 at the age of seventy-two.

She had learned well from a husband who worked hard as long as he lived. Nat Francis continued to buy land opportunistically: by 1840 he had amassed 1,600 acres, and by 1847 he had increased his holdings to almost 3,500 acres, most of it in the same general area and much of it connected. His slave property increased steadily too, from thirteen who were more than twelve years of age in 1837 to twenty-nine of all ages (including eight adult males) in 1840 to thirty-seven (including thirty-two who were more than twelve years of age) just before his death in 1849. At no time during his career as he steadily accumulated property in land and slaves did trumpets blow and a voice from on high proclaim him "planter"—this only happened in works of scholarship, not real life. From beginning to end Nat Francis remained what he had always been, a sturdy bourgeois farmer.

His economic success was accompanied by considerable wheeling and dealing, another trait of the American middle class. He sometimes speculated in land and he used credit freely. Fairly often he loaned sizable sums of money to neighbors who put up land as collateral. Sometimes these deals got complicated, and occasionally they led to court cases. In a hearing in the Superior Court, described in Thomas C. Parramore's *Southampton County, Virginia,* he was accused of being "notorious for his love of money" which, with allowances for courtroom dramatics, was not too far off the mark and certainly did not remove him from the middle-class mainstream. Indeed, the fatal illness he contracted in 1849—probably pneumonia—resulted from an arduous trip to Mississippi to collect overdue debts.

Nat Francis prospered in many business activities, but he concentrated on agriculture. Like his father and most of his neighbors, he practiced diversified farming. He tended a few apple orchards and produced some cider and brandy, and he raised some food crops like potatoes and beans. He raised some cattle and sheep and many hogs, and he cultivated cotton and corn in large quantities. Like so many other Southern agribusinessmen, he emphasized a combination of corn and hogs, but he also

had a small cotton gin, a small brick kiln, a small tannery and several spinning wheels, and he operated a functional carpentry shop and a well-
equipped blacksmith shop. He owned a good number of work animals,
wagons, carts, and farm tools. He ran an efficient agribusiness with adequate amounts of capital, equipment, and labor and even more know-how
and energy.

Though not well educated, he was thoroughly literate. He strongly
supported local education efforts, and one community school operated in
his home for many years. Like his father, he saw that his children received
a better education than he had, and his eldest son even briefly attended
Randolph-Macon College. Though most of the family's funds were invested in business operations, the Francis home gradually acquired a few
refinements—some nice wainscoting, some sturdy furniture, several plain
but handsome mantels, and other "store bought" accessories such as mir-
rors, a pair of silver candlesticks, and a few books. The Francises were not
intellectuals, but several of these volumes received constant attention, especially a large, expensive family Bible (complete with a list of births and
deaths in the front) and Adam Clarke's four-volume revision of the Reverend Thomas Harmer's *Observations on Various Passages of the Bible.*

Nat and Lavinia were staunch Methodists, members of nearby Clarks-
bury Church which, next to their home and business, attracted their
greatest commitment. Nat served as one of the trustees who purchased the
church land, and he also taught Sunday school for many years. Like black
Nat, white Nat was a dedicated Christian. Black Nat showed his commitment by trying to liberate his people while white Nat showed his commitment by leading a proper, respectable private life and striving to succeed
at his calling.

Nat Francis was also a staunch Democrat. In 1845 he remembered "Old
Hickory" living out the last months of his life in Tennessee and named his
seventh child Andrew Jackson Francis to honor the man who had shaped
the Democratic party. In *The American Political Tradition and the Men Who
Made It,* Richard Hofstadter described Jackson as a leader who championed "the classic bourgeois ideal, equality before the law, the restriction
of government to equal protection of its citizens" and thus attracted the
"rising middle class," the "expectant capitalist" and indeed "a host of 'ru-

ral capitalists and village entrepreneurs' " all over America. This char-acterization of Jacksonian Democrats perfectly suited a Southern agribusinessman like Nat Francis, who died only four years after his polit-ical hero.

A good family man as well as a good businessman, Nat Francis pre-pared well for his death at the age of forty-three. His complicated will carefully divided up his large estate, which required a bond of $70,000. His wife Lavinia received the family home, 637 surrounding acres, and one-third of the slaves. Each of four living sons received sizable farms, and all of the children shared in the distribution of most of the rest of the estate, including the remaining two-thirds of the slaves. Like his father and most other middle-class farmers, Francis made no attempt to keep his estate in-tact; no kind of manorial or seigneurial mentality existed. Instead each male heir received a considerable grubstake and encouragement to go out and expand his business just as "paw" had done, and the girls (or their fu-ture husbands) got a nice slice of the pie too.

Nat Francis's two eldest sons soon settled down on the land, following in the footsteps of earlier generations of the family. The old story of hard work and gradual prosperity repeated itself. Then catastrophe struck again when the Civil War erupted only thirty years after Nat Turner's revolt. The eldest son William stayed home to look after the whole family's ex-tensive business interests, but the next two sons, twenty-seven-year-old Nathaniel Thomas ("Tinker") and twenty-one-year-old John Wesley marched off with the Southampton County "Rough and Ready Guards" and both fought through the war with Lee's army. Young John remained a private, but Nathaniel rose to become captain of Company G of the Third Virginia Infantry Regiment. He was never a real hero, but like his father and namesake, he did what had to be done when the fighting started. A typical middle-class man in the middle echelons of the army, he followed his new calling conscientiously, helping to mold the Army of Northern Virginia into one of the most efficient killing machines of the nineteenth century.

The Confederate war effort was essentially a middle-class operation, and it needed middle-class leadership. In the madness of battle, com-manders like the otherworldly "Stonewall" Jackson and the aloof Lee could be very effective, but the commander in chief, the president of the whole Confederate nation, had to stir the bourgeois instincts of the people. In this respect Jefferson Davis failed. Industrious, intelligent, and patriotic, he still could not rally and inspire the white masses. This son of a dirt farmer from Georgia was too aristocratic to lead a middle-class war effort. Clement Eaton's *Jefferson Davis* did not capture the real man nor did his earlier biographers, and he seemed just as distant and remote to his contemporaries. In the initial stampede to form a new nation, the Confederates selected a strong, forceful leader, but they wandered too far from the Southern mainstream in their quest and came up with a real loser. They would probably have lost anyway, given the overwhelming resources of the North, but the Francis boys and their comrades in the trenches and millions more on the home front carried the fatal burden of an ineffective president. Many Confederate congressmen and governors were well tuned to the bourgeois masses, but all too often they were the very people Davis antagonized the most. Increasingly isolated and unpopular, he eventually lost control of his own people, and only the martyrdom of postwar imprisonment restored his tarnished image.

The mismanaged home front began to deteriorate first, and soon Lee's veterans also began to waver under the relentless attacks of the enemy, but they fought on to the end at Appomattox. As luck would have it, Captain Francis and his troops were overrun and captured at Five Forks, only eight days before the final surrender, which meant that he was shipped north to a prisoner-of-war camp rather than being immediately paroled with the last remnants of Lee's army.

But finally the Francis boys and their surviving comrades came home—thoroughly whipped. Quickly thirty-two-year-old Nathaniel returned to his old agricultural calling, trying to make up for lost time and lost slave property (with no compensation this time). Revolutionary change seemed to have occurred; the Confederacy was gone with the same wind that carried away slavery and so many Johnny Rebs. Yet down at the grassroots level local records tell a story of basic continuity. A vigorous new generation of war children and war babies closed the terrible gaps in the white population. The blacks escaped slavery, but soon the freedmen returned to labor on land still owned by whites like Nathaniel Francis; radical measures like land redistribution had no more appeal to the victorious middle class in the North than to the defeated middle class in the South. Reconstruction passed quickly all over the South, and whites retained their traditional dominance over blacks for almost another century. The Southern, middle-class way of life survived though sorely tried, and ex-rebels like Nathaniel Francis again worked hard as agribusinessmen, progressing surely but more slowly than in prewar days. The sons and grandsons of these postwar farmers scattered out in all directions, often settling in growing cities all over America. The rhythm of life changed, but the old middle-class ground rules remained the same. No matter how sophisticated and technical their new occupations, no matter how many depressions hit, no matter how often over the generations they marched off to distant corners of the earth to fight as "Yanks," no matter how many years separated them from their antebellum ancestors, fundamentally they remained much the same as the Samuel and two Nathaniel Francises and other antebellum farmers who sired them; their tap roots still ran back straight to the soil of places like old Southampton County.

By the 1840s and 1850s this bourgeois mentality permeated the rural South. Whether it originated there or in the towns and cities is a chicken-or-egg riddle, for outside of isolated backwashes, the whole white South was dominated by a bourgeois mentality. One sign of this was the persistent push for formal education. The majority of the redneck masses scattered over the countryside could read and write, and many whites living in more populated areas had the equivalent of high-school educations. Richard Beale Davis's encyclopedic, three-volume *Intellectual Life in the Colonial South* has described the impressive foundations antebellum Southerners had to build upon. After the Revolution state governments had grown and matured slowly, operating with limited budgets financed by very low property taxes on land and slaves. By the 1830s these governments began to furnish new social services like insane asylums, institutes for the deaf, dumb, and blind, and penitentiaries for hardened criminals. Most governments had also been trying for some time to subsidize at least partially some sort of limited education for poor whites, but not enough money accumulated in state treasuries to finance real public school systems. By the 1850s some states such as North Carolina and Virginia had plans ready, and Georgia even started funneling profits from the state-owned Western and Atlantic Railroad into a nascent system when the Civil War intervened, but the South, like the West, still trailed the Northeast in educating the white masses.

Generally education was a private family matter, but in a bourgeois environment that was sufficient for great progress—or, by world standards, phenomenal achievement. Some urban areas and well-populated counties had made independent progress toward public education, but most Southern whites sent their children to some sort of private school—perhaps a distinguished academy but more likely a less formal "old field school," a community operation set up in a cabin on worn-out land or in the home of a patron (like Nat Francis) and financed by small tuition payments from the students. Most parents had large enough incomes (and small enough tax obligations) to afford such opportunities, and down at the grassroots level all kinds of obscure schools flourished. Often such activities are recorded only in crumbled old receipts for fees, financial records of obscure families that seldom find their way into formal archives. A few samples from eastern North Carolina tell the story:

April the 30th 1858

Joseph Wells Jr. To Isaac J. Newton for 45 days Tuition
Three Dollars & sixty five cents

I. J. Newton

Feb. the 14th 1868

Joseph Wells Jr. To L. F. Johnson
Lo 85 Days Schooling @ $8\frac{1}{2}$¢ per day =   6.92
1 Mental Arithmetic   .32
                                                                 ――――
                                                                 7.24

Dec the 13th 1868

Uncle Joseph you are due me $5.85 cts. for tuition and due Uncle Davy $2.40 cts for board whole amount is $8.25 cts

P. W. Alderman

This was not a very neat, precise system, and it looked weak on the state level, but remembering the rural nature of much Southern life, it functioned pretty well, even after the disruption of the Civil War. Down at the grassroots level, white boys and girls usually received a basic education. This patchwork system worked because the individualistic people, though opposed to "big government," strongly believed in education as a religious and economic necessity in their middle-class Protestant culture.

Higher education received strong support too. The South had a very large number of active, little colleges, and the nation's first chartered state universities began in Georgia and North Carolina. Some of these institutions offered much high-school-level work, but most of them lived up to the academic standards of the time. Small, sectarian colleges flourished, and many rising new state universities fell under the influence of the churches too. In Macon the Georgia Female College emerged in 1836 as one of the nation's earliest institutions of higher learning for women. Taken over by the Methodists in 1843 and renamed Wesleyan Female College, its enrollment of 173 was the highest in the state by the time the Civil War started, and for the next four years it was the only real college operating in Georgia. In the 1850s the University of Georgia usually enrolled around a hundred students while further north the University of Virginia usually enrolled about 550 and even further north mighty Harvard attracted less than 400 students. Overall the Southern system allowed middle- and upper-class parents a chance to give their brightest children an advanced education, and a brilliant young man from the backwoods such as John C. Calhoun of South Carolina might even cap off his education at Yale University and Tapping Reeve's law school in nearby Litchfield, the best the new nation had to offer.

Northerners seldom came south even to the best schools, but the supposedly provincial South did not hesitate to send promising students north to elite institutions such as Harvard, Yale, and Princeton. The two sons of wealthy Charles C. Jones of Georgia got along fine in the North as Robert Manson Myers's *A Georgian at Princeton* demonstrated. Charles Junior went on to get his law degree at Harvard, and the younger Joseph went on to obtain his advanced degree at the Medical College of the University of Pennsylvania, another favorite of Southerners. They had a few surprises, like bloody town-versus-gown clashes far worse than anything they saw earlier at South Carolina College and quaint Irish servants who seemed much like quaint Negro servants back home, but generally Southerners like the Joneses fit right in and continued to go north to school in large numbers until the eve of the Civil War. Indeed, one of the most melancholy omens of the coming war was the spectacle of trainloads of cheering Southern students returning home from their studies in the North as storm clouds gathered. The melancholy lingers on at Yale where plaques commemorate students who fell in the Civil War—fifty-five gray as well as 113 blue—and, in a sense, at Harvard too, where the Memorial Hall erected to commemorate the school's Civil War dead makes no mention at all of the sixty-four former students who died for their Southern homeland.

Another sign of the bourgeois nature of Southern society was the steady emergence of technology and industry in a region long committed to profitable agriculture. One of the pioneers of this industrialism, described in Broaddus Mitchell's *William Gregg: Factory Master of the Old South*, operated in four different states during his spectacular career. Born in 1800 in Monongalia County on the rugged Virginia frontier, Gregg moved in with an uncle in Alexandria when he was about ten, and there he learned the rudiments of watchmaking and the manufacture of textile machinery. Soon his uncle moved to central Georgia and established one of the first textile factories in the cotton belt, and Gregg worked with him. When the factory failed after the War of 1812, his uncle sent him to Lexington, Kentucky, where he worked as an apprentice watchmaker and silversmith, and in 1821 he moved to Petersburg, Virginia, for further training. His busy, nomadic youth left little time for formal schooling, but like most whites, he acquired basic literacy within the grassroots educational system. Mostly he learned on the job in what today would be called vocational training.

In 1824 he moved to Columbia, South Carolina, and became a diversified businessman. He married in 1824, and by 1834 he had made a fortune and retired. But soon he returned to work as a pioneer in the South's developing textile industry. He also became a silent partner in a jewelry store in Charleston, but primarily he championed Southern industrialization by word and action. In 1846 he established the Graniteville Manufacturing Company near Aiken. One of the South's first cotton-mill towns grew up around the massive stone plant. Hiring only poor whites, Gregg soon had a work force of 300 and a mill village of almost a thousand. He took an active part in every aspect of the operation, and by the 1850s the company was paying handsome dividends averaging twelve percent annually. Specializing in coarse cotton fabrics, Graniteville flourished, and even today it turns out "blue gold," the tough fabric for blue jeans. A strict, straitlaced, paternalistic boss, Gregg oversaw the health, education, and moral development of his workers and their families—whether they liked it or not. But as Anthony F. C. Wallace's *Rockdale: The Growth of an American Village in the Early Industrial Revolution* emphasized, this kind of paternalism was highly developed in the North too. Like many other Southern industrialists, Gregg rose from a humble background, but some other country-born Southerners who pioneered in industry had a better start in life.

Cyrus Hall McCormick came from a more settled and affluent area of Virginia than Gregg. Born into a middle-class Scots-Irish family in 1809, he grew up in the rolling farmland of the Shenandoah Valley not far from Lexington. His father Robert possessed about 1,200 acres of land, nine slaves, twice that many horses, and a passion for tinkering with machinery. Young Cyrus received the usual limited but functional education, but he inherited his father's talent for inventing. Continuing one of his father's abandoned efforts, in 1832 he perfected the first mechanical wheat reaper. He continued to tinker with his new machine, patented it in 1834, and began to manufacture it commercially in the Valley. He also licensed some Northern manufacturers to build his reaper, but their product did not meet his high standards of performance. Finally, in the 1840s he decided to move north to the rough little city of Chicago and concentrate the whole manufacturing operation under his own supervision.

Gregg had just started his textile mill down in South Carolina, but could a Virginia farmboy go north and compete against the legendary hardworking, sharp-practicing Yankee? Daniel Pratt, a New England farmboy with the same kind of limited education as McCormick, had just established a flourishing mill town near Montgomery, Alabama, and many other Yankees had come south and done well in manufacturing, railroading, and other commercial pursuits, but could a redneck from a supposedly slowpaced region hack it in the dynamic North?

To make a long story short—no problem. McCormick concentrated his resources in Chicago, and his new International Harvester Company prospered. A master nineteenth-century capitalist, he successfully defended his patent rights in the courts, continued improving his machine at the factory, and aggressively marketed his product at home and abroad. He pioneered new sales techniques such as field trials, guarantees and warranties, and installment buying, and soon he emerged as one of antebellum America's first self-made millionaires, a Northern captain of industry from the South.

McCormick was a staunch Presbyterian and a loyal Democrat, and like most businessmen, he deplored the disintegration of the Union. His own experiences showed that Northerners and Southerners were basically the same bourgeois folk, but suddenly they had turned upon one another. During the war he traveled frequently abroad, but as soon as the Confederacy collapsed he tried to help his old home state by funneling funds to the Union Theological Seminary at Hampden-Sydney College, a Presbyterian bastion in Southside Virginia, and to Washington College in Lexington. This little school was not destroyed by Union troops like the adjoining Virginia Military Institute and the nearby home of Governor John Letcher, but it still had a difficult time reopening and returning to normal even under the leadership of an ex-soldier named Robert E. Lee, and McCormick's assistance was vital. Today on the campus of Washington and Lee University the Lee Chapel and the McCormick Library stand near one another, fitting memorials to two great men who shared the agony of being both Southern and American during a time of terrible troubles.

Aggressive capitalists such as McCormick and Gregg were more representative of the Old South than Lee, but the general, a first-rate engineer, shared their technological skill. The South welcomed science and technology and eagerly exploited the latest machinery such as cotton gins, complex vacuum-pan apparatuses for refining sugar, steam engines and systems for harnessing water power, and all manner of gadgets for mills and factories. The Curtwright Factory, constructed in central Georgia in the 1840s to manufacture cotton cloth, was a model of modern technology and, though it was virtually unknown until recent archaeological excavations of an area of Greene County now under the water of a new dam, it was by no means unusual in the South. Even more complex technology such as railroad and telegraph systems penetrated the South just as quickly. Bourgeois Southerners did not see these new inventions as threats to their way of life but rather as obvious improvements that would increase efficiency and profits. As Thomas Cary Johnson, Jr.'s *Scientific Interests in the Old South* demonstrated, they were also receptive to scholarly and theoretical experts such as chemist J. Lawrence Smith, oceanographer Matthew Fontaine Maury, geologist William B. Rogers (who later founded the Massachusetts Institute of Technology), botanist H. W. Ravenel, botanist-astronomer Louis R. Gibbes, medical scientist Bennett Dowler, geologist Joseph LeConte, and his brother, physicist John LeConte (who later helped establish the University of California). Even more significantly, many more creative scientists and a great number of skilled but obscure technicians found a hospitable home in the antebellum South.

During the Civil War these experts and technicians forged a lethal arsenal of secret weapons that rivaled the North's efforts in this aspect of modern warfare. Hydrographer John M. Brooke of Florida designed powerful new cannons for coastal defense, but his main challenge to the Union navy came early in the war when he supervised the construction of a revolutionary new warship. Taking the Union ship *Merrimack*, which was scuttled at Portsmouth, Virginia, he turned his skilled workers loose in it; and after many delays due to technical difficulties, in March 1862 the powerful ironclad *Virginia* moved slowly into Hampton Roads and destroyed two large wooden ships of the Union fleet. Northern coastal cities suddenly seemed very vulnerable, but the next day the Union's new ironclad *Monitor* arrived in Hampton Roads. The two iron monsters closed and blazed away at each other at ranges as short as a hundred yards, but neither ship suffered serious damage. Finally, after four hours, the two ships drew apart and the battle ended inconclusively, but the age of armored warships had dawned and the South had drawn first blood. Skilled Confederate workers built other ironclads such as the mighty *Tennessee*, but over time they could not match the production of Northern shipyards.

Ingenious rebel technicians unleashed other "infernal machines" at the Union navy. Low-slung little torpedo boats caused much concern, and one of them seriously damaged a large Union warship off Charleston. Even more disturbing was the rebels' most dramatic secret weapon, the submarine. Horace L. Hunley of New Orleans designed this lethal little ship, which was finally constructed in machine shops in Mobile and then shipped by rail to Charleston. The revolutionary little vessel submerged better than it resurfaced, and before it was ready for combat it had drowned several nine-man crews, including its inventor Hunley. Finally, early in 1864 another band of volunteers squeezed into their posts, and the *Hunley* attacked and sank the Union warship *Housatanic* but went down with her victim, never to rise again. Confederate authorities gradually lost interest in this new weapon, which was so dangerous for friend as well as foe. Still, like the ironclad, the U-boat was a weapon with a future.

A much more serious challenge to the Union navy came from Matthew Fontaine Maury's "torpedoes" (anchored naval mines), which kept blockading ships at bay off Southern ports. These new devices did not always explode properly after prolonged exposure to salt water, and Admiral David G. Farragut successfully defied them ("Damn the torpedoes, full speed ahead") when he drove his fleet into Mobile Bay in the summer of 1864; but he paid a price when his lead ship, the monitor *Tecumseh,* ran afoul of a live mine and went down like a rock with almost a hundred of its crew. If other rebel mines had detonated properly, Farragut, a Tennessee Yank with a son in the rebel navy, might have been one of the goats of the war, but luck sailed with the Union fleet that day, and Mobile Bay became a Yankee pond.

Confederate inventors also tinkered with observation balloons, and they produced all sorts of new or renovated firearms. Some were spectacular successes, but some failed completely, such as the double-barreled cannon designed to fire simultaneously two balls connected by a chain that would mow down the enemy. Slow-burning powder made it impossible to fire both balls at the same time, and after a few unsuccessful test firings the whole idea was abandoned. But Confederate technicians kept at it, and over the course of the war they came up with many improvements and breakthroughs. Also, obscure middle-class mechanics and craftsmen in the factories developed all sorts of new devices and procedures for increasing production. Overall, the bourgeois Confederacy effectively exploited its pool of technicians and skilled labor. Only a few nations on earth could exceed the technological ability of the Confederacy, which just happened to be fighting one of them—the Union.

But as in the North, the advance of science and technology did not undermine the powerful religious commitment of the masses in the antebellum South. Back in the 1830s de Tocqueville in *Democracy in America* had observed that "although the Anglo-Americans have several religious sects, they all regard religion in the same manner." During the next generation disputes over slavery split most of the major denominations along sectional lines. Despite this, Northerners and Southerners continued to practice the bourgeois Protestantism of their fathers, and during the Civil War both sections responded to the same kind of religious stimulation, with the Yankees increasingly committed to destroy slavery with a "terrible swift sword," and the rebels perhaps even more motivated to preserve the Confederacy.

In the late antebellum South where the Protestant majority was massive and where the defense of slavery encouraged internal unity, the religious scene emerged the clearest. A good number of Southerners belonged to no formal church and others had only a superficial commitment, but Donald G. Mathews in *Religion in the Old South* correctly stressed evangelical Protestantism as the essence of Southern religion. He emphasized its powerful appeal to a rising lower middle and middle class seeking identity and solidarity, and he further insisted that this evangelical spirit was powerful not only among Baptists and Methodists and Disciples of Christ but also within the more formal Presbyterian and Episcopalian churches. Not all members of these groups were real Evangelicals—far from it—but the evangelical spirit radiated out in all directions. It permeated, if it did not always conquer, most Protestant congregations. It strongly appealed to white women who were excluded from many intellectual and spiritual activities but became a majority of the evangelical multitude, and it also had a great impact on the slave community.

And why not? Evangelical Protestantism had a powerful appeal all over antebellum America. The dramatic, direct action of the Holy Spirit one-on-one with a miserable sinner, the deep, emotional experience of being "born again" as an adult, the emergence of a new and better person as part of the community of the elect—all of this had stirred many Americans all the way back to the early Puritans. Local church records in the South reveal the power of this Evangelicalism, its ability to unleash new energies while imposing new restraints and to alter and discipline the personalities of even some of the grandest hell-raisers. Of course, many "backslid," but they often returned to the fold again, and fresh masses of reinforcements were periodically gathered at revivals and camp meetings, which sometimes attracted thousands of participants.

Even the most middling farmer, lower middle class at best, would defer to no man after he had been born again and joined the elect—the real elite. Indeed, he would have to struggle to resist the sin of vanity in order to avoid lording it over the poor, unredeemed sinner who happened to own a lot of land and slaves. Destined to be the equal of other whites when he emerged from his mother's womb, he became the superior of the unsaved masses when he accepted sweet Jesus as his master. The born-again Christian walked humbly with his God, but he stood tall among his fellow mortals.

This born-again minority helped inject a powerful dose of optimism into Southern culture. In an age of dynamic capitalism, middle-class America generally radiated an optimism that startled the rest of the world, including other emerging bourgeois democracies in the Western world. Mother Europe had spawned the revolutionary idea of progress and the eighteenth-century Enlightenment with its onward-and-upward philosophy, and such ideas had intensified as they crossed the Atlantic Ocean. Foreign visitors like de Tocqueville often commented on the booming confidence of all antebellum Americans, but as with some other national characteristics, optimism emerged a little more forcefully in the sunny South, which floated not only in the mainstream but on the very crest of American culture.

It may well be, as Lionel Tiger speculated in *Optimism: The Biology of Hope,* that positive thinking has been bred into human beings over the ages as a trait that promotes survival. Regardless, it is certainly true that an instinctive, robust optimism helped found and preserve the first English settlement at Jamestown where America began. Naive visions of forests saturated with gold and broad rivers flowing straight to the rich markets of Asia soon died—along with many who sought them—but the vision of limitless land was accurate enough to fuel a relentless optimism, especially in the agricultural South. The westward drive toward new and better land became almost a pilgrimage for Southerners who envisioned a better day beyond the horizon. In 1796 Yankee Moses Austin stood at the Cumberland Gap and watched in awe as Virginians and Carolinians poured westward toward their own Beulah Land:

> Can anything be more Absurd than the Conduct of man. Here is hundreds Traveling hundreds of Miles they know not for what Nor Whither, except its to Kentuckey, passing land almost as good and easy obtained . . . but it will not do, its not Kentuckey its not the Promised land its not the goodly inheratence the Land of Milk and Honey, and when arrivd at this Heaven in Idea what do they find? a goodly land I will allow but to them forbiden Land.

But Austin, a good American, caught the bug too a little later when it was diagnosed as "Manifest Destiny," and he ended up with his Southern-born son promoting the settlement of Texas, another "Land of Milk and Honey," which attracted thousands of gringos, mostly Southerners.

This American *drang nach Westen* that began at Jamestown helped trigger the Revolutionary War, the first great challenge to European colonialism. Rational rebels are more optimistic than desperate; they are willing, as one Southerner put it, to risk their lives, fortunes, and sacred honor for an ideal. Revolution flared all along the coastal colonies, but the South furnished its share of budding rebels, men who had a dream, who believed that a ragtag uprising on the fringe of a wild continent could prevail against the mightiest empire on earth. After the shooting started, the loudest and most confident shout of defiance came from Southerner Thomas Jefferson. His leading biographer, Dumas Malone, in an interview in *Newsweek* in December 1978, labeled him "an excessive optimist," and surely only a super son of the Enlightenment could have shaken the world with his call for not only life and liberty but also, incredibly, for the pursuit of happiness. Such optimism might have come from New Englanders such as the Adams boys or much more likely from an expatriate such as Ben Franklin, but in fact it did come from the South where the skies always seemed a little brighter.

What was most incredible of all, the American rebels actually won their independence in battle and went on to build a mighty new nation under the leadership of a series of confident Southern presidents from Washington to Jackson. Spurred on by young Southerners like John C. Calhoun, a real mover and shaker in his early days in Washington, and Henry Clay, perennially optimistic about his career and his nation, the United States forged ahead, sometimes too swiftly. They were two of the most fiery "War Hawks" who pushed the unready nation into a second war against the old mother country. Luckily the new, upstart nation emerged from this un-necessary struggle with its borders intact, giving additional credence to the old saying that "God looks after fools, drunkards, and the United States."

But greater troubles lay ahead. Old man Clay never lost his optimism even as sectional tensions grew ominously and his own crusades for the presidency failed. But old man Calhoun was a different story. His national ambitions frustrated and his state's future clouded by a black majority within and an abolitionist minority without, he lost his exuberance and became, by American standards, an extreme pessimist. This swing from one extreme to another occasionally happened with Southerners and other Americans hooked on something as volatile as optimism, but invariably the doomsayers have failed to hold the allegiance of the masses for long. Some other antebellum Southern politicians joined Calhoun's dreary cru-sade, but the bourgeois masses were wary of these prophets of doom and gloom. Most Southern politicians were content to denounce outside crit-icisms and to champion their native region in the manner of modern chamber of commerce spokesmen. Indeed, these traditional optimists held back secession sentiment for a whole generation, until the election of Lin-coln and the firing on Fort Sumter spawned enough hysteria to drive the Northern and Southern people into a war neither had wanted.

Suddenly the tensions of decades of snarling between the sections ended, and the South mobilized for war with a surge of emotional opti-mism. This initial euphoric stampede to the slaughter is a hallmark of modern war, and it occurred in the North too, but nowhere—not New York and Boston in 1861 or London, Paris, and Berlin in 1914—did con-fidence flair so fiercely as in the South at the beginning of the Civil War. Southerners now saw themselves building a new nation just as their fore-fathers had in 1775. The war was a great crusade, the bright beginning of the new Confederacy, not the sad end of the old Union. Some Southern-ers grieved silently, but the vast majority were swept along in the romantic enthusiasm of the moment. All over the Southland eager "troops" marshaled for action. One Confederate officer, a professional soldier named Braxton Bragg, could hardly believe what he saw in the training camps: "Our troops are raw volunteers, without officers, and without discipline, each man with an idea that he can whip the world."

This traditional Southern optimism, further stimulated by wartime patriotism, fueled Johnny Reb's élan and the headlong infantry assaults that became his trademark. And when the Confederate experiment in rebellion collapsed four years later, the exuberant Robert Toombs of Georgia spoke for many Southerners at one psychological level when he explained to a Yankee soldier that they had never really been defeated: "We just wore ourselves out whipping you."

But the reality of defeat could not be avoided; the South had lost a war it had never doubted it could win. This was the cruelest aspect of Reconstruction, the admission of defeat by a people born and bred to optimism. Other Americans such as blacks and Indians knew the feeling well enough, and many mainstream Americans had more than a passing acquaintance with failure too, but few had experienced such a massive, total defeat. Yet Southern optimism was too deeply rooted to die, and it soon flowered again in the rich ashes of Reconstruction as the scars of the war slowly faded from the Southern psyche. In a historical sense the South wavered only an instant before surging forward again; indeed, the old optimism even increased as blacks, as Southern as whites, were now free to seek their own destiny and lunged eagerly for civil and political equality and their share of the economic pie—at least "forty acres and a mule" at first. The collapse of Reconstruction temporarily dampened the blacks' fiery optimism just as the collapse of the Confederacy had temporarily dampened the whites' fiery optimism, but by that time—the late 1870s—the old momentum had been regained and the exuberant age of the "New South" had dawned.

Even in Southern history few leaders could rival the spokesmen of the New South in raw optimism; yet this New South with its constant heralding of material prosperity actually began at Jamestown, not Atlanta or Birmingham. Basically it was only an extension of the Old South's onward-and-upward spirit, which had been briefly interrupted by the "late unpleasantness." The emphasis on industrial and commercial expansion only echoed William Gregg, James D. B. De Bow, and other antebellum boosters. No matter that the New South was not really new in its ideals nor especially successful in its efforts; it both reflected and revived the old hell-for-leather optimism that had always motivated the region, and the people of the South, including many who did not really benefit, responded as enthusiastically as they always had. The New South credo was only part of the mythology of the Gilded Age, which closed out the nineteenth century with a surge of industrialization; but nowhere in the nation could the champions of bourgeois capitalism outdo the sheer exuberance of Atlantan Henry Grady and his many imitators in the booming cities of the South.

The old agrarian spirit lived on, however, and before the end of the century Southern farmers, driven to desperation by the economic status quo, joined their Western comrades in a headlong political attack on the dominant business interests. This movement soon closed ranks under the banner of the Populist party, and it was most dynamic, most hopeful, and often most successful in Dixie. Southern populists unleashed an optimistic—sometimes even revolutionary—rhetoric that rivaled the euphoric outbursts of their New South opponents. They really expected to overcome the enormous obstacles facing any regional, third-party movement within the American political system. Again, it was a cocky but futile charge up Cemetery Ridge, but even though the Populist party disintegrated, many of its relatively radical proposals were eventually incorporated into the American system. And the Southern optimism that had helped power this crusade survived to become part of the rising Progressive movement.

This loosely knit, broadly based, bourgeois-dominated Progressive movement replaced Populism as the main challenge to the political and economic establishment by the turn of the century. The Progressives also wanted significant reform, and the Southern wing of the movement furnished at least its share of raw optimism. It was altogether appropriate that Progressivism reached its peak under the leadership of Virginia-born, Carolina- and Georgia-bred Woodrow Wilson. Molded by a peculiar blend of Calvinism and optimism—a uniquely American and especially Southern psychological mix—Wilson led his people to considerable reform at home and then hurled them into a great crusade to make not just the United States, nor the Western Hemisphere, but the whole wide world safe for democracy. Southerners stampeded to the forefront of this most idealistic crusade in the nation's history. The first Southern president since the 1840s had fired the can-do spirit of the American people, and the Southern masses rallied quickly, not simply because they yearned to show their national patriotism nor because they loved a good fight, but because they understood all too well the language of optimism.

The "Yanks" poured into France and turned the tide in the last great battles of the First World War. Many heroes emerged, including a hillbilly rifleman from Tennessee named Alvin York, but more than 100,000 American soldiers did not live to celebrate the final Allied victory. Immediately Wilson pushed for the League of Nations, the international organization he confidently expected to usher in his brave new democratic world. The failure of this grand design crushed the idealistic Wilson and sapped the customary optimism of the whole nation. Southerners were as disappointed as anyone else, but despite the ravages of the boll weevil and the Great Depression, optimism remained alive and well in Dixie. Sometimes diverted into twisted crusades like the Ku Klux Klan, Southern optimism awaited only the right leader to bring it to full flower again.

Many political messiahs arose in the troubled times of the 1930s, and one of the most colorful and perhaps most capable was Huey Long, a good ole boy from rural Louisiana who with typical enthusiasm promised to turn the ailing economy around and make every man a king. Finally, however, presidential leadership fell to another politician who resembled the Dixie Kingfish only in his booming optimism. Franklin D. Roosevelt, a product of the mighty Northeastern aristocracy, took power with a broad grin and the observation that all Depression-ridden America had to fear was fear itself. The Southern people supported this Yankee president not just because they were desperate and Democratic, but because he was one with them in his invincible optimism.

Much like Wilson, Roosevelt first achieved some domestic reform and then hurled the American people into another bloody crusade for a better world. Of course, the South rushed to arms, again fired with confident idealism. Again many heroes emerged (including a tough little Texan named Audie Murphy, who looked like a Confederate drummer boy) and this time more than 300,000 fighting men never came back home. Again military victory failed to fulfill the hopes and dreams of the American people, and again a period of disillusionment followed and then intensified under the leadership of a Southern president who characteristically underestimated the impossible by trying to right every domestic wrong and at the same time win a major war on the Asian mainland. The tragedy of this brilliant, cocky Texan plunged the nation into an unnatural period of pessimism that was prolonged by the Watergate debacle. But even as the gloom intensified, a supremely confident politician from south Georgia challenged all conventional political wisdom and won the presidency. Once again the South's ancient optimism paid off as another native son took up the increasingly impossible challenge of leading the turbulent nation. After three tough years as president, the little Georgian was still cocky enough to dismiss the challenge of a powerful rival with the offhand promise to "whip his ass."

Modern Southern optimism runs directly back to the antebellum period when it was concentrated in the sprawling middle class. Daniel R. Hundley, who had a good deal to say about rednecks, also examined the Southern middle class in detail in his 1860 book. With more than a touch of condescension, he first compared the upstart bourgeoisie with his own elite class of Southern gentlemen which, he concluded, in its purest form was of aristocratic parentage and possessed a "lithe, airy, and graceful carriage" and "compactness and delicacy of muscle" (like, for example, one Daniel R. Hundley). But then he confessed that "intermarriages" with the middle class had bred many exceptions, like "Mr. Jefferson himself . . . [who] while his mother was a Randolph, his father was only a worthy descendant of the sturdy yeomanry of England."

Then Hundley got directly to his subject, contending that "the middle class of the South constitute the greater proportion of her citizens including farmers, planters, traders, storekeepers, artisans, mechanics, a few manufacturers, a goodly number of country school teachers, and a host of half-fledged country lawyers and doctors, parsons and the like." He saw them as proud, independent, generous, hospitable, and straightforward but often bigoted in religion, inadequately educated, and provincial. The women he found particularly admirable:

These, almost without exception, are worthy of our admiration and respect. Modest and virtuous, chaste in speech and manners; they are, besides, very industrious housekeepers, kind-hearted mistresses, and the most devoted of wives and mothers; although, we are free to confess, they are not infrequently quite simple and unsophisticated, easily gulled or deceived, knowing at best but little of the world and its manifold follies, and caring even less for its empty vanities and trumpery shows. The labors, indeed, of such a Southern matron are onerous in the extreme. Besides the cares of a mother, the anxieties of a house-keeper, and the wants of her husband, she has also to look after the wants of the blacks [Hundley thought that most of the middle class owned slaves]. . . . No wonder, therefore, that such a Southern matron is ever idolized and almost worshipped by her dependents, and beloved by her children, to whom no word ever sounds half so sweet as *mother,* and for whom no place possesses one half the charms of *home.* She lives indeed only to make home happy. She literally knows nothing of "woman's rights," "or free love," or "free thinking"; but faithfully labors on in the humble sphere allotted her of heaven— never wearying, never doubting, but looking steadfastly to the Giver of all good for her reward; and she is to-day the most genuine pattern and representative of the mothers of our Revolutionary history, to be found any where in the land. . . .

In most instances the daughters of such a Southern matron resemble their mother, save that they possess a little more modern polish and culture, and hanker more eagerly after the vanities of the world; but even the daughters are often quite uneducated in the current literature of the times, and in all things else evince a simplicity of mind and character altogether refreshing. Sometimes, 'tis true, they are sent to Boarding-Schools, (which are becoming more common in the South of late years), are there exposed to a false and shallow system of hot-bed culture for a few sessions; and emerging therefrom in due time make their debût in life, possessed of full as much pride and affectation, as well as conceit and vanity, as of artificial graces of person and manner; and boasting a superficial knowledge of twenty different branches of learning, but in reality having a perfect mastery and comprehension of none. Southern young ladies of this character, however, are usually the daughters of tradesmen, village storekeepers, and the like, who constitute a pretty fair proportion of the Southern Middle Class. . . .

Hundley described a wide variety of bourgeois men. He felt that city folk, especially merchants, were much alike in the North and the South, and Southern planters with some slaves seemed to him very much like well-to-do New England farmers. Southern "middle class lawyers, doctors, schoolteachers, parsons, and the like" were more irritating:

> Happy, jovial, well-contented blades! Each one fancies he carries the world in a private sling of his own, somewhat as David carried the pebble with which he slew the giant; with this difference only, that each flatters himself he is a veritable Goliah of Gath, instead of a very, very small David, indeed! . . . If we may be indulged to use a vulgar saying, *they just think they know it all.* Thus they very often render themselves quite ridiculous in the eyes of persons who have seen more of the world; particularly so when, while entertaining the pleasant conviction that they are the most notable individuals in the society in which they move, they solemnly and seriously declare to you that said society is the most refined, the purest, and the perfectest every way in the whole world! O ye pretty fellows, what a nice set of country cockneys you are indeed!

Other bourgeois types who, in Hundley's opinion, bore watching were the rural and small-town merchants.

> These storekeepers generally keep on their shelves a miscellaneous assortment of goods, groceries, hardware, cutlery, hats, caps, shoes, agricultural implements, and, in fine, almost any thing you can name "in their line." While many of them are gentlemanly and honest, the major portion (as we think, if we don't say so) are shrewd, sharp, cunning fellows; glib of tongue, full of their own conceit, but prodigal of bows and compliments, and always smiling of countenance, yet, did one credit their own most solemn asseverations, always selling every thing at a "most tremendous sacrifice." . . . for the small huckster, particularly the country haberdasher of either a New-England village or Southern cross-roads, is sure to be jewed and worried past endurance any how, by his fourpenny customers, who will never consent to purchase any thing save at a reduction from the price first demanded; and hence the seller has to swear that he paid fabulous sums for his goods, but "as it's you" he will part with them for once "at a sacrifice." Certainly, all country store-keepers are not of this stamp, but we apprehend that a majority of them are not overburdened with conscientious scruples; we do not care what their parentage may be, or in what climes they may have their local habitation. Lying and cheating, as well as jewing down a seller and disparaging that which one wishes

to buy, are neither sectional nor national peculiarities—they are human and world-wide.

The reader will understand us, therefore, when we tell him that Southern Store-keepers (we do not speak now of the city merchants) are pretty much like all other shopmen the world over. They certainly do possess some marked peculiarities, but aside from those which are mainly due to local surroundings, they differ but little from any ordinary shop-keeper in New England or the North-West. They generally, in all the States, spring from the thrifty middle classes; and their heads are much more constantly occupied with how they may turn an honest penny, than with politics, or science, or religion. . . .

If a respectable farmer of the middle class in the South, has a son who early evinces a fondness for trade, by eternally swapping jack-knives with his school companions, or exchanging marbles, or fish-hooks, or puppies, or any thing else, and always making a "good thing" by the operation, even if it be at the expense of a few white lies; this hopeful juvenile is very soon installed behind some merchant's counter, and the doting parents consider that their youthful prodigy's fortune is already made. And the youthful prodigy entertains the like conviction, and determines that the old folks shall one day see him the owner of a store; and dressed in broadcloth every day, and a black satin vest, and big gold watch with a heavy gold chain; and owning a white painted house "in town," with an immense portico in front, and making semi-annual visits to New-York or Philadelphia after goods; and coming in a carriage with servants in livery, to see the old homestead every Christmas; and having the seat of honor awarded him on such occasions, while he makes the eyes of all to stare in awe and wonder at the marvellous yarns he spins out concerning the sights to be seen in the metropolis. . . .

Hundley looked even closer at retailing in the Old South, denouncing the "Model Clerk" who could never be trusted and then describing the "honest, homely lad" who worked right beside his crooked colleague and, through frugality and hard work, succeeded in becoming the "Honest StoreKeeper":

Though not much read in books [he] is remarkable for hard common sense—what the country people vulgarly call *horse-sense*—and this prevents him aping the manners of those whose superior advantages have rendered them more elegant and refined than himself. Hence he is truly a gentleman at heart, and rarely given to any kind of vulgar ostentation; but, instead of a showy house, luxurious furniture, liveried domestics, and extravagance in dress, so soon as he finds himself possessor of more cash capital than his business requires, he invests it in a suburban farm—small at first, but enlarged and added to from year to year, until after a while it assumes the stately proportions of a plantation, to which the thrifty owner retires in his old age, . . . leaving his sons or sons-in-law to carry on his former business. Such storekeepers are always deservedly respectable and well thought of; and their children in most cases being properly educated and well-bred, have the *entree* of the best society, and usually conduct themselves worthily in every relation of life, whether civic or social.

'Tis most true, however, that the Honest Storekeeper does not always succeed in acquiring a fortune, but in a majority of cases dies with the harness on, and goes to receive, in a better country than this, the rewards due a life of honest toil and unflinching integrity.

In many ways Hundley admired the massive, vigorous Southern middle class, but he showed concern too. The bourgeoisie was just too confident, even cocky; too many thought they carried "the world in a private sling." They failed to defer to their betters—Hundley's class of Southern gentlemen—and in truth they often ignored such class concepts, which ran counter to their belief in white male equality. They were ambitious and aggressive. Their children often attended school with the offspring of the elite and mixed socially. Inevitably this led to considerable "intermarriage," which diluted the purity of the upper class and caused all sorts of other significant consequences (like, for example, Thomas Jefferson). Hundley longed for an earlier golden age of the elite that in his imagination had taken place sometime after the Norman Conquest and before the late antebellum period. Despite his romanticism and snobbishness, he did see that, although the South seldom used the term *middle class*, it was the dominant group in the late antebellum period.

Despite his hang-ups, Hundley saw much of the essence of the Southern bourgeoisie. Hard-working, family-oriented folk, they led proper but far from flawless lives. In general they were "respectable" people who obeyed the law, owned property, paid taxes, and attended church. They believed in white equality and freedom and individuality, and they tolerated eccentricity as long as it did not threaten the security of the community. They championed education and a souped-up version of the nineteenth-century belief in progress. Even more in a mental than a physical sense, they encompassed the great majority of the white population, including most of the so-called aristocrats and rednecks. Some poor or trashy whites at the bottom and fewer pure snobs at the top did not really belong, but even they were powerfully influenced by the ideas and ideals of the bourgeoisie. The middle class dominated, and its influences radiated in every direction, even down into the black population at the bottom of Southern society.

CHAPTER 4
THE BLACKS

The roots of modern black America run straight back to the virgin soil of the New World. The main title of Lerone Bennett, Jr.'s *History of the Negro in America* spelled it out: *Before the Mayflower.* Blacks lived in Virginia a year before the Pilgrims headed for the same colony and ended up landing in New England a decade before the vaunted Puritans established the Commonwealth of Massachusetts. The individual stories of these original black pioneers have largely faded away in the mists of early Virginia, but the collective odyssey of this handful of Africans can be pieced together tentatively from surviving bits and pieces of early colonial records. The complete story has vanished with most of the original records, but the general outline of an early American tragedy emerges all too clearly.

The first few blacks arrived in Virginia unexpectedly—probably dumped at Jamestown as part of the loot seized by a Dutch (or English) ship that had raided Spanish commerce. Perplexed colonial authorities had no experience with black settlers. Slavery had thrived in the older Spanish and Portuguese colonies to the south for a century, and these blacks may well have been originally destined for a lifetime of brutish labor on a Latin American plantation. Mother England still retained some oppressive features of old feudalism, but she had no system of slavery and her children clinging to the Virginia coast had no personal experience with such a system. So the Virginia authorities offhandedly and pragmatically

assigned the few "negars" to the same status that encumbered so many
white immigrants to the new colony; they became indentured servants for
a specified number of years. Thus the English again "muddled through"
with a temporary expedient.

But this original solution did not hold. The English in Virginia were
still a provincial, island folk, late surging out into the broad world. Englishmen everywhere believed that the "frogs" and "wogs" began at Ca-
lais, just across the Channel from the mother island. They just did not like
foreigners, and black Africans were about as foreign as you could get. Englishmen also belonged to a broader Western European culture, but as David Brion Davis's *The Problem of Slavery in Western Culture* demonstrated,
this too boded ill for the tiny black minority in Virginia. Color conscious-
ness and racial concepts were deeply ingrained in the European psyche,
and slavery was an ancient institution that had taken on new life as Europe began to colonize much of the rest of the world. The idea of enslaving
other peoples had created some tension in European intellectual life all
along, but generally it had been justified and rationalized over the centuries from the ancient tribalism of the Hebrews and the Greeks through
the accommodations of Christianity right up to the emerging science of
the early modern era—so much so that the gradual development of an abolition movement in the eighteenth century came as more of a historical
surprise than the continuation of old slave systems in the New World well
into the nineteenth century.

From the start the first blacks in Virginia were "niggers"—inferiors and
heathens in the eyes of the English majority. Too few to defend themselves and too different in color to assimilate quickly, black Virginians
gradually were drawn into the kind of slave system other English colonies
were adopting. Ironically, only Georgia, the last and the most Southern
of the thirteen original American colonies, briefly outlawed slavery.

Through the 1620s and 1630s Virginia blacks hung on in a period of
flux, but by the 1640s some had become servants for life, slaves in every
practical sense. Here and there a black might remain free—or half free in
white man's country—but surviving county records show a clear trend toward black bondage. In 1640 a county court found three servants guilty of
running away from their master. All three received thirty lashes; the two

whites also received three additional years of servitude, but the lone black was made a servant for life. Occasionally whites began to record in deeds the sale of blacks "for the rest of their lives." In 1652 the final touch was officially revealed when one white recorded the sale to another white of "one Negro girle named Jowan; aged about Ten yeares and with her Issue and produce duringe her (or either of them) for their Life tyme. And their Successors forever." Yet a year later free black Anthony Johnson had no difficulty taking whites George and Robert Parker to court and winning possession of a disputed piece of property. Ironically, though, the property involved was another black man, John Casor, who was ordered to serve Johnson (not the two whites) for life while Robert Parker was ordered to pay all court costs.

For a generation Virginia blacks lived in a schizophrenic world of freedom, temporary servitude, and slavery, but by the 1660s the muddling ended and black freedom was through. The colony's laws began to forge permanent shackles for blacks and by the turn of the century a complete slave code had evolved that would bind them down for more than a century and a half. Perhaps a few of the descendants of sturdy farmers such as Anthony Johnson escaped slavery over the years, for free blacks never entirely vanished from the Old South, but the great mass of blacks was trapped. And after the turbulence of Nathaniel Bacon's rebellion of 1676 subsided and tobacco rooted in deeply as a money crop, the importation of African slaves began in earnest, not just in Virginia but all along the Southern seaboard. Eventually approximately 427,000 were shipped into the South, including around 54,000 after the international slave trade was officially outlawed by the federal government in 1808; but as Philip D. Curtin's *The Atlantic Slave Trade* pointed out, this was a small fraction of the millions and millions of blacks pumped into Latin America, more than 3,500,000 into Brazil, and even more into the Caribbean islands.

Almost all slave importations into the British colonies along the coast of North America flowed into the Southern areas where climate and soil invited large-scale cultivation of tobacco, rice, indigo, and long-fiber cotton. The Northern colonies had very few opportunities to exploit masses of slave laborers on the land; they could afford to yield to the idealism of the Revolutionary War era. Slavery faded away in the North, but its small black minority continued to face massive discrimination. In the South slavery became an integral part of the booming economy, and idealism yielded to profits. Within the new nation blacks constituted more than a third of the Southern population, and in some plantation areas they greatly outnumbered whites. Afro-Americans would remain a significant part of the Southern population and a permanent minority within the nation as a whole.

America's destiny as a multiracial society was sealed early in the colonial South by a movement that began "before the Mayflower" as a trickle and then swelled into a powerful current and eventually tapered off rapidly as the new nation matured. Blacks were caught in a slave system that severely hampered their development, but even so, by the end of the antebellum period they had laid the foundations of black culture in the South, their new homeland. Whites were free to lay much firmer foundations for the future, but blacks too jelled as a people. By the 1830s, at the very latest, both white and black Southerners had become native Americans in the profoundest sense, lost forever to old worlds on the other side of the broad Atlantic Ocean.

By this late antebellum period blacks had become a thoroughly mixed folk, no longer just African or Negroid. Over the generations they blended with other ethnic groups in the South. Blacks and Indians mixed sporadically but seldom attained real harmony. Blacks usually feared red power as much as whites, but occasionally blacks and reds groped toward some sort of coexistence or even alliance against relentless white power. Such an awkward alliance developed when Indians in northern Florida gave refuge to some runaway slaves. Here reds and blacks fought shoulder to shoulder, waging guerrilla warfare, but inevitably the long, brutal Seminole War ended in 1842 with another white conquest.

Blacks interbred much more extensively with the whites they lived among continuously. The white man's law and religion and customs forbade miscegenation—a terrible word in the vocabulary of the ruling race—but, of course, as James Hugo Johnston's *Race Relations in Virginia and Miscegenation in the South: 1776-1860* proved, largely with local documents, it occurred frequently anyway. Usually free white males mated with dependent, vulnerable female slaves in relationships that varied all the way

from rape to enduring love but usually fell somewhere in between, especially with vigorous youngsters just beginning to feel the sap flow. Inter-
course between male slaves and free white females was much rarer, yet
despite the terrible risks, it occurred enough to generate considerable gossip. Down at the grassroots level people behaved as they always had; the
two races lived apart, maintaining their separate identities, but also together, blending often and mingling blood and genes over the generations.

As time passed many "whites" acquired "black" or "red" blood, and a
plethora of "blacks" acquired "red" and especially "white" ancestors—so
much so that they evolved into a new colored folk difficult to label or classify. If the concept of "hybrid vigor" has any validity in the family of man,
then surely antebellum Southern blacks were a dynamic people. First the
international slave trade disrupted ancient tribal ties and jumbled together Africans from homelands scattered over more than half a continent. Then in America many Indian tribes and many more European and
Euro-American tribes contributed to the increasingly complex ancestry of
the slaves, who finally became perhaps the most "all American" of the nation's people with roots running back to all three of the traditional major
races. Never mind that this complex new folk could be dismissed simply
as "niggers" throughout most of America's history; they along with the
rednecks and the Indians have the best claim to the title of the "old stock"
of the American population. Now as blacks merge more completely into
the American mainstream than ever before, they show a natural curiosity
about their ancestral past.

The psychological force of this yearning surfaced dramatically in the
overwhelming popular response to Alex Haley's *Roots*, the story of an
American family from the proud Mandingo tribe on the coast of West Africa in the eighteenth century to the proud black bourgeoisie in Tennessee
in the twentieth century. This moving story of one modern man's search
for his ancestral past stirred the whole nation, for many Americans long
to untangle their complex genealogy and find their real roots. Properly
done, genealogy can meet a real need in every person, and it can also be
a very useful tool for scholars. They too often have dismissed it as an ego
trip for little old ladies in tennis shoes who make too much noise in state
archives buildings all over the nation.

Haley's book had special appeal for black Americans who had for so long been denied their rightful place in the history of a nation they did so much to build. But even as blacks finally began to receive more recognition as a people, they were still deprived of any individual identity as part of a specific family stretching back through the generations. Haley offered just this possibility as he traced one branch of his family back seven generations to the proud African warrior Omoro and his sturdy wife Binta and their son Kunta Kinte, discovering along the way an Indian great-great-grandfather and a redneck great-great-great-grandfather named Tom Lea and offhandedly mentioning a collateral line that ran back to old Alabama and included a well-to-do planter named James Jackson and an overseer named Jim Baugh.

But as Haley himself said, his famous book was "faction," part fact and part fiction, and the scholar must insist on putting the emphasis on the last syllable of this new word. *Roots* relies primarily on a family's oral traditions handed down over generations, not hard evidence: essentially it should be read as a historical novel, especially after the television adaptation dwarfed the more balanced and less stereotyped original book. Haley's great leap backward across the Atlantic Ocean to the precise ancestral village of Juffure in Gambia, supposedly the home of Kunta Kinte, raises the most questions of all. Genealogically it is the equivalent of a proud white American claiming direct descent from the Emperor Charlemagne or some other giant far back in the mists of early Europe.

Actually, American blacks cannot return to their ancestral villages and tribes nor tread the land of their African forebears; their ancestral roots were wrenched out of Africa and obliterated long ago. With luck, blacks may be able to trace back several generations, perhaps even to Reconstruction or maybe even a little farther if their ancestors were free before the Civil War. But for most blacks the curtain must fall with slavery. Local Southern records that describe whites in such detail give little sustained information on individual slaves who did not even have permanent, legal names. The early federal censuses refer to blacks only as property, giving their age (approximate) and sex and color ("b" for black and "m" for mulatto). County records treat slaves similarly, and even wills and petitions usually list only black first names, which could change at the whim of a new master. Newspapers, journals, correspondence, and other bits and pieces from the past generally do no better for blacks in a culture in which only dramatic figures such as Nat Turner received detailed public scrutiny. The black masses simply fade away into the long night of slavery, at best fleeting shadows in a bleak landscape.

Occasional exceptions do not negate the general rule. Herbert G. Gutman's *The Black Family in Slavery and Freedom,* which probed deeply into the slave past but only briefly examined the post–Civil War experience, unearthed family and kinship relationships among a few black communities that lived over several generations on stable, large plantations such as Good Hope in South Carolina where detailed records and journals and even a few photographs have survived. But even in these ideal circumstances, only a bare-bones story of the resident slaves emerged. This had to be fleshed out with imaginative and innovative research and interpretation, and much remained unanswered.

Sometimes a standard American biography inadvertently backtracked into the murky world of slavery and the even obscurer tangle of miscegenation. In 1954 Jesuit Albert S. Foley authored the orthodox biography of a distinguished Catholic priest. His *Bishop Healy: Beloved Outcast* simply told the life story of James Augustine Healy, who died the second bishop of Maine in 1900. The first chapter routinely presented the early life of Healy, but this turned out to be a far from routine story of the bishop's roots in the Deep South.

Young Michael Morris Healy, a native of Catholic Ireland and a veteran of the British army, joined kinsmen in Georgia soon after the War of 1812. He worked hard as a farmer and plowed his profits into land and slaves. Finally he settled for good near Macon, in the heart of the cotton belt. An exceptional man described in detail in local records and accounts, Healy prospered, accumulating sixty slaves and a 1,600-acre plantation—half in woods and half in cultivated fields. He also held other scattered pieces of land and quite a few mortgages on property of neighbors who had borrowed money from him. Much like the ambitious young Irishman in Cash's *Mind of the South,* he rose rapidly from immigrant redneck to prosperous planter in the booming cotton economy of the Deep South. Proud and independent, he defied custom and took as his wife the beau-

tiful mulatto slave girl Mary Eliza. This union had no legal basis in antebellum Georgia, but it was much more than just another lustful dalliance
in "the quarters." Michael and Mary Eliza were husband and wife in the
profoundest sense, and their happy union produced ten children over the
years.

The first child, James Augustine, was born in 1830 and spent his early
years roaming the lush countryside with a young slave companion and
guardian. Little "Jeems" learned to love his native land, running and riding across the open fields, swimming in the gleaming streams, and ex-
ploring the mysterious woods—as the old Southern song put it, "in the
pines where the sun never shines." But his father knew that the stern realities of the slave South would soon intrude upon paradise: "Jeems" was the
son of a slave woman and thus a "nigger" and also technically a slave. So
in 1837 planter Healy took his young son north to seek a free destiny. He
had great difficulty finding a school for him in New York—"Jeems" was a
"nigger" there too—but finally a Quaker school in Flushing accepted him.
The father returned home to the South, and the son's Georgia life ended
forever. The long road to the priesthood and prominence began. Eventually Bishop Healy became famous, and his obscure early life in Georgia
surfaced almost by accident, throwing another brief flash of light back into
the dark world of slavery. His father's lineage can be traced a little farther
back to County Roscommon in Ireland, but his mother remains a mystery,
just another slave with no certain roots.

The great majority of antebellum blacks simply faded into the obscurity of slavery, and they can be studied only with great difficulty, using
special sources and techniques. In recent decades many scholars have tried,
and three have had considerable success. Sociologist George P. Rawick
concentrated on a rich lode of interviews with elderly black people begun
in the 1920s by Fisk University in Tennessee and Southern University in
Louisiana and then expanded greatly by the Federal Writers' Project of the
Works Progress Administration during the Depression as a white-collar
operation within a much broader range of "make-work" programs designed to relieve massive unemployment.

The interviewers, usually white and often women, were not professionally or psychologically prepared to extract the maximum amount of

information from the dependent and deferential old blacks they talked with—too many old barriers remained. Some interviews became rituals, with poor blacks fearful of losing government benefits telling privileged, official-looking whites what they wanted to hear about Dixie's "old times . . . not forgotten," or more significantly, not telling them what they did not want to hear. The blacks' memories of Reconstruction and later periods shone forth the clearest, but old people often retain or regain clear memories of early childhood, and this stage, when slavery rested the lightest on blacks, often surfaced too. Sometimes when black testimony did get brutally frank and drifted away from the traditional image of antebellum paternalism, uneasy whites simply deleted offending passages. Nevertheless, some of the harsh reality of slavery still emerged from these interviews, especially in the Virginia operation, which employed many black interviewers. Slavery was quite similar in all of the Southern states; it just seemed harsher in Virginia because old blacks there spoke more candidly to black interviewers, who in turn felt no need to soften the truth when they turned in their work.

These interview programs operated erratically on the state level. Many interviews never reached the Library of Congress in Washington, including, not surprisingly, the bulk of the work done in Virginia, which was only recently retrieved by Charles L. Perdue, Jr., Thomas E. Barden, and Robert K. Phillips and published under the title *Weevils in the Wheat*. Soon the federal government lost interest and abandoned the whole program which, despite its weaknesses, had begun to tap and accumulate valuable information about the black heritage in America.

Professor Rawick tirelessly tracked down these interviews scattered over twenty-one states, and he published them throughout the 1970s in forty volumes under the general title *The American Slave: A Composite Biography*. In 1972 he also wrote a short, introductory volume entitled *From Sundown to Sunup: The Making of the Black Community*, which summarized his interpretations and conclusions based on years of work with these grassroots interviews and other sources. His book also encouraged more recent evaluations of these interviews, such as Paul D. Escott's *Slavery Remembered*, a study including considerable quantification.

In the same year Rawick's little volume appeared another prominent scholar, Yale historian John W. Blassingame, published *The Slave Com-

munity: Plantation Life in the Antebellum South. He considered the W.P.A. interviews unreliable and concentrated instead on another unique, eye-witness source, the numerous published memoirs of fugitive slaves. These daring people, usually from the upper South and often illiterate and almost always male, were certainly not a representative sampling of the slave masses, and abolitionist publishers often edited their testimony for educated, middle-class readers in the North. Still, these fugitive slave narratives presented a clear view of slavery by the people who knew it best. The abolitionist obviously used these works as antislavery propaganda; however, after a huckster named James Williams tricked John Greenleaf Whittier into publishing a bogus narrative and proslavery writers had a field day picking it apart, they became very cautious in screening runaways and authenticating their stories before going to press. After all, plain, unvarnished truth made the best propaganda anyway. Inevitably the literary and moral ruffles and flourishes of that Victorian age crept into these autobiographies, but their strength was simple, direct testimony about the South's "peculiar institution," which always fascinated and often appalled Northern and foreign readers.

More than seventy of these authentic, full-length memoirs were published before and after the Civil War, and as Blassingame demonstrated in his more recent *Slave Testimony,* voluminous other eyewitness testimony by blacks exists in letters, speeches, articles, short memoirs, and various kinds of interviews. In this massive volume published in 1977 and in the second, extensively revised edition of *The Slave Community* published in 1979, Blassingame accepted the W.P.A. interviews with elderly slaves that he had rejected in his first edition, but he properly warned that they had to be used with caution and sensitivity. In addition, historian Leslie Howard Owens, following in the footsteps of Rawick and Blassingame and benefiting from their pioneering efforts, produced in 1976 *This Species of Property: Slave Life and Culture in the Old South,* which utilized the W.P.A. interviews and the fugitive slave narratives. Like his predecessors he used many other sources as well, and like them he published a solid study of the murky world of slavery.

All three of these recent works agreed on one main point: the slaves molded a life and culture of their own, especially after working hours in the privacy of their own quarters. Rawick called this a "syncretic" culture—a new blend that was not simply African and not just Southern white either. All three authors stressed African retentions within this new American black culture, especially in music, dancing, folktales, and religion. They exaggerated this somewhat by placing too much emphasis on the New Orleans area and isolated pockets of black development along the Atlantic coast in places such as the sea islands of Georgia and South Carolina. As generations passed, the overwhelming mass of black slaves moved farther and farther inland, and fewer and fewer native Africans remained. The slaves became less and less African and more and more Southern, and on the eve of the Civil War they were more American than ever before.

The African heritage never vanished completely. Black music and dancing obviously went far beyond mere imitation of white models, and some African folktales and religious beliefs survived too, but white culture generally predominated. The wide varieties of black and white Christianity that entangled the Old South like a host of kudzu vines cannot be neatly unraveled and dissected. Donald G. Mathews argued in *Religion in the Old South* that whites and blacks shared words, images, and rituals and continuously interacted upon each other within a common milieu powerfully influenced by evangelical Protestantism. Nonetheless, since the social status of the two groups varied so much, so too did their religious experiences. He also emphasized that black preachers often hailed bourgeois virtues such as self-discipline, pride, respectability, sobriety, perseverance, and honesty that whites admired too; and he concluded that the oppressed blacks may well have developed a more worthy religion than the white Protestantism of their masters. He and Eugene D. Genovese in *Roll, Jordan, Roll: The World the Slaves Made* recognized considerable African influence in black religion, but both also stressed the harsh reality of slavery, which led blacks to hope for freedom and equality in this world as well as salvation in the next.

Mathews and Genovese placed a little too much emphasis on the independence of black religion, and Blassingame went a little farther in his examination of general beliefs within the slave community. In order to justify his assertion that the most powerful and influential person on a

plantation was often the conjurer, he turned to the fugitive slave narrative
of Henry Bibb of Kentucky:

> I got myself into a scrape at a certain time, by going off in this way,
> and I expected to be severely punished for it. I had a strong notion of run-
> ning off, to escape being flogged, but was advised by a friend to go to one
> of those conjurers, who could prevent me from being flogged. I went and
> informed him of the difficulty. He said if I would pay him a small sum, he
> would prevent my being flogged. After I had paid him, he mixed up some
> alum, salt, and other stuff into a powder, and said I must sprinkle it about
> my master, if he should offer to strike me; this would prevent him. He also
> gave me some kind of bitter root to chew, and spit towards him, which
> would certainly prevent my being flogged. According to order I used his
> remedy, and for some cause I was let pass without being flogged that time.
> I had then great faith in conjuration and witchcraft. I was led to be-
> lieve that I could do almost as I pleased, without being flogged. So on the
> next Sabbath my conjuration was fully tested by my going off, and staying
> away until Monday morning, without permission. When I returned home,
> my master declared that he would punish me for going off; but I did not
> believe that he could do it, while I had this root and dust; and as he ap-
> proached me, I commenced talking saucy to him.

Blassingame ended the story here, in mid-paragraph, but Bibb had a good
bit more to say:

> But he soon convinced me that there was no virtue in them. He be-
> came so enraged at me for saucing him, that he grasped a handful of
> switches and punished me severely, in spite of all my roots and powders.
> But there was another old slave in that neighborhood, who professed
> to understand all about conjuration, and I thought I would try his skill.
> He told me that the first one was only a quack, and if I would only pay
> him a certain amount in cash, that he would tell me how to prevent any
> person from striking me. After I paid him his charge, he told me to go to
> the cow-pen after night, and get some fresh cow manure, and mix it with
> red pepper and white people's hair, all to be put into a pot over the fire,
> and scorched until it could be ground into snuff. I was then to sprinkle it
> about my master's bedroom, in his hat and boots, and it would prevent
> him from ever abusing me in any way. After I got it all ready prepared, the
> smallest pinch of it scattered over a room, was enough to make a horse
> sneeze from the strength of it; but it did no good. I tried it to my satisfac-
> tion. It was my business to make fires in my master's chamber, night and

morning. Whenever I could get a chance, I sprinkled a little of this dust about the linen of the bed, where they would breathe it on retiring. This was to act upon them as what is called a kind of love powder, to change their sentiments of anger, to those of love, towards me, but this all proved to be vain imagination. The old man had my money, and I was treated no better for it.

One night when I went in to make a fire, I availed myself of the opportunity of sprinkling a very heavy charge of this powder about my master's bed. Soon after their going to bed, they began to cough and sneeze. Being close around the house, watching and listening, to know what the effect would be, I heard them ask each other what in the world it could be, that made them cough and sneeze so. All the while, I was trembling with fear, expecting every moment I should be called and asked if I knew any thing about it. After this, for fear they might find me out in my dangerous experiments upon them, I had to give them up, for some time being. I was then convinced that running away was the most effectual way by which a slave could escape cruel punishment.

Bibb himself said of the slaves that "many of them believed in what they call 'conjuration,' tricking, and witchcraft," but obviously he was not the only black who became "satisfied that there is no virtue at all in it." Blassingame is not the only recent scholar who has strained a little to discover African retentions among the American slave masses; indeed, in the wake of the civil rights crusade of the last generation and the ongoing drive for black pride and identity, this was virtually inevitable. The time ripened for such an interpretation, and scholars, like Supreme Court justices, do respond to election returns and other popular trends. Besides, they were at least indirectly reacting to an influential little book published way back in 1959.

Three years earlier in 1956 Kenneth Stampp's *The Peculiar Institution: Slavery in the Ante-Bellum South* prepared the way by giving the post–World War II generation of Americans an up-to-date volume to replace older works such as U. B. Phillips's *American Negro Slavery*, which was based on traditional assumptions of black inferiority. In contrast, Stampp "assumed that the slaves were merely ordinary human beings, that innately Negroes *are*, after all, only white men with black skins, nothing more, nothing less." Over time this attitude brought down upon him condemnations ranging from "integrationist" to "racist," but nevertheless, his book has remained the best treatment of slavery for more than three decades, the solid foundation for a deluge of newer studies.

Then, only three years after Stampp's work appeared, came Stanley M. Elkins's *Slavery: A Problem in American Institutional and Intellectual Life*, another influential work. A white native of Boston with degrees from Harvard and Columbia and a professorship at elite Smith College, Elkins brought impeccable credentials to his task; he also presented a series of hypotheses that drew the attention—and relentless scrutiny—of a generation of rising young scholars. Elkins emphasized the concept that antebellum Southern plantations were enough like twentieth-century Nazi concentration camps to totally control and subordinate the black masses and thereby infanticize many of them, creating hordes of scratching, shuffling Sambos, pathetic creatures happy in their degradation. A brilliant, innovative thinker, Elkins ranged widely over the published wisdom of his age and concentrated on new wrinkles in the burgeoning field of psychology, all the while ignoring the original grassroots records of the region he was studying. The result was an intellectual tour de force, a seminal work that analyzed the mentality of the slave in new ways—and missed the mark by a mile.

Some Sambos did emerge among the slave population, pitiful people broken by oppression, but the vast majority of blacks avoided this zombie fate described so graphically by Elkins. They knuckled under well enough, as defeated folk always do in the face of overwhelming force. Indeed, every living person, black or otherwise, should if not honor, at least understand his humble ancestors who bent with the wind, yielded to raw power, and thus survived long enough to pass on life and hope to the next generation. Every tribe needs heroes, but survival over time requires masses of ordinary people who "hunker down" and "get by" the rough times. For every heroic Joan of Arc or Nat Turner or "Stonewall" Jackson who carries the flag into the enemy hosts, hundreds of thousands of others must toil away their lives in obscurity, simply carrying on in a harsh world. Such folk demonstrate a kind of heroism themselves, and even in an oppressive environment such as slavery they do not become simple Sambos. They certainly learn to appreciate the old adage "discretion is the better part of valor," but they do not just degenerate.

As Elkins exaggerated the number of Sambos, other works such as Herbert Aptheker's *American Negro Slave Revolts* exaggerated the number of rebel martyrs like Nat Turner, Gabriel Prosser of Richmond, and Denmark Vesey of Charleston. The Sambos and the Nats were the extremes, the exceptions to the general truth that lay in between in a huge middle group composed of a bewildering jumble of black individualists.

Many of these black people in the middle absorbed some and often many of the middle-class values of their white masters. Fogel and Engerman's *Time on the Cross* concluded that many great planters such as Bennet H. Barrow of Louisiana successfully imbued many of their slaves with the Protestant work ethic, and much evidence of this exists down at the grassroots level where it occurred just as often with middle-class redneck farmers who worked more closely and lived more intimately with their slaves. So often pictured as irreconcilable enemies, "rednecks 'n' niggers" often cooperated in a rough, unequal kind of harmony that forged the tough, enduring core of Southern life.

The whites had the power and usually the numerical edge, but this cultural interchange was never just a one-way flow. Peter H. Wood's *Black Majority* showed that slaves from West Africa were accustomed to hard, disciplined labor and that they brought valuable expertise in rice cultivation to colonial South Carolina and also made significant contributions to fishing, basket weaving, and other economic activities in the struggling young colony. Though sometimes distorted, some African music and dancing seeped into white culture; from Stephen C. Foster to Elvis Presley and beyond it never ceased. Many young whites listened to the stories and legends of the slaves, and one, Joel Chandler Harris, published many of them as his "Uncle Remus" stories, which have delighted a century of young readers. Folktales share many common themes the world over. Hence by the time Harris was listening to black spellbinders as a teenager in Georgia in the 1860s, these particular stories may well have absorbed some white or red ideas and incidents as the South's complex culture evolved rapidly, but Harris left no doubt that his own direct debt was to ordinary, articulate black slaves.

Other whites were less pleased with the black influence on Southern culture. An old complaint surfaced again as late as 1925 in the *Scrap Book*

of Miss Mildred Rutherford, principal of an exclusive prep school for white
ladies ("an ideal school for ideal women," as she put it) that was located
not far from where Harris had soaked up black folklore. She complained
that white children nursed by "Africans" went around saying things such
as "she'll hoodoo you," "make a cross and spit on it," "I heard a creech
owl last night, mighty bad luck," "don't you start a journey on Friday,"
and "watch out, she'll conjure you." Black servants certainly influenced
white children, but as with the Uncle Remus tales, the origins of super-
stitions were quite complex. The Indians who first settled America and
the Europeans who came later both brought their own vast tangles of belief and superstition, some of which were similar to West African concepts; from hoodoos and curses to conjurers and witches the fertile
imagination of the South drew from many sources. Doubtlessly some black
adults marveled at the strange ideas their children sometimes picked up
playing with local "Buckra" (known more formally as Anglo-Saxons, Celts,
whites, etc.). Similarly the Southern accent—or more accurately, the numerous regional versions of English spoken through the broad Southland—reflected many influences but was often strongly affected by the
Afro-Americans who first began to wrestle with and contribute to English
even "before the Mayflower," long before waves of other immigrants began the same struggle to absorb and affect the American language.

Blacks influenced whites in many obvious ways and uncounted subtle
ways, but overall, white influence was overwhelming. By the late antebellum period blacks spoke only English, Southern-style with their own
variations; they could not hope to communicate with their distant cousins
on the shores of Africa. Many blacks embraced Protestant Christianity,
again with some variations of their own. They would have considered West
Africans the rankest heathens, and even those who rejected the white
man's religion retained only bits and pieces of the religions of Africa. Furthermore, most American blacks had become noticeably lighter in skin
color than their kinsmen across the Atlantic Ocean.

Most important of all, like it or not, consciously or unconsciously, the
slave masses were powerfully influenced by the middle-class mentality,
which dominated the white world around them. Slaves did partially shape
their own culture with their own values and customs; but more than they

themselves realized, more than many of their masters comprehended, and more than most modern scholars will concede, the black masses were shaped by the dominant white majority. In short, they were not Samboized or radicalized but, to a significant degree, "bourgeoisized." This process cannot be measured precisely within the obscure slave masses where even the best recent scholars have been able to throw only a few beams of light into the darkness. Still, special sources such as the W.P.A. interviews with elderly ex-slaves and the fugitive slave narratives reveal some evidence of this rising bourgeois spirit among the black masses. The slave system frustrated many black talents and ambitions like a huge dam holding back a mighty river, but many weaknesses developed in the system—the strict slave codes were not fully enforced—and blacks seized every opportunity, just as a rising river spurts through every crack in a dam. This minority of blacks who to some degree beat the system reflected the restless spirit of the repressed black masses, and their unique, sometimes startling accomplishments often appeared in the orthodox grassroots records of the white world, clearly documenting the rise of a black bourgeoisie in the Old South.

The lumber industry thrived over much of the South and employed many slaves. Often they worked right alongside whites, sometimes in positions of responsibility and authority. In the headlong drive to hire and reward efficient workers, the profit motive sometimes nullified both the spirit and the letter of the slave codes. John Hebron Moore's article in the *Mississippi Valley Historical Review* in December 1962 documented the case of "Simon Gray, Riverman: A Slave Who Was Almost Free." A native of Natchez who somehow acquired literacy and a slave hired out to work for a lumber company, Gray began as a common laborer in a sawmill. Able and industrious, he was soon put in charge of a crew rafting logs downriver to the mill, and he also routinely handled many cash and credit transactions for his white employers. As the company flourished so did Gray, who was as bourgeois as his bosses. He became a skilled flatboat captain directing white as well as black crewmen, and he wheeled and dealt with a wide variety of white entrepreneurs—wholesalers and retailers and everyone in between—in a wide-open, highly competitive American business operation.

Lumbermen were free spirits, and Gray had his quirks like the rest of them, but despite the hostility of some whites who felt he had forgotten "his place," he more than held his own in the rough-and-tumble competition as he operated all the way from Natchez to New Orleans. By the mid-1850s he and his family lived like free blacks though they were technically still slaves. Like any good American, Gray was hooked on work; he stayed on the job despite deteriorating health and disappeared from the company's record books only when invading Union soldiers disrupted the whole economy. Other skilled slave employees of the company, like Jim Matthews, operated in the same quasi-free atmosphere. All over Dixie lumber companies that ranged widely up and down the rivers and deep into the sprawling forests required workers with endurance and resourcefulness, and they offered some slaves a chance to develop specific skills and a general bourgeois attitude.

Other Southern industries also allowed and even encouraged slave development as Robert S. Starobin's *Industrial Slavery in the Old South* pointed out. More specifically, Charles B. Dew's study of slave ironworkers in the *American Historical Review* in April 1974—based mainly on the voluminous records of William Weaver's ironworks in the Shenandoah Valley of Virginia—described the emergence of skilled, sophisticated, self-confident slave workers. They felled trees and produced charcoal, manned the blast furnaces, and transported pig iron to nearby cities for final manufacturing, and they also raised their own food in slack seasons. Sometimes owned by the manager but more often hired when needed, they, not free whites, furnished the majority of the labor force in the antebellum Southern iron industry. As they developed valuable skills, they began to acquire informal privileges that almost became fixed rights, and in turn this led to all sorts of ongoing adjustments and accommodations between bosses and workers. The whip was still used, and in extreme cases recalcitrant slaves were still sold south to the cotton fields, but ordinarily compromise and conciliation predominated, hardly the procedures promulgated by the slave codes.

As some of the slave ironworkers "got ahead," they developed middle-class habits. Pay bonuses coaxed some into supervisory positions, and many did overtime for extra pay in cash or goods. Some bought food, tobacco, and clothing at the company store, others bought time off to visit their families and friends back home, and all acquired a more independent, self-confident attitude. Over the years skilled slaves saved hundreds of dollars, and Sam Williams even opened a savings account at a bank in nearby Lexington.

This sort of thing was not supposed to happen in the slave South, but right in the same town an eccentric professor at the Virginia Military Institute also bent the rules to the breaking point. In spite of warnings from local lawyers about "unlawful assembly," he ran a Sunday school for black children. Thomas Jonathan Jackson believed that the demands of his Presbyterian God came first, so he ignored the grumbling of townspeople who finally just ignored the thriving operation that attracted almost a hundred youngsters. The South had its share of the nation's sublime eccentrics and, after all, what could you do with the kind of humorless, by-the-book teacher who bored most of his V.M.I. students to stupefaction and then turned right around and greeted his slave students with a rhythmless version of the hymn "Amazing Grace"—never wavering for an instant from what he considered his Christian duty.

Only a few years later "Stonewall" Jackson slaughtered invading Yankees with the same determination, and the slave Sam Williams continued putting money in his savings account like a good Calvinist too. When freedom came in 1865, he and his wife Nancy and most of the other artisans and skilled workers at Weaver's ironworks stayed on the job and continued their usual work as freedmen under formal contracts.

Less than fifty miles south of Lexington a mulatto slave boy was born in 1856 and named Booker Taliaferro by his mother Jane, who had high ambitions for all of her children. By the time the Civil War started an estate inventory listed him as simply "Booker" and valued him at $400. He was already learning the strict work routine of the plantation and farm, and as he later recalled in his autobiography *Up from Slavery*, he never had time for sports and games but "occupied most of the time in cleaning yards, carrying water to the men in the fields, or hauling to and from the mill"; then when he got big enough, he went "to the 'big house' at meal-times to fan the flies from the table by means of a large set of paper fans operated by a pulley." Soon after the war ended his whole family moved to West

Virginia and he started school. It was also at this time that he added Washington to complete his name. After further training back in Virginia at Hampton Institute, he launched a career that made him the leader of the black masses for an entire generation and a thoroughgoing advocate of the traditional American work ethic. What is revealing is that it all started with the hard lessons of a slave childhood.

Earlier generations of blacks had learned the same lessons, and many adult slaves had sought a better life through hard labor like many other Americans. Most had to settle for very limited gains, but some—Simon Gray and Sam Williams, for example—achieved considerable success against odds that other Americans could hardly imagine. These favored few who advanced dramatically even in slavery demonstrated a significant spirit among the slave masses who, when given half a chance, acted suspiciously like their middle-class masters.

Even before the antebellum period many blacks were working hard to improve their lot within the confines of slavery as Gerald W. Mullin demonstrated in *Flight and Rebellion,* a study of the evolution of slavery and slave resistance in Virginia during the eighteenth century. Early in that century "outlandish" African immigrants offered some resistance by loafing or running away in groups and other communal acts, but most came from work-oriented cultures, and generally they labored efficiently for their masters on isolated plantations. Gradually these planters became diversified businessmen who encouraged the development of skilled slaves for the increasingly complex economy, and by the end of the century many artisans had emerged from the slave masses on the land. These elite slaves were thoroughly acculturated; they spoke English well and many could read and write too. Frequently town dwellers, these hardy individualists operated confidently in the white world; yet, ironically, of all the slaves they became the most acutely aware of the injustices of the system and thus the most disaffected, the most likely to run away or even rise up in rebellion. And, the greatest irony of all, when some of this black elite did plot rebellion in 1800 under Gabriel Prosser, a Richmond blacksmith, they found themselves too advanced and sophisticated to rally the ordinary black masses in the countryside. These privileged houseservants, ironworkers, waiters, janitors, warehousemen, boatmen, miners, and blacksmiths lived too far above the field hands, and the whole plot collapsed of its own top-heavy weight, a clear case of too many chiefs and not enough Indians.

Gabriel's insurrection shook the white world briefly, but masters continued to encourage the development of skilled slaves even as the cotton kingdom began to flourish. In 1822 Denmark Vesey sent another tremor through the South. A native West Indian slave who was brought to Charleston, he soon purchased his own freedom after winning a lottery. He made a good living as a carpenter who, according to court records, could read and write "with great facility." He was eventually detected trying to organize a massive slave revolt as again privileged, urban instigators failed to mobilize the rural masses effectively. As happened previously, the vision of great profits overcame the whites' fears of slave revolts, and some antebellum slaves continued to acquire valuable skills, though manumission became much more difficult.

More and more blacks drifted into the growing towns and cities where opportunities seemed the greatest. Richard C. Wade's *Slavery in the Cities: The South 1820-1860* described the advantages of urban life for blacks. The small, free minority that had a choice flocked to cities such as Baltimore, Richmond, St. Louis, Charleston, Savannah, and New Orleans, and runaway slaves often found a haven there too in nascent ghettoes. Slaves tried to wheedle an urban assignment, and many skilled slaves found work in commercial and industrial centers, some owned by urban masters and others hired out from the boondocks. Many unskilled blacks also found work in cities that needed hewers of wood and drawers of water just like rural areas. Some slaves went a giant step farther by working out a deal that allowed them to go on their own to town and find their own employment and periodically split the take with the master back home. These blacks sometimes irritated whites with their aggressiveness as they adopted the wheeling-and-dealing techniques of white entrepreneurs. They cried all the way to the bank like rich planters and moaned and groaned about hard times while privately conceding that they were doing "jes fine" like small-time white capitalists. These blacks were nimble and quick jacks-of-all-trades, and they quickly learned to evade most white harassment. Articulate, opportunistic, and much admired by the black masses, they would be natural leaders of their people when freedom came.

George Teamoh, who left a handwritten autobiography, was just such a black. Raised a slave in the Norfolk-Portsmouth urban area, he became a caulker in local shipyards, escaped to the Northeast in the 1850s, and came back to Virginia after the Civil War and served as a legislator until Reconstruction collapsed. An able, industrious, middle-class, Christian Southerner who happened to be black, he and many others like him simply lacked a fair chance in nineteenth-century America, even in the more advanced urban areas.

Blacks became a significant part of antebellum urban life, and women far outnumbered men in this relatively new phase of the black experience in the South. These tough, independent women worked as domestic servants, seamstresses, laundresses, and in other service occupations. Some · drifted into prostitution, but whites usually dominated that specialty. All over the urban South a petit bourgeoisie of black men and women painfully evolved, just waiting to break free of all the shackles of slavery and to compete against other Americans on equal terms.

Occasionally talented free blacks actually succeeded despite long odds and great risks. William Johnson of Natchez was one who prospered by anyone's standards. Legally freed by his master when he was around eleven years old, Johnson learned the barber's trade (a black monopoly before the Civil War) from his brother-in-law, James Miller, who soon moved on to booming New Orleans. Young Johnson stayed in Natchez, and for the rest of his life he enthusiastically engaged in a variety of business activities. His barbering business expanded and flourished, catering exclusively to whites and employing exclusively blacks. Almost all of his barbers were free blacks who came to him as young apprentices to learn the trade, and some later struck out on their own with their boss's blessing. He employed only two slaves, but Charles—hired out by a white master—proved very able and soon managed one of Johnson's small, branch shops, while Jim—owned by Johnson himself—also did well. Johnson's barber shops offered shaves for twelve cents and haircuts for a quarter and operated seven days a week (and sometimes even on Christmas). His customers included many distinguished citizens, who could obtain for a fee all kinds of extra goods and services such as perfumes, hair oils and soap, and could even rent private "shaving boxes" for a quarter a month. Johnson's customers went first-class, and in 1834 he added another refinement, a bathhouse (cold baths, fifty cents, hot ones, seventy-five cents from April through September).

Five feet seven inches tall and weighing only 140 pounds, Johnson was a dynamic, ambitious businessman who continually expanded and diversified his operations. He successfully speculated in real estate and housing, profitably rented several buildings, ran street watering and hauling businesses for a while, and frequently lent money at interest to whites. The Mississippi Rail Road Company went bankrupt soon after he purchased $2,000 worth of its stock, but generally he invested his money shrewdly and profitably. Like most successful Southern businessmen, he also invested in land and slaves. Late in his career he started accumulating tracts for farming and lumbering, and by the time of his death in 1851, he owned more than 1,500 acres. His estate also included fifteen slaves valued at $6,075—from the barber Jim valued at $1,000 down to Old Rose who was worth only $25 on the open market. Johnson knew how to manage the slave system to maximum effect, hiring out some of his laborers in slack periods and hiring extra hands when his own operations expanded. His rags-to-riches story matched the careers of many prominent Southerners; indeed, a summary of his life, omitting all mention of race, sounds like the story of a typical bourgeois businessman of the time.

Johnson also led the kind of social life so many other successful Southerners enjoyed. A restless extrovert, he delighted in the company of all sorts of people. He gambled a good bit, especially on card games and horse races, but also on cockfights and boat races and just about any other kind of contest. He enjoyed hunting and attending the theater. Though no intellectual, he accumulated a respectable library and subscribed to many magazines and journals, and he saw that each of his ten children received a functional education. He built a fine home and filled it with nice furniture, and for the last sixteen years of his life he kept a detailed business and personal diary and also saved all of his records and many miscellaneous papers and documents. His descendants faithfully preserved everything, and in 1951 William Ranson Hogan and Edwin Adams Davis edited and published the diary under the title *William Johnson's Natchez*, reinforcing the unique journal with orthodox records from the white world. Three years later they followed this up with a biography entitled *The Bar-*

ber of Natchez. Thus was resurrected an exceptional black man who somehow lived out the American dream in the slave South.

Yet even Johnson could not ignore the reality of his color. Despite all
of his achievements he was still basically a "nigger" in Mississippi. He could
not vote or hold office or serve on a jury or participate in a militia drill.
He had to sit in the balcony reserved for blacks when he attended the theater, and he could not hope to belong to the prestigious social clubs. He
tried to be a decent master to his own black slaves, but he had to play by
the general rules of the game. He sold a few of them over the years (always
for a profit), but he never split up a family by sale. In the privacy of his
diary he sometimes railed against the whole system of slavery and discrimination, but what could he do openly? He had already pushed to the very
limits of a system designed to keep blacks down, and finally in 1851 his
luck ran out. He was murdered in cold blood by a neighbor named Baylor
Winn, legally a white man but possibly a mulatto. The only witnesses were
black, so they could not testify against the culprit, and after several years
of hearings and trials Winn was acquitted.

Some whites considered blacks such as William Johnson a threat; yet
he accepted and indeed embraced the bourgeois values of white society.
Though not very religious, he lived the Protestant work ethic as truly as
any of his white neighbors. He and friends William Miller and Robert
McCary and other free blacks who prospered in barbering and related
businesses really were a threat in the sense that they showed that blacks
could rise above slavery and compete in the free world of whites. They
were ready and willing to plunge into the American mainstream; all they
needed was a decent chance.

An even more dramatic success story evolved in the interior of antebellum South Carolina. A young mulatto slave named April gained his
freedom from his master who was almost certainly also his father. Taking
his former owner's name of William Ellison, he prospered as a repairer and
manufacturer of cotton gins. Eventually, like many self-made whites, he
became a planter with 900 acres of land and sixty-three slaves (all
"blacks"). He and his large family lived the upper-middle-class life-style
to the hilt though, like the Johnsons in Mississippi, they faced many racist
restrictions, and some of his children married into the thriving mulatto

middle class in Charleston. This rags-to-riches story reads like an implausible novel, but Michael P. Johnson and James L. Roark have sifted through grassroots records and thoroughly documented the Ellison saga in two books, *Black Masters: A Free Family of Color in the Old South* and *No Chariot Let Down: Charleston's Free People of Color on the Eve of the Civil War.*

The handful of free blacks (of whatever color) like Johnson and Ellison who overcame tremendous odds demonstrated the validity of the introductory remarks in E. Franklin Frazier's *Black Bourgeoisie,* which vaguely traced the roots of the modern Negro middle class back to antebellum free blacks in the North and South. As Ira Berlin's *Slaves without Masters* indicated, the great majority of the South's 262,000 free blacks (a small group compared to the almost four million slaves in 1860) could not match the performances of Johnson and Ellison and barely eked out marginal existences. Most were small-time operators, but some—farmers, fishermen, artisans, and entrepreneurs—adopted as much of the bourgeois way of life as the dominant whites would allow, much more than is generally recognized.

Frazier's book not only underestimated the bourgeoisization of the free black minority; it completely ignored this same trend among the slave masses. Skilled slaves like ironworkers demonstrated middle-class values most openly, but this was only the tip of the iceberg. Down among the obscure slave masses many men and women were touched by this American fever, which involved much more than simple pride in a job well done. The shadows of slavery obscure much of this middle-class mentality, which cannot be precisely measured even among the free white population, but it existed to a significant extent, and it often surfaced without warning.

The voluminous records of the American Colonization Society contain many letters from bourgeoisized American blacks. Supported by prominent Americans such as Thomas Jefferson, Andrew Jackson, and Henry Clay and formally established in 1817, this unique organization strove to emancipate slaves and colonize free blacks in Africa. It stressed emancipation in the free North and colonization in the slave South, operating schizophrenically in a shadow world between the increasingly quarrelsome sections of the country. It received the most support in the upper South where many free blacks lived, but nowhere did it find massive

backing, and it started to fade rapidly in the 1830s as the abolition movement emerged in the North.

But the Colonization Society did not fail completely; by the time the
Civil War began more than 15,000 American blacks had landed on the
coast of West Africa and established the nation of Liberia. The overwhelming majority of Southern slaves had no chance for this new life across
the ocean; only a few had masters—usually motivated by Christian conscience—who gave them the choice of slavery at home or freedom in distant Africa. These fortunate few almost always chose freedom away from
home, and some later wrote letters back to America to friends, kinsmen,
and former masters. Bell Irvin Wiley's *Slaves No More: Letters from Liberia,
1833-1869* presented a sampling of these letters from black pioneers in Africa who remained very much Americans.

Some letters from these black pioneers reflected the middle-class attitudes that had developed in the slave community. Like European colonists who landed in America, the "Americo-Liberians" (as they called
themselves) found it difficult to adjust to an alien continent, and many
suffered greatly in the early days. Some farmed and a few even developed
large plantations, but the soil and climate were not attractive for agriculture—at least as far as native Americans were concerned. Most of the
American Negro colonists plunged enthusiastically into trade and commerce, and many did quite well in the buying and selling that only white
men could do with complete freedom back home. Gradually Liberia sta-
bilized and began to expand at the expense of neighboring African tribes.
The Americo-Liberians did not hesitate to stomp native Africans who began to refer to the aggressive newcomers from America as "white men."

These transplanted Americans generally were much paler than native
Africans, and besides, they certainly did act like "white men," that is,
Southerners or Americans. They preferred the corn and pork of the old
country, eating native foods only as a last resort. Their early defenses cop-
ied the pioneer stockades of early America. They continued to speak a
Southern version of English, and they patterned their government and legal system after American models. Some tried to spread Christianity among
the heathen, but most committed themselves primarily to the pursuit of
profit, just like middle-class Americans on the other side of the ocean. A

tiny handful of Americo-Liberians such as Jefferson Waters of Georgia returned home to slavery—much to the delight of proslavery propagandists who spread the word far and wide—but the overwhelming majority remained free in their new home in Liberia, though it took them a long time to acclimate to Africa. America, the land of their degradation, was also the land of their ancestors; their Americanness was more than just skin-deep.

In this respect they resembled the approximately 10,000 embittered white Confederates who fled to Latin America at the end of the Civil War to escape Yankee "despotism." These white refugees from America also found it difficult to blend into a new, alien world, and they too held on to many old ways of the old country, including a determination to "get ahead" and prosper among their less aggressive neighbors. Soon the word drifted south that the conquering Yankees were neither willing nor able to impose a permanent tyranny, and the vast majority of the refugees came home where they, unlike the Americo-Liberians, could be certain of freedom and equality. Even the small pockets of refugee rebels who refused to return remained hopelessly American. One of the most distinct settlements of these diehards survived and prospered eighty miles inland from São Paulo, Brazil, with some pioneers cultivating large crops of watermelons with "rattlesnake" seeds brought originally from their homeland to the north. Even in this distant land the Confederate settlers christened their new home "Villa Americana"—a name that told all too clearly what even the most unreconstructed Southerners were at heart. Their descendants live on today, proud to be Brazilians but proud too of their Southern ancestors. Like the original Americo-Liberians, these Confederate immigrants carried some bitter memories of the old country, but their Americanness remained more than just skin-deep too.

The Americo-Liberians were the fortunate few blacks who could escape slavery through the cooperation of their masters and the American Colonization Society. Some other American blacks tried desperately to follow them but faced insurmountable barriers. Letters in the files of the Colonization Society tell this sad story of highly Americanized blacks trying to escape slavery and oppression by returning to the alien land of their ancestors.

At the same time Jefferson Waters returned to Georgia from Liberia, young William H. Moss was trying desperately to go the other way to freedom. Examined in detail in James M. Gifford's article, "Black Hope and Despair in Antebellum Georgia," in the fall 1976 edition of *Prologue*, Moss's persistent correspondence with Colonization Society officials represented a relatively sophisticated, middle-class attempt to reach Liberia. Though only seventeen years old when he wrote his first letter in 1853, Moss kept hammering away over the years, trying to borrow enough money from the society for traveling expenses. Claiming to be free and "out of my appri[n]tisship" but possibly still a slave, he regularly read the society's journal, the *African Repository*, and played every angle. Finally after much fruitless manipulating, he made a supreme effort in the spring of 1857. In several letters he described himself as a "Boot Maker by trade" who had studied "Spelling & reading the English grammar Arithmetic & Geography & English language Analysis & Physiology & Hygiene & botany & parkers philosophy & I can teach Chemistry veary good . . . & I have started into Geology But I can Not do much with it yet." He also conceded that he could "not Remember long at the Time." He claimed to be able to "teach music . . . and Spelling & reading," to "garden as well as anyone at the North," and to have continued his studies with work in "Chemistry and Natural & Experimental philosophy." He stated further that he knew "Mechanics, hydrostatics hydraulics acoustics Electro magnetism & magnet Electricity." To top it all off, he claimed to have been studying medicine for some time under Dr. William R. Moseley.

The officials of the Colonization Society probably had trouble deciding whether to laugh or cry over such pompous boasting by an obscure young black man, but, as kind and gentle men, they did not break off the correspondence. Then on 2 May they were astonished to receive a letter from Dr. Moseley, a respected member of the white community and the medical profession. Moseley strongly recommended Moss, who was indeed studying medicine under his direction, and he concluded unequivocally: "I have to say that I am of the opinion by next fall he will be competant bothe for admitence into College and for the preactice of medicine *in Liberia*. His habits *are good* and he is a very moral young man."

Young Moss did get a little carried away in some of his desperate letters trying to win the support of the Colonization Society, but he was indeed a bright, hardworking, ambitious young black man on the make for a better life. Stuck away in a small town in central Georgia, just another black in a sea of faceless slaves, he had somehow become more bourgeois than many whites in his neighborhood. With the encouragement of some blacks and the quiet help of a few whites, he had already entered the middle-class world of striving for achievement and recognition. Against great odds he became literate and even partially educated. His young life had all the ingredients of a classic American success story as he struggled to soar as far as his abilities would carry him—if not in America, then in Liberia. Ironically, the system that suppressed him had also infected him with bourgeois ideas.

A unique individual, William H. Moss fought the system valiantly— and lost. He never made it to Liberia; his letters stopped coming to the Colonization Society and he simply disappeared. He may have died in a smallpox epidemic in his hometown in 1857 or he may have been sucked back into the dark world of slavery. He was far more ambitious and accomplished than most blacks, but thousands and thousands of others— free and slave—had also absorbed much of the bourgeois mentality that permeated the white South and trickled steadily down to the slave masses. Slavery was indeed a "peculiar institution" that affected each black person in a very distinct manner. Some blacks drifted into bourgeois ways and many others leaned in that general direction, but a few such as John Glasgow were brutally herded in the opposite direction.

Born free in British Guiana, young Glasgow became a sailor, and soon he was working the Atlantic routes, often operating out of Liverpool, one of England's busiest ports. There he met a Lancashire girl from a nearby farm, and soon they married. Illiterate but intelligent, he was a personable fellow, large and well built and "black as a coal." His English neighbors remained much like the seventeenth-century Englishmen who landed at Jamestown and much like the Anglo-Americans still living across the Atlantic: they had little use for "niggers" and no sympathy for miscegenation. Still, the happy young couple was tolerated as they settled down quietly near Liverpool. Glasgow continued to earn a living as an able-bodied seaman in the British merchant marine, his calling, while his wife continued the farm work she had done all her life. Soon they had two children, and Glasgow decided to spend more time at home, gradually learning the agrarian way of life and going to sea only to earn needed cash. Aided by his father-in-law, he obtained a small farm, and with his seaman's earnings he bought three horses, a cart, and a plow. Gradually he began to make his mark as an independent man. By 1830 he had almost completely abandoned the sea, but needing more funds for the farm, he signed on at Liverpool for a voyage to Savannah to pick up a cargo of rice.

The voyage was uneventful, but the twenty-five-year-old Glasgow ran into trouble as soon as he stepped ashore at Savannah, a Southern city with tough rules and regulations about blacks—any blacks. Southern free blacks, men such as William Johnson, were considered a nuisance or embarrassment by many whites; free black outsiders were generally considered a menace. Such fellows coming ashore as hearty, confident sailors might plant dangerous ideas in the minds of Southern blacks. Hence in the wake of Denmark Vesey's insurrectionary plot in 1822, South Carolina enacted legislation to restrict their movements. In the port of Charleston free black seamen who came ashore were interned in the local jail until their ships departed. The British government protested that this procedure violated treaty agreements between the United States and Great Britain. Federal officials did not deny the legitimacy of the complaint but pleaded their inability to force South Carolina compliance. Pressure by Secretary of State John Quincy Adams had no lasting effect, and even a stern lecture by a Supreme Court justice could not deter the Carolinians: they considered their new regulations essential for public safety—a matter of life and death—and hence more important than constitutional quibbles about treaties being "the supreme law of the land." Besides, any good American enjoyed twisting the British lion's tail and listening to him roar, and no good American favored forcing an explosive constitutional confrontation over a few people who were both "furriners" and "niggers." A few years later in 1833 the federal government under President Andrew Jackson moved to the brink of civil war to end South Carolina's nullification of a federal tariff, but that state's first defiance of federal authority in the 1820s went unchallenged, and nobody moved a muscle to help John Glasgow in 1830.

By this time Savannah had adopted regulations much like Charleston's, so Glasgow was routinely interned in the city jail. Doing time there was no picnic, and Glasgow became uneasy as well as uncomfortable when his ship stayed on and on in the harbor waiting for a full cargo of rice. Finally after some weeks of waiting—and rising "room and board" charges on the jail's ledger—the vessel was loaded. Then suddenly it departed, leaving Glasgow alone in "the land of the free." Perhaps the captain wanted to avoid paying Glasgow's jail fees and salary or maybe he resented a black shipmate with a white wife and mulatto children back in England. Whatever the reason, he simply left Glasgow to the tender mercies of Georgia law.

The law spoke clearly in such cases. Glasgow was sold at auction to the highest bidder like any other piece of private property. Suddenly Glasgow became an American slave. He retained his name (unofficially) but little else as he disappeared into the booming cotton fields of central Georgia. There he toiled for a driven and hard-driving planter on the make named Thomas Stevens. Glasgow did not adjust: he could not forget his free life, his wife and children back in England, his dream of working his way up into the secure ranks of the Lancashire yeomanry. He too had been a man on the make, striving to "get ahead," but now he was just another field hand. He bucked the system enough to provoke a harsh master determined to break his spirit. Another slave described the climax of a series of brutal punishments.

> The unfortunate fellow was taken to the whipping-post, which on Stevens' estate consisted of two solid uprights, some ten feet high, with a cross-beam at the top, forming a kind of gallows. Along the cross-beam were three or four massive iron cleats, to which pulleys were fixed, having a fine but closely-twisted cord passing over them. John Glasgow having been stripped, as on the previous occasion, the end of one of these cords was tightly fastened round his wrists. His left foot was then drawn up and tied, toes downward, to his right knee, so that his left knee formed an angle by means of which, when swung up, his body could conveniently be turned. An oaken stake, about two feet long, was now driven into the ground beneath the cross-beam of the whipping-post, and made sharp at the top with a draw-knife. He was then hoisted up by his hands, by means of the pulley and rope, in such wise that his body swung by its own weight, his hands being high over his head and his right foot level with the pointed end of the oaken "stob" or stake.

I may here state that this punishment is called the picket, and by being swung in this manner, the skin of the victim's back is stretched till it shines, and cuts more readily under the lash: on the other hand, if the unhappy sufferer, swinging "between heaven and earth" as it is called, desires to rest, he can do so only by placing the foot that is at liberty on the sharp end of the stake. The excessive pain caused by being flogged while suspended, and the nausea excited by twirling round, causes the victim of the "picket" to seek temporary relief by staying himself on the "stob." On his doing so, for ever so brief a space, one of the bystanders taking hold of the bent knee, and using it as a handle, gives the unfortunate a twirl, and sends him spinning round on the hard point of the stake, which perforates the heel or the sole of the foot, as the case may be, quite to the bone.

John Glasgow thus suspended was flogged and twisted for an hour, receiving "five licks" or strokes of the raw cowhide at a time, with an interval of two or three minutes between, to allow him "to come to, and to fetch his breath." His shrieks and groans were most agonizing, and could be heard, at first, a mile and a quarter off, but as the punishment proceeded, they subsided into moans scarcely audible at the distance of fifty paces. All Stevens' slaves were made to stand by during the infliction of the torture, and some of them took turns at the whipping, according to the instructions of their master, who swore he would serve them the same if they refused, or ever disobeyed him as "that cussed nigger there had done." At the end of the hour he was "dropped from the gallows," his back being fearfully lacerated, his wrists deeply cut with the cord, and his foot pierced through in three places. Beneath the beam there was a pool of coagulated blood, whilst the oaken stake was dyed red with that which had streamed from his foot. He could not stand, much less walk, so they carried him to his quarters, where the usual application of salt and water, and red pepper, was made to his wounds, and he was left to die or to recover, as might be. It was a month before he stirred from his plank, five months more elapsed ere he could walk. Ever after he had a limp in his gait.

Slavery broke Glasgow. Two years after the "picket" his right leg was shattered by a falling tree—perhaps he still limped too much to get out of the way—and he spent the rest of his days an invalid, shelling corn and doing other light chores, at best half a hand and half a man. The psychological damage to this subject of Queen Victoria at least equaled the physical damage; he had known freedom and suddenly lost it. Elkins's *Slavery* did not concern itself with real individuals such as John Glasgow, but he more than most slaves endured trials similar to the sudden, massive horror experienced by victims of Nazi concentration camps. Even Glasgow was not completely Samboized, however. The spirit of freedom still flickered in him, and he passed it on to a fellow slave named Fed.

Born around 1810 in Southampton County, Fed experienced a real slave childhood. His father Joe lived on a nearby plantation, but was soon carried away by a migrating master. Fed saw him only once and remembered very little, only that his father was very black and the son of an Ibo tribesman. Fed's mother Nancy, alone with three children, was forced to take another man, Lamb, by whom she bore three more children. Fed's childhood on the farm was not too bad, even with a stern mistress named Betty Moore who always carried a light whip that the slaves called the "blue lizard." Then, about ten years before Nat Turner's revolt erupted in another part of the county, Elizabeth Moore's estate was divided among her six children in the usual middle-class manner, and Fed and his mother moved south into adjoining Northampton County, North Carolina, to become the property of Moore's son-in-law, James Davis.

Small and wiry, energetic and ambitious, Davis worked his slaves hard. Too young to do a man's work, Fed still put in a full day on his new master's farm, handpicking worms off tobacco plants and doing other chores, but he remained there only eighteen months. Soon Davis needed more cash to build a new home, so he simply sold the black youngster to Sterling Finney, who was speculating in slave property as he moved south to Georgia. Stunned with grief, Fed marched away with a coffle of slaves, bound for the booming Georgia market. He never saw his mother or kin or friends again; he simply vanished from their lives.

He was taken to Milledgeville, the capital of Georgia, and there he was sold to Thomas Stevens, an enterprising farmer. Fed grew to manhood on Stevens's fast-growing farm. He labored in the fields and also learned basic carpentry from his master and participated in many other of his diversified business activities. Inevitably Fed absorbed some of his master's bourgeois attitudes as the years passed. In 1830 John Glasgow joined Stevens's growing gang of slave laborers, and he and Fed quickly became fast friends. Older and more cosmopolitan and sophisticated, Glasgow was like a much older brother or even an uncle to the shy young Virginian who never tired of hearing stories of the great outside world of freedom. As Fed later put it: "To John I owe a debt of gratitude, for he it was who taught me to love and to seek liberty."

Glasglow planted the idea of freedom in Fed's head and heart where it flowered, and he also shaped a powerful image of England as a refuge for oppressed American blacks. Not the North nor Canada nor Liberia but golden England would be Fed's ultimate beacon and his last hope. Increasingly restless, Fed took to hiding out in the woods and swamps to escape the relentless grind of hard labor. Sometimes he laid out for weeks, only to return to a brutal whipping, but he could not bring himself to make the long run for freedom. It was, without question, a fearful gamble for a life-long slave stuck away in a remote corner of the Deep South. Finally he was talked into running away by a white man who led him into Tennessee, where he discovered his "nigger stealing" accomplice had been jailed. He brought the confused Fed back to his master and graciously accepted a thirty-dollar reward for recapturing a "runaway." Catching on at last, Fed talked fast, swore never to run away again, and miraculously avoided another whipping.

When old Stevens died in 1839, his estate was divided among his heirs in the usual manner, and Glasgow and Fed went to different sons. "Decatur" Stevens was no better than his father as far as the slaves were concerned, so Fed, lonely and restless, ran for freedom again, this time entirely on his own. He still had not the foggiest idea how to get to England, and he only got as far as Tennessee before he was captured. He managed to escape, but disoriented and discouraged, he returned to his master in northwest Georgia, and again he received "a dreadful flogging."

Things went from bad to worse for Fed. One day his master became enraged at him and leaped on him, calling for another slave to bring his gun. Reflexively Fed threw him off, and Stevens hit the ground hard, injuring his neck. Fed ran off in a panic and hid in the woods for three days, but then a slave patrol with dogs ran him down. Like his friend Glasgow, Fed now felt the full weight of the slave system.

> . . . at this moment, Billy Curtis, a planter, who was one of the party, and who was well mounted, rode up and struck me on the head with a dogwood club. The blow felled me, as though I had been shot, completely stunning me. When I recovered, I found myself stretched on the ground,

my head bleeding fearfully, and my master standing over me, with his foot on my forehead. The scar that blow made, I retain to this day.

I was now forced to get up, when they drove me to where I had seen the posts. Here they tied my hands and feet together, and passing the rope through the block and pulleys, hoisted me up and began to swing me backwards and forwards. Billy Curtis stood on one side, with a bull-whip in his hand, and David Barrett on the other, with a cowhide. My master stood a little further off, laughing, and as Curtis and Barrett could not whip and swing me too, a negro was set to keep me going. As I swung past them, these men hit me each a lick with their whips, and they continued doing so until I fainted, when I was taken down.

But I was not done with yet. . . .

To prevent my running away any more, Stevens fixed bells and horns on my head. This was not by any means an uncommon punishment. I have seen many slaves wearing them. A circle of iron, having a hinge behind, with a staple and padlock before, which hang under the chin, is fastened round the neck. Another circle of iron fits quite close round the crown of the head. The two are held together in this position by three rods of iron, which are fixed in each circle. These rods, or horns, stick out three feet above the head, and have a bell attached to each. The bells and horns do not weigh less than from twelve to fourteen pounds. When Stevens had fixed this ornament on my head, he turned me loose, and told me I might run off now if I liked.

I wore the bells and horns, day and night, for three months, and I do not think any description I could give of my sufferings during this time would convey any thing approaching to a faint idea of them. Let alone that their weight made my head and neck ache dreadfully, especially when I stooped to my work, at night I could not lie down to rest, because the horns prevented my stretching myself, or even curling myself up; so I was obliged to sleep crouching. Of course it was impossible for me to attempt to remove them, or to get away, though I still held to my resolution to make another venture as soon as I could see my way of doing it. Indeed, during those three long months, I thought more of John Glasgow, and getting off to England, than I had ever done all the time before, with such a firm purpose. I collected and arranged in my mind all the scraps of information I had been able to procure from others, or that I had acquired myself; and concealed, in the trunk of an old tree, a bundle of clothes and a flint and steel and tinder-horn: for though my case seemed desperate, I clung to hope, with a tenacity which now surprises me.

Finally the bell was temporarily removed, and Fed, now more afraid to stay than to run, took off again. More knowledgeable now but still confused about geography, he headed north into western Kentucky and then down the Mississippi River to New Orleans, which he understood to be "just across the water" from England. Quickly sucked into the great city's slave pens, he soon found himself hard at work on a dreary cotton plantation in Mississippi. After a few months he ran again, knowing now to follow the great river north to free country.

This time he made it, passing through Illinois and Indiana and on into Michigan. He received some help from sympathetic Northerners, black and white, but generally he did it on his own, demonstrating what Larry Gara's *The Liberty Line: The Legend of the Underground Railroad* later stressed: the heralded underground railroad was actually not very extensive or well organized, so that runaway slaves generally had to find their own freedom. Fed was headed for Canada, the next best thing to glorious England, but he remained for a year in Marshall, Michigan, doing construction work with other runaways. Then he moved on to Detroit where he joined a group of Cornish miners, good Englishmen, and worked with them in northwestern Michigan for eighteen months. Finally he crossed into Canada and stayed briefly at Dawn Institute, a vocational training center for fugitive American slaves. Then at last he took his savings and bought passage on a steamer to England, where he rejoined his miner friends at Redruth in Cornwall.

Now with the free name of John Brown—common enough in England—he moved around some, working at the carpenter's trade he had learned in slavery; but he was handicapped by his foreign accent and his foreign skin. Finally in 1851 he moved to London, took a room in an inexpensive boarding house, and contacted officials of the British and Foreign Anti-Slavery Society. They were fascinated by his life story, but they checked up on him very carefully; like American abolitionists, they had been embarrassed by phony fugitive slaves a couple of times. Soon they were convinced that this plain black man and his story were authentic, and they dispatched him on a speaking tour.

Brown just told it like it was for him in American slavery, and he effectively reached his middle-class and well-to-do audiences. Gradually learning the tricks of oratory, he sometimes lectured for an hour and a half, and soon he was collecting enough in fees to cover many of his living expenses. Invariably audiences were moved by the story of his friend John Glasgow, a British subject swallowed up by slavery. Brown concentrated on this episode, and soon it was being published as an independent story. The British and Foreign Anti-Slavery Society's *Anti-Slavery Reporter* ran his account of Glasgow on 1 July 1853, and other English newspapers and journals followed suit. The Leeds Anti-Slavery Series published it as tract number eighty-nine and distributed it widely. The story spread to Europe and America where a few abolition journals reprinted it, including *Frederick Douglass' Paper*, which gave it front-page coverage on 1 October 1854.

Brown and his abolitionist friends also saw that Glasgow's story was properly recorded and witnessed by a notary public in London. The Glasgow tragedy was neatly written out in longhand on nine large sheets and officially witnessed by Alexander Ridgway in London on 1 May 1854, and that document, crudely signed by John Brown, remains today in the archives of the British and Foreign Anti-Slavery Society in Rhodes House at Oxford University. The British abolitionists also carried the story to the British Foreign Office with a demand that an investigation begin. Obviously the mistreatment of a British subject in Savannah in 1830 could not be remedied a quarter of a century later, but the British government was still trying to end the internment of black seamen in Southern cities such as Charleston and Savannah, so the consuls at these two seaports were dutifully and rather unenthusiastically instructed to investigate the Glasgow affair. They found out nothing, of course. Just as Glasgow had been swallowed up by Georgia slavery, the whole matter was filed and forgotten in routine Foreign Office records, which now rest securely at the Public Record Office in London.

But the British and Foreign Anti-Slavery Society did not give up. In 1855 it published John Brown's autobiography, which included a whole chapter on his friend Glasgow. Brown had been making some effort to learn to read and write, but this small volume, *Slave Life in Georgia*, was actually penned by Louis Alexis Chamerovzow, the society's tireless secretary. In the manner of many athletic and theatrical stars, Brown told his story to a professional writer, who then recorded it in standard middle-class English for the reading public. *Slave Life* was, of course, abolition propaganda; but when checked against various grassroots records from the antebellum South, as was done by F. N. Boney in a 1972 reissue of the volume, it passed muster. Brown had been a slave certainly, and his memoir remains at least as reliable as any white reminiscence about the good old days on the plantations. Occasionally polemical, it was still potent antislavery propaganda because it remained a basically accurate description of slavery from the perspective of a former slave. Its value was enhanced because the vast majority of runaways came from the upper South, and only a very few of the really reliable fugitive slave narratives described slavery in deep Southern states such as Georgia.

Slave Life sold well enough to run a second, limited edition, and before the year ended it was translated into German and, altered slightly and weighed down with a ponderous, Teutonic introduction, published in Stuttgart. It received only limited notice in an America already quite familiar with fugitive slave narratives, but overall it helped provide John Brown with some funds to supplement his lecture fees and occasional income from carpentry work.

Brown had not adjusted easily to life in free England. He accepted the mores of the middle-class capitalistic society, the whole work ethic of striving and succeeding that he had already been exposed to in the slave South. Nevertheless, like many white Americans and Englishmen who also accepted this creed, he simply did not succeed. He did not totally fail either, for he kept plugging along. As his work as a writer and lecturer tapered off, he concentrated more on carpentry, but he had never been more than a journeyman in this field, and he barely got by. He planned to go to the West Indies or Liberia to teach free blacks to cultivate cotton profitably, but he never saved enough money to try. Or perhaps he hung back for fear of failure, much as he had hung back so long before running from slavery in Georgia. Soon the Civil War ended slavery in America, but by this time Brown had no desire to go home. He had made his peace with England, another white man's country. Late in life he married an Englishwoman and began to eke out a modest living as a "Herbalist" (herb doctor) in a working-class area of London. There he died quietly in 1876, as forgotten in his native land as his friend John Glasgow had been in his.

Brown of Georgia died in obscurity, still a marginal man in free England, but many fugitive slaves prospered and thrived in freedom. As a group they were exceptional people who challenged long odds to win the liberty white Americans took for granted. Many quickly accepted the capitalistic system of the North. This same middle-class system functioned in the South, where it dominated the whites and powerfully influenced many slaves too, inadvertently preparing them to operate more effectively as free people.

The dramatic life of Frederick Douglass, one of the most famous runaways, demonstrated this clearly. His *Narrative of the Life of Frederick Douglass, An American Slave, Written by Himself*, 1845, and other writings now being published by the Yale University Press described his life as a young slave in detail. Born on the Eastern Shore of Maryland around 1818, he was christened Frederick Augustus Washington Bailey by his proud mother, but people just called him Fred. A mulatto, his father may have been his first master, Aaron Anthony, but he never knew for sure, and his mother soon faded away too. As he put it: "My mother and I were separated when I was but an infant—before I knew her as my mother. . . . I never saw my mother, to know her as such, more than four or five times in my life; and each of these times was very short in duration, and at night."

On his own, young Fred soon learned all about the relentless Southern work ethic. His first master was an ambitious, energetic bourgeois type who ended up owning three farms valued at $8,500 and thirty slaves and serving as what Douglass called "clerk and superintendent . . . overseer of the overseers" for a wealthy planter named Edward Lloyd who owned several hundred slaves. Adult slaves worked very hard on Lloyd's vast holdings. As a child of about six, Fred lived on Lloyd's home plantation (which alone employed 167 slaves), but he had only chores to do: "The most I had to do was to drive up the cows at the evening, keep the fowls out of the garden, keep the front yard clean, and run errands for my old master's daughter." Still, like young Fed and young Booker T. Washington, he remembered well the no-nonsense work discipline that permeated every level of the slave-labor system.

After several years young Fred was sent across the Chesapeake Bay to live with Mr. and Mrs. Hugh Auld in Baltimore, and there he remained for a few years. With occasional help from whites, but mostly on his own, he learned to read and write—and to thirst for knowledge and freedom.

Then at about eleven years of age he was sent back to the Eastern Shore where he settled down to a harsh work routine under Mr. and Mrs. Thomas Auld in the little town of St. Michaels. Soon he was rented out to Edward Covey, a renowned "nigger breaker." An ambitious man who rented land and slaves and perpetually drove himself and his workers, he taught young Fred the real meaning of hard labor and slavery. The blacks called him "the snake" because he constantly popped up unexpectedly, eager to punish slackers in the fields.

By this time Fred had grown large and strong as a lad of about sixteen, and he began to defend himself against physical abuse almost like a free man. Then in 1834 he was assigned to work for William Freeland, who lived near St. Michaels. A decent fellow, Freeland believed in middle-class ways too. He owned two slaves and rented three others and, as Douglass put it: "He worked us hard, but always between sunrise and sunset. He required a good deal of work to be done, but gave us good tools with which to work." After about a year with Freeland, Douglass and some friends decided to run for freedom, but like Fed in Georgia and many other slaves, he wavered. Success meant the fearful unknown, and failure meant terrible punishment, including the distinct possibility of a one-way trip to the cotton fields of the Deep South. An inadequate knowledge of geography further handicapped the plotters who delayed too long, aroused white suspicion, and ended up in jail.

Then Fred was returned to Hugh Auld in Baltimore where he was hired out to work in William Gardner's shipyard as an apprentice. There he worked at a feverish pace, having little time to think of his future. After about eight months some white apprentices beat him up severely, so he was then hired out to work as a caulker in Walter Price's shipyard. Learning fast and working hard, he was soon bringing home to Auld nine dollars in weekly wages. Then, gaining confidence as well as skill, he began to hire himself out for top dollar, wheeling and dealing, making more money while working fewer hours.

Suddenly, after a clash with Auld, he was jerked back into his old routine and returned to a regular job at another shipyard. Frustrated and disgusted, free of all family ties, he finally made his run for freedom in September 1838. He reached New York City without difficulty, married

Anna Murray, a free black woman who came north to join him, and moved on to New Bedford, Massachusetts, where after some deliberation, he assumed the free name of Frederick Douglass.

He had learned a stern work ethic in slavery—the hard way—and now he applied it with a vengeance in freedom. Hostile white workers blocked his efforts to pursue his calling as a caulker, so he labored (and almost slaved) away at any job he could find. As Douglass explained: "There was no work too hard—none too dirty. I was ready to saw wood, shovel coal, carry wood, sweep the chimney, or roll oil casks—all of which I did for nearly three years in New Bedford, before I became known to the antislavery world."

Then Douglass launched a spectacularly successful career. Intelligent and articulate and industrious, he attacked slavery in the South and racial prejudice in the North. He wrote and spoke widely as the abolition movement grew steadily in the North. In 1847 he began his own antislavery newspaper, first named the *North Star* and later known as *Frederick Douglass' Paper*. In this field he was a radical, advocating violence to eliminate slavery. He supported John Brown, the white abolitionist, in his attack on Harpers Ferry, and when the Civil War started he was prominent among those who pushed Lincoln to go all out to crush the slave South. He vigorously recruited black troops for the Union army and rejoiced when Lincoln finally made emancipation a primary objective of the war effort. After victory he championed Radical Reconstruction as the only way to eliminate the stubborn vestiges of the old slave regime.

But beyond the question of slavery, Douglass eagerly accepted the traditional American economic system. When speaking to black audiences, he stressed self-help, and he eagerly plunged into the bourgeois mainstream himself, moving ahead rapidly. He succeeded in the business world and also became a significant figure in the Republican party, holding several patronage posts over the years. A representative black American of the nineteenth century, he hated the slave system that had abused him, but once that was gone, he embraced the dynamic capitalism that permeated the North and the South. Eager and ambitious, he fit right in as soon as the American system allowed him access.

Other fugitive slaves traveled the same rough road. William Wells Brown's career closely resembled Douglass's. Born in Kentucky around

1815, the son of a white planter and a slave mother, he was hired out to work on a steamboat and in a printer's shop in St. Louis. He was introduced to education as well as hard labor while still a slave, and his career blossomed in freedom. He pursued formal education, including the study of medicine, but mainly he established himself as a professional writer. Prolific and versatile, his work ranged from poetry and the novel to travel literature and biography. He concentrated on black history, and his most notable contribution was his own Southern autobiography, *Narrative of William Wells Brown, A Fugitive Slave, Written by Himself,* published in 1847, only two years after Douglass's story.

Similarly, another runaway slave, William W. C. Pennington, was born in 1809 in Douglass country, on the Eastern Shore of Maryland. First hired out as a stonemason, he later followed the trade of blacksmith until he ran away at the age of twenty-one. He eagerly pursued formal education in the North, published his *Fugitive Blacksmith* in London in 1849, and became a prominent minister in churches in New York City and New England. And William and Ellen Craft, slaves in Macon, only about thirty miles from John Brown's slave home in Georgia, did quite well for themselves in England. There in 1860 they published *Running a Thousand Miles for Freedom,* which told a lot about their escape but very little about their lives in slavery. They returned to America after the Civil War and, Southern to the core, they ended up back in Georgia in 1870. They settled near Savannah, ran a school for blacks of all ages, and operated a large plantation that used to be owned by whites but now was cultivated by families of black tenant farmers. Free of slavery's chains, the Browns, Penningtons, and Crafts of the South quickly and successfully adopted the American way of life; all they had ever needed was a chance. Many other fugitive slaves with less talent and ambition than these exceptional blacks also made the transition from slavery to freedom and managed to hold their own in the competitive American system; they too had lacked only a chance to show that they belonged in the mainstream of national life.

The great majority of Southern slaves had no real chance to escape to freedom, but they too were affected by the pervasive middle-class mentality of white America. In the free world the competitiveness of the system created some rogues—slippery fellows who lied, cheated, stole, or even murdered to get ahead. Within the tense, "uptight" world of slavery, middle-class values were sometimes even more strained and distorted. Some ruthless operators within the slave community preyed unmercifully upon their own people, much like pimps and pushers in modern ghettoes. Most blacks had to walk a narrow line between their masters and their fellow slaves; and cooks, mammies, other house servants, skilled laborers, and other privileged slaves had to perform a particularly delicate balancing act. Even the best of them drifted over to the white world occasionally, lured by calculated self-interest, absentminded affection, and other complex, partly unconscious motives that affect human beings under pressure. The worst of them crossed the line with a vengeance, willing and even eager to get ahead at the expense of other blacks.

This black exploitation of blacks could even be murderous. Solomon Northup, a former slave, described such an incident in his *Twelve Years a Slave*. Born free in New York, he lived a normal life with his wife and three children until 1841. About thirty years old and a carpenter and musician by trade, he went to Washington, D.C., to play the violin for a circus troupe, and while there he was shanghaied into the slave pens of the nation's capital. The slave trade operated efficiently, and soon he was shipped to New Orleans and sold to a planter in central Louisiana. Like John Glasgow, Northup had difficulty making the sudden adjustment to the world of black slavery, and like John Brown, he was a long, long way from free country. But finally he got word out to Northern friends who instituted legal proceedings that gained him freedom. He joined John Brown and the Crafts as one of the tiny handful of slaves who escaped slavery in the Deep South and lived to write about it. He began free life anew in New York, and in 1853 with the collaboration of a lawyer-writer, he published his story, including the epic of Lew Cheney, who manipulated his way to freedom over the broken bodies of his friends.

> The year before my arrival in the country there was a concerted movement among a number of slaves on Bayou Boeuf, that terminated tragically indeed. It was, I presume, a matter of newspaper notoriety at the time, but all the knowledge I have of it, has been derived from the relation of those living at that period in the immediate vicinity of the excitement. It has become a subject of general and unfailing interest in every slave-hut on the bayou, and will doubtless go down to succeeding generations as their

chief tradition. Lew Cheney, with whom I became acquainted—a shrewd, cunning negro, more intelligent than the generality of his race, but unscrupulous and full of treachery—conceived the project of organizing a company sufficiently strong to fight their way against all opposition, to the neighboring territory of Mexico.

A remote spot, far within the depths of the swamp back of Hawkins' plantation, was selected as the rallying point. Lew flitted from one plantation to another, in the dead of night, preaching a crusade to Mexico, and like, Peter the Hermit, creating a furor of excitement wherever he appeared. At length a large number of runaways were assembled; stolen mules, and corn gathered from the fields, and bacon filched from smokehouses, had been conveyed into the woods. The expedition was about ready to proceed, when their hiding place was discovered. Lew Cheney, becoming convinced of the ultimate failure of his project, in order to curry favor with his master, and avoid the consequences which he foresaw would follow, deliberately determined to sacrifice all his companions. Departing secretly from the encampment, he proclaimed among the planters the number collected in the swamp, and, instead of stating truly the object they had in view, asserted their intention was to emerge from their seclusion the first favorable opportunity, and murder every white person along the bayou.

Such an announcement, exaggerated as it passed from mouth to mouth, filled the whole country with terror. The fugitives were surrounded and taken prisoners, carried in chains to Alexandria, and hung by the populace. Not only those, but many who were suspected, though entirely innocent, were taken from the field and from the cabin, and without the shadow of process or form of trial, hurried to the scaffold. The planters on Bayou Boeuf finally rebelled against such reckless destruction of property, but it was not until a regiment of soldiers had arrived from some fort on the Texas frontier, demolished the gallows, and opened the doors of the Alexandria prison, that the indiscriminate slaughter was stayed. Lew Cheney escaped, and was even rewarded for his treachery. He is still living, but his name is despised and execrated by all his race throughout the parishes of Rapides and Avoyelles.

In 1968 scholars Sue Eakin and Joseph Logsdon reissued Northup's story with an introduction and a series of footnotes citing original Southern documents to verify his narrative. In the published *Acts of the Second Session of the Thirteenth Legislature of the State of Louisiana,* they discovered that Lewis, a slave of David Cheney who lived in the Bayou Boeuf area, was freed by an act of the legislators in 1838. Cheney received $1,500 for his lost property, and Lewis received $500 for his heroic services. In the same act five other local slaveholders received compensation for their seven slaves who were executed for plotting insurrection. Thus did Lew Cheney earn his freedom and turn a neat profit—more than the traditional thirty pieces of silver.

Like collaborators in occupied nations and informers in prisons, blacks could be corrupted and perverted by the slave system. White oppression of blacks encouraged black oppression of blacks, and the slave masses paid the price. Slavery was a harsh system; it inflicted physical and psychological damage on all blacks, some much more than others. Whippings, family separations, sexual abuses, and general humiliation and degradation all took their toll, directly or indirectly. Sometimes tension and fear over time could devastate a victim worse than one sudden, brutal onslaught, but every slave bore some scars, visible or invisible. At the same time that slaves were absorbing some middle-class values, they absorbed much punishment too. Of all the diverse American people, blacks found it the most difficult to really belong; certainly the slaves "paid their dues."

Slaves might fall victim to grotesque, sadistic abuses, but for economic as well as moral reasons, such incidents were rare—or at least rarely reported. Yet questionable and disquieting occurrences did surface occasionally. Some medical scientists seeking abstract truths and pragmatic cures found blacks very convenient guinea pigs; the slave system created unique temptations and unique opportunities. Thomas Jefferson, a great and good man as the world goes, first inoculated his slaves against smallpox by an unreliable, dangerous technique called variolation, but at the same time he exposed his own family to the same treatment. In 1801, when Jenner's safer and more effective technique was available, he vaccinated about 200 slaves—some his and others belonging to neighbors—with successful results. Soon thereafter Jenner's vaccination was accepted in Virginia as a legitimate medical procedure, but few realized the vital role slave guinea pigs had played.

A much more aggressive experiment was conducted by Dr. J. Marion Sims who told all in his autobiography, *The Story of My Life*, edited and published by his son in 1884. Born on a farm near Lancaster, South Carolina, in 1813, Sims graduated from South Carolina College in 1832 and then studied medicine in Charleston and Philadelphia. Finally he settled in Montgomery, Alabama, in the 1840s and established a thriving medical practice, specializing in surgery.

He became intrigued by the female problem of vesico-vaginal fistula, a cleft between the bladder and the vagina that allowed the unimpeded flow of urine. A rare and nonlethal defect that usually developed after childbirth, it was in Sims's view "loathsome," and victims certainly experienced constant discomfort and humiliation. They simply could not control the flow of urine out of their bodies and thus became freaks and pariahs and, worse yet, no doctor could help them.

After encountering this condition for the first time in the slave Anarcha after delivering her baby, Sims determined to develop a surgical procedure for sealing the cleft between the bladder and the vagina. Among the slave masses of central Alabama he found an adequate supply of experimental patients, and to their owners he made a proposition:

> If you will give me Anarcha and Betsey for experiment, I agree to perform no experiment or operation on either of them to endanger their lives, and will not charge a cent for keeping them, but you must pay their taxes and clothe them. I will keep them at my own expense.

So the great work began with Anarcha, Betsey, and Lucy, a third slave, as the subjects of a series of new operations. Anesthetics were not yet used in surgery, and the patient suffered greatly. Lucy went first in December 1845, and she ran into real trouble, as Sims described clinically:

> At the end of five days my patient was very ill. She had fever, frequent pulse, and real blood-poisoning, but we did not know what to call it at that day and time. However, I saw that everything must be removed; so I cut loose my sutures, which had been held by a peculiar mechanical contrivance which is not necessary here to detail. Then I attempted to remove the little piece of sponge from the neck of the bladder. It was about two inches long. One inch occupied the urethra, half an inch projected into the bladder, and half an inch into the meatus. As soon as it was applied, the urine came dripping through, just as fast as it was secreted in the bladder, and so it continued during all the time it was worn. It performed its duties most wonderfully; but when I came to remove it I found what I ought to have known, that the sponge could not rest there simply as a sponge, but was perfectly infiltrated with sabulous matter, and was

really stone. The whole urethra and the neck of the bladder were in a high state of inflammation, which came from the foreign substance. It had to come away, and there was nothing to do but to pull it away by main force. Lucy's agony was extreme. She was much prostrated, and I thought that she was going to die; but by irrigating the parts of the bladder she recovered with great rapidity, and in the course of a week or ten days was as well as ever. . . . It took Lucy two or three months to recover entirely from the effects of the operation.

Betsey went next and then Anarcha. On and on it went for four years. Gradually other doctors lost interest (and hope) and stopped assisting Sims, who then had to perform "operations only with the assistance of the patients themselves." His friends warned him that he was working too hard and "breaking down," but they made no mention of Lucy, Betsey, and Anarcha and three or four other slave women he experimented on over the years. Finally in 1849 Sims succeeded. By relentless trial and error he developed an effective surgical technique for stitching up the cleft or fissure with fine silver wire, and the long-suffering black women were finally made whole again and returned to normal lives (as slaves).

Completely worn out and besieged by diarrhea, Sims decided to move north to a more healthy climate. He sold all of his possessions in Montgomery, including a dozen slaves, some of whom were already hired out in town as "cooks, waiters, and body-servants." Settling in New York City, he established the Woman's Hospital of the State of New York and frequently remedied the once-hopeless vesico-vaginal fistula by his new surgical procedure. Soon his operation became routine in advanced American medicine, and he also demonstrated his special surgery in Europe where he was widely acclaimed. He continued his distinguished career until he died in 1883, full of fame and honors, or, as the citation at the beginning of one of his articles put it:

> Author of "Silver Sutures in Surgery," "The Sims Operation for Vesico Vaginal Fistula," "Uterine Diseases," "History of the Discovery of Anaesthesia" Etc., Etc. Member of the Historical Society of the City of New York; Surgeon to the Empress Eugenie; Delegate to Annual Conference of the Association for the Reform and Codification of the Law of Nations, 1879; Founder of the Woman's Hospital of the State of New York, and formerly Surgeon to the Same; Centennial President of the American

Medical Association, Philadelphia, 1876; President of the International Medical Congress at Berne, 1877; Fellow of the American Medical Association; Permanent Member of the New York State Medical Society; Fellow of the Academy of Sciences, of the Academy of Medicine, of the Pathological Society, of the Neurological Society, of the County Medical Society, and of the Obstetrical Society of New York: Fellow of the American Gynaecological Association; Honorary Fellow of the State Medical Societies of Connecticut, Virginia, South Carolina, Alabama, and Texas; Honorary Fellow of the Royal Academy of Medicine of Brussels; Honorary Fellow of the Obstetrical Societies of London, Dublin and Berlin, and of the Medical Society of Christiania; Knight of the Legion of Honor (France); Commander of Orders of Belgium, Germany, Austria, Russia, Spain, Portugal and Italy, Etc., Etc., Etc.

Lucy, Betsey, and Anarcha died in obscurity somewhere in the Deep South.

They had had no real way to resist the painful, prolonged experiments that were conducted upon their bodies, but at least they were finally cured of a "loathsome" disorder. Some other Southern slaves did not fare that well at the hands of curious physicians. John Brown grimly recalled one phase of his slave life in Georgia when his master paid off a debt by loaning him to Dr. Thomas Hamilton. A graduate of the University of Pennsylvania Medical School and a trustee of the Medical College of Georgia, Hamilton was among the scientific elite of the state and, according to Brown, he conducted a series of experiments on him. Brown spelled it out in detail:

> Yet, it was not without curiosity I watched the progress of the preparations the Doctor caused to be made. He ordered a hole to be dug in the ground, three feet and a half deep by three feet long, and two feet and a half wide. Into this pit a quantity of dried red oak bark was cast, and fire set to it. It was allowed to burn until the pit became heated like an oven, when the embers were taken out. A plank was then put across the bottom of the pit, and on that a stool. Having tested, with a thermometer, the degree to which the pit was heated, the Doctor bade me strip, and get in; which I did, only my head being above the ground. He then gave me some medicine which he had prepared, and as soon as I was on the stool, a number of wet blankets were fastened over the hole, and scantlings laid across them. This was to keep in the heat. It soon began to tell upon me; but though I tried hard to keep up against its effects, in about half an hour I

fainted. I was then lifted out and revived, the Doctor taking a note of the degree of heat when I left the pit. I used to be put in between daylight and dark, after I had done my day's work; for Stevens was not a man to lose more of the labor of his slaves than he could help. Three or four days afterwards, the experiment was repeated, and so on for five or six times, the Doctor allowing me a few days' rest between each trial. His object was to ascertain which of the medicines he administered to me on these occasions, enabled me to withstand the greatest degree of heat. . . .

Having completed his series of experiments upon me, in the heated pit, and allowed me some days' rest, I was put on a diet, and then, during a period of about three weeks, he bled me every other day. At the end of that time he found I was failing, so he left off, and I got a month's rest, to regain a little strength. At the expiration of that time, he set to work to ascertain how deep my black skin went. This he did by applying blisters to my hands, legs and feet, which bear the scars to this day. He continued until he drew up the dark skin from between the upper and the under one. He used to blister me at intervals of about two weeks. He also tried other experiments upon me, which I cannot dwell upon. Altogether, and from first to last, I was in his hands, under treatment, for about nine months, at the end of which period I had become so weak, that I was no longer able to work in the fields.

Some exploitation of this sort was bound to occur in the slave South; blacks made ideal guinea pigs. Whites had always been fascinated by the Negro's skin color. Jefferson speculated on it in his *Notes on the State of Virginia,* and a generation earlier Dr. John Mitchell of Tidewater Virginia had experimented on living subjects. Later in 1796 Henry Moss, a free black from Virginia who was turning white, allowed Dr. Charles Caldwell to conduct experiments on his skin in Philadelphia. And Dr. Hamilton of Georgia may have continued his experiments too. He eventually moved to the town of Rome in the northwestern part of the state where he died in 1859. On 29 March 1861, the *Daily Sun* of Columbus, Georgia, briefly mentioned him in a short entry entitled "A Curious Freak of Nature":

> There is a negro woman belonging to the estate of Dr. Hamilton, late of this place deceased, says the Rome Courier, who was formerly very *black* but is now of tawny *white* color. We understand the change occurred gradually in this way: small white spots appeared, and these enlarged until they ran into each other and spread over her entire body.

This slave may have been no more than "a freak of nature" like Henry Moss, an extreme victim of a disease known as vitiligo, but it is at least possible that the distinguished doctor continued the kind of experiments he had performed earlier on John Brown. Nobody bothered to ask the "negro woman belonging to the estate of Dr. Hamilton."

A much more "curious" and disturbing announcement appeared daily on the front page of the *Charleston Mercury* from 6 October to 8 November 1838, as part of a large advertisement for Dr. T. Stillman's Medical Infirmary for Diseases of the Skin:

> TO PLANTERS AND OTHERS.—Wanted, fifty Negroes. Any person having sick Negroes, considered incurable by their respected Physicians, and wishes to dispose of them, Dr. S. will pay cash for Negroes effected with scrofula or king's evil, confirmed hypocrondraism, apoplexy, diseases of the liver, kydneys, spleen, stomach and intestines, bladder and its appendages, diarrhrea, dysentary, &c. the highest cash price will be paid on application as above.

Not just in the South, but all over America, doctors and medical schools needed bodies for dissection, and grave robbers ("resurrectionists") stayed busy. Sometimes the bodies of the distinguished dead were dug up and hauled off to the dissection laboratories, but the corpses of the poor and humble were usually the best bet. Obviously slave bodies would be the easiest of all to obtain, either for dissection after death or examination and experimentation while still alive. Such actions were not widespread or highly organized; moreover, they were seldom publicly recognized and never officially condoned. But occasionally, for a fleeting instant, Stanley Elkins's concept of the similarity between antebellum plantations and Nazi concentration camps springs to mind as blurred previews of the twentieth century flash briefly across the pages of old newspapers and autobiographies.

Slavery was a harsh system with some razor-sharp edges, but the masses of blacks did not become childlike Sambos. Most did the best they could within the repressive system, which constantly evolved with the times. Change accelerated during the Civil War. Under the strain of modern warfare cracks widened in the never-monolithic system as Clarence L. Mohr's *On the Threshold of Freedom* demonstrated for Georgia, and grassroots realities showed more clearly than ever. Some slaves became more assertive during the war; others were carefully controlled and held to hard labor on the home front. The surging martial spirit and the presence of Confederate troops actually tightened the screws on some blacks, and many black workers responded to the new environment with prodigious, though increasingly involuntary, efforts.

James H. Brewer's *The Confederate Negro* documented the tremendous achievements of blacks in wartime Virginia. With increasing numbers of white men marching off to fight the Yankees, black Virginians carried more and more of the load on farms and in factories. They labored in the Confederate commissary, quartermaster, ordnance, and naval departments, and they were essential in maintaining roads, canals, and railroads and in operating fast-growing military hospitals. They also erected most of the massive fortifications that shielded Virginia's vitals. Expanding their prewar role, more and more blacks labored as blacksmiths, teamsters, porters, cooks, packers, caulkers, tanners, miners, laundresses, nurses, woodchoppers, and indeed as every conceivable sort of skilled and unskilled laborer. Joseph Reid Anderson, owner of the massive Tredegar Iron Works in Richmond, had long used black workers "whom he brought up to be puddlers, heaters and rollers," and during the war he conceded that these men were "as a choice set equal to any white hands." Not just in Virginia but all over the Confederacy black workers were absolutely essential to the rebel war effort.

Slaves had penetrated most areas of the antebellum economy, and Confederate blacks steadily expanded their economic activities, especially in the crucial industrial sector. As the war ground on and on and white casualties mounted, blacks became more and more essential. Finally, on 20 March 1865, only three weeks before Appomattox, the Confederacy began to recruit black soldiers for the army with the understanding that honorable military service would lead to postwar freedom. Robert F. Durden's *The Gray and the Black: The Confederate Debate on Emancipation* documented the slow, grudging drift of Jefferson Davis and the other rebel leaders toward this radical policy, which the Yankees began as early as the spring of 1862. The rebels waited far too long to try to mobilize black manpower for combat, but their hesitancy was understandable. As Confederate General Howell Cobb warned the secretary of war: "If slaves will make good soldiers our whole theory of slavery is wrong."

The concept of black inferiority undergirded the entire slave system, and recruiting blacks for the high calling of combat in defense of the Southern homeland would undermine the rationale of the system. If thousands of slaves served honorably in the Confederate army and returned home proud and free, they and their wives and children could never be held down again. But even the conservative Confederates finally realized that only black troops could fill the decimated ranks of the rebel armies and bring victory over the hated Union forces, which now included almost 200,000 blacks who were mostly former slaves, that is, Southerners.

A pragmatic determination to win at all costs finally prevailed over tradition, but few Southerners, black or white, had any illusions about the motivation of the Confederate leadership. Earlier the wartime North had been won over to the use of black troops partly by the idealism of abolitionists like Frederick Douglass, but cold-blooded pragmatism had played a role there too, as William Hanchett's *Irish: Charles G. Halpine in Civil War America* documented. A professional writer, Halpine joined the government's campaign to sell the idea of black soldiers to Northern whites. He invented a humorous Irish immigrant soldier named Miles O'Reilly and let him present the case for blacks in the Union army in a manner that would amuse everyone but blacks:

> Some tell us 'tis a burnin' shame
>   To make the naygers fight;
> And that the thrade of bein' kilt
>   Belongs but to the white:
> But as for me, upon my sowl!
>   So liberal are we here,
> I'll let Sambo be murthered instead of myself,
>   On every day of the year.
>
> On every day in the year, boys,
>   And in every hour of the day;
> The right to be kilt I'll divide wid him,
>   And divil a word I'll say.
>
> In battle's wild commotion

I shouldn't at all object
If Sambo's body should stop a ball
    That was comin' for me direct;
And the prod of a Southern bagnet,
    So ginerous are we here,
I'll resign, and let Sambo take it
    On every day of the year.

On every day in the year, boys,
    And wid none o' your nasty pride,
All my right in a Southern bagnet prod,
    Wid Sambo I'll divide!

The men who object to Sambo
    Should take his place and fight;
And it's better to have a nayger's hue
    Than a liver that's wake and white.
Though Sambo's black as the ace of spades,
    His finger a trigger can pull,
And his eye runs sthraight on the barrel-sights
    From undher its thatch of wool.

So hear me all, boys darlin',
    Don't think I'm tippin' you chaff,
The right to be kilt we'll divide wid him,
    And give him the largest half.

When the Confederate leaders finally decided to follow suit and recruit blacks, they too worked diligently to swing white public opinion behind this last desperate experiment in rebellion. They championed the concept of black troops almost like they were running for office, speaking out forcefully. On 9 February 1865, Secretary of State Judah P. Benjamin publicly advocated the new policy for the first time at a mass meeting in Richmond. This great planter from Louisiana offered to give his last bale of cotton to the cause and asked his audience, "Has any man the right to hold a bale of cotton from his country?" The enthusiastic crowd roared "No!" and cheered his calls for more sacrifices for victory.

> I want more. I want all the bacon—everything which can feed the soldiers—and I want it as a free gift to the country. Talk of rights! What right do the arrogant invaders leave you!

I want another thing. War is a game that cannot be played without men. (Cheers.) Where are the men? I am going to open my whole heart to you. Look to the trenches below Richmond. Is it not a shame that men who have sacrificed all in our defence should not be reinforced by all the means in our power? Is it any time now for antiquated patriotism to argue a refusal to send them aid, be it white or black?

Then a lone white shouted "Put in the niggers," and the crowd cheered and cheered. This exhorter and the rest of the white audience had much in common with Private Miles O'Reilly and most Northern whites; they shared the same pragmatic, even cold-blooded rationale for using black troops.

As usual, nobody bothered to consult with the blacks. By early 1865 they would hardly have been enthusiastic about service in the rebel army; they certainly had no illusions about a change of heart among the whites. Why should they risk death in the slaveholders' army to obtain a freedom already guaranteed by a Union victory? As the war had unfolded over four long years, the black masses had demonstrated repeatedly that they understood what was at stake and favored a Northern victory. Many blacks, such as Booker T. Washington's mother, secretly prayed for the Union, but others had a chance to show their feelings more openly.

Whenever Union armies drew near, great crowds of blacks flocked toward these forces of liberation. Even early in the war, before emancipation became the official Northern policy, blacks favored the blue. Even in states such as Georgia, which for a long time remained far behind the main battle lines, some blacks were quick to vote with their feet for Union victory. Clarence L. Mohr's *On the Threshold of Freedom* described their efforts to thwart tightening Confederate controls and reach freedom along the seacoast where Union forces had seized the isolated sea islands. He estimated that at least a thousand Georgia blacks reached these little havens of freedom before Sherman's army marched through the heart of the state late in 1864. Sherman's invasion gave many more Georgia blacks the chance to choose between the blue and the gray, and hordes of them flocked to join the Yankees. In states such as Mississippi, Union invasion came much earlier and so did the great folk migrations of blacks toward freedom. In William Faulkner's novel *The Unvanquished,* Drusilla, a tough young Confederate lady, described this graphically:

They began to pass in the road yonder while the house was still burn-
ing. We couldn't count them; men and women carrying children who
couldn't walk and carrying old men and women who should have been at
home waiting to die. They were singing, walking along the road singing,
not even looking to either side. The dust didn't even settle for two days,
because all that night they still passed; we sat up listening to them, and
the next morning every few yards along the road would be the old ones
who couldn't keep up any more, sitting or lying down and even crawling
along, calling to the others to help them; and the others—the young strong
ones—not stopping, not even looking at them. I don't think they even
heard or saw them. "Going to Jordan," they told me. "Going to Jordan."
. . . They just pass here without food or anything, exactly as they rose up
from whatever they were doing when the spirit or the voice or whatever
it was told them to go. They stop during the day and rest in the woods;
then, at night, they move again.[1]

This great surge of hopeful people resembled the hordes of whites Moses
Austin described pouring westward through the Cumberland Gap almost
seven decades earlier: "hundreds Traveling hundreds of Miles they know
not for what Nor Whither, except its to Kentucky . . . the Promised Land
. . . the goodly inheratence the Land of Milk and Honey."

The slaves voted with their feet for Northern victory even though they
often faced all-too-familiar racial hostility and discrimination within Union
lines. Yet they were Southerners too, no matter how marginally they had
existed in the South, and some were inextricably entangled with the whites
around them. Faulkner's novel dramatized this closeness in the friendship
between Bayard, the white boy, and Ringo, the slave boy. Too young to
fight, they were inseparable comrades, playing at war games, both want-
ing to be the Johnny Reb good guy who whipped the Yankees. As Bayard
explained it, they were more than just brothers.

. . . Ringo and I had been born in the same month and had both fed
at the same breast and had slept together and eaten together for so long
that Ringo called Granny "Granny" just like I did, until maybe he wasn't
a nigger anymore or maybe I wasn't a white boy anymore, the two of us

---

[1]William Faulkner, *The Unvanquished* (New York: Random House, 1938)
103-104.

neither, not even people any longer: the two supreme undefeated like two moths, two feathers riding above a hurricane.[2]

Simple, gut feelings such as personal affection and sense of place could swing some blacks to the Confederate cause as J. K. Obatala indicated in his article, "The Unlikely Story of Blacks Who Were Loyal to Dixie," in the March 1979 issue of *Smithsonian*. Not every black who worked for the Confederacy had to be compelled: Bill Doins cooked for rebel troops; Josephus Black played the music they marched by; Tom and Overton joined them in the fight at Brandy Station; and body servant James Jones stayed with Jefferson Davis until the bitter end.

But the great majority of Southern blacks resembled Frederick Douglass. Though born-and-bred Southerners who had absorbed much of the way of life of their masters, they still insisted on the abolition of slavery, a radical change that had to precede more moderate future accommodations. The Confederate government was too conservative and traditional to consider seriously this radical change until it was far too late to have any impact on black Southerners. The Rebel South fought without the free, voluntary support of its large black minority, and finally the divided Confederacy came crashing down.

Overwhelming Union victory in 1865 gave Southern blacks their first real chance to become complete Americans. Leon F. Litwack's *Been in the Storm So Long: The Aftermath of Slavery* movingly described their optimistic rush into the age of Reconstruction. They were determined to get a fair shake at last, but with slavery gone, most of their objectives were relatively moderate. They strived desperately to obtain a functional education—the traditional reading, 'riting, and 'rithmetic of the middle class— and they made a significant contribution to the establishment of modern, statewide public school systems throughout the South. They yielded on the explosive issue of school integration rather than jeopardize the whole new education system. Besides, whether they had learned it from the whites or from their experiences with whites or simply carried it in their bones like so many other peoples, many blacks sympathized with the concept of racial separatism; they were willing and even eager to go it alone in the

[2]Ibid., 7-8.

schools and churches and in many other areas of day-to-day existence. But all blacks agreed on the necessity of some sort of education, and by the thousands and the tens of thousands they trooped into little schoolhouses, determined to better themselves and their people as quickly as possible. Old and young, men and women, they struggled to make up for two centuries of lost time—operation bootstrap, nineteenth-century style.

Even more important than education for most adult blacks was land, the essence of the Southern economic system. Largely an agrarian folk like the whites, they had labored for others for generations. They had learned the ways of the soil and the climate the hard way. Like the whites, they were, in the words of a rebel war song, "native to the soil." They had worked free of charge all their lives, and now they wanted a small delayed payment, compensation for a lifetime—many lifetimes really—of hard labor in slavery. The cry went up: "forty acres and a mule"—a small yeoman farm and some equipment to work it. From the black viewpoint this was not radical or unreasonable. The freedmen simply sought admission to the free-enterprise, private-property world of white America. Willing to begin at the bottom as the humblest kind of petite bourgeoisie, they asked only for the chance to rise or fall on their own like other Americans.

But to Southern whites and most Northern whites this was radical, even revolutionary. To take one person's land and give it to another— that was strong medicine, even for defeated rebels. Many Northerners who had opposed slavery and rejoiced in its destruction drew the line here. Confiscating or liberating slave property was a very special case— Southern whites themselves conceded that slavery was a "peculiar institution"—and only the heat of battle drove Northerners to tamper even with that unique species of property. But confiscating and redistributing land, the foundation of the American way of life, was an altogether different matter. Ironically, the bourgeois spirit that helped drive blacks to seek their own land also drove whites to reject this desperate effort to enter the American mainstream.

Northern and Southern whites agreed on the sanctity of private property, especially land; even the Civil War did not really divide them on this fundamental middle-class belief. The freed blacks did not get their own land. Here and there in the confusion of the crumbling Confederacy a few

acres came under the control of blacks, and they held on to them tenaciously, but overall the mass of Southern blacks remained landless and thus
very vulnerable economically.

Perhaps it was just as well. Massive land redistribution would have
generated another whole layer of hatred and bitterness among the beaten
white majority while the blacks may well have received little lasting benefit. Hard times lay ahead for Southern agriculture. Family farms did not
fare well in the last decades of the nineteenth century. Many yeoman
whites with generations of experience as independent farmers slipped into
the bleak world of sharecropping and tenancy where most blacks were already trapped. A great mass of new, less experienced black yeomen would
doubtlessly have suffered the same fate, generating even more bitterness
and frustration. Yet despite all the practical considerations, the vision remains of former slaves asking only to be allowed to become more Southern
and more American, seeking to better themselves in the way they knew
best, and finally being forced to settle for not half a loaf but only a few
crumbs.

The newly freed blacks sought in other ways to break with their slave
past. Many left their old farms and plantations, at least temporarily. Un-
derstandably they wanted to escape the old slave environment, and besides, they were often seeking kinfolk who had been shipped far away. Most
black slaves had adopted white family life as best they could, but the economics of slavery often shattered these fragile structures and dispersed lov-
ing families in all directions. The strong tendency of middle-class
slaveholders to divide all their property equally among their children accelerated the disruption of black families. Thus many youngsters like Fed,
who became John Brown, and Fred, who became Frederick Douglass, grew
up without the benefit of a real family. Slave parents often married without the benefit of clergy and always without official recognition. The same
blacks who took to the road to try to reunite their families and kinfolk often
took great pains to have their marriages properly recorded in freedom; they
wanted to "make it legal."

Education, property, and family were all essential for "respectable"
middle-class life, and many blacks tried to conform to these standards.
They also plunged eagerly into the political whirl. This too was part of

the American way, but it was also essential for ex-slaves who hoped to hold their own in the "land of the free." They had to defend themselves against the Southern whites and a growing number of Northern whites who felt they lacked the capacity for full-scale participation in democratic government.

Much like the hordes of Irish immigrants in the Northeast, Southern blacks took readily to politics and thus antagonized the old electorate and traditional politicians. Some effective black leaders emerged as well as a handful of boobs and charlatans. Again like the Irish, all of these new politicians were denounced by their opponents as unreliable and dishonest, but in general they handled themselves reasonably well. Political corruption did not begin in New England with the Irish nor in the South with the freedmen; both regions had been perfectly capable of producing sleazy politicos long before the arrival of the new voters.

Blacks found allies in "carpetbaggers" from the North and native white "scalawags"—a mixed bag of fellows, some high-minded and well intentioned and others cynical and corrupt. Regardless, outside of Mississippi and South Carolina, blacks simply lacked the numbers to control state governments, and even there they could not establish permanent power. During the rather brief postwar period described in works such as John Hope Franklin's *Reconstruction After the Civil War* and Kenneth M. Stampp's *The Era of Reconstruction, 1865-1877,* the Union army occupation was some comfort as blacks learned to play "hardball" with their political opponents. However, the blue army demobilized in victory almost as rapidly as the Confederate army had disintegrated in defeat. Even for the few years that the Union army remained in the South, it was spread very thinly and only really effective in major towns and cities where most Southerners did not live. Down at the rural grassroots level, life did not change a great deal; blacks were free but not equal or propertied. Soon the army left and native white Southerners regained political control in order to muscle blacks out of meaningful political participation for several generations.

No real revolution occurred, even in the midst of Reconstruction. Many blacks began drifting back to the old home areas to rejoin those who had never left. They went back to work on the land, somebody else's land, now as day laborers or contract workers instead of slaves. This was an im-

provement but far from what they had envisioned. Black talent had a better chance to rise, but the obstacles were still formidable. A little higher
percentage of blacks could now "do their thing," but no sweeping breakthrough occurred. Blacks hunkered down for a long, drawn-out battle for
equality, still determined to be Americans in spite of America itself, which
remained a white man's country.

Their leader well into the twentieth century was Booker T. Washington. The little slave boy from Virginia had grown up fast, but he never
forgot the lessons in hard labor he learned in his youth. Educated and further indoctrinated in the Protestant work ethic by former Union General
Samuel Chapman Armstrong at Hampton Institute, he then moved on to
Alabama in 1881 and established Tuskegee Institute, a pioneer black
school that taught vocational education and preached self-help. A realist,
Washington did not defy white power but rather concentrated on training
young black men and women in basic skills that were needed in the South.
Nowhere in America were poor folk taught more scrupulously about working hard, getting ahead, and attaining security and respectability—and
nowhere did more students get the message.

Blacks heard other more ideological and radical leaders such as W. E. B.
DuBois of Atlanta University, but they really listened to Washington,
a hard-working, self-made American if there ever was one. A pure Southerner, half white and half black and all "Negro," he set realistic goals for
his people and yielded to the formal, legal system of segregation that was
sweeping through the South late in the nineteenth century. Behind the
scenes "the Wizard," as he was known, maneuvered to remain the black
leader of his time and also to coax favors and concessions for blacks out of
the great white men of business and politics. A tireless worker, in 1915 he
finally succeeded in working himself to death like any good middle-class
American. He left his people in a troubled time of rising white hostility
to blacks. Some of the skilled work once open to slaves had been segre-
gated beyond the reach of free blacks, and lynchings had become painfully
common. Yet despite everything, Washington had built firmly on the
foundations laid way back in slave times; and blacks, stubborn Southern
optimists, were preparing for better times, pushing tentatively for justice
and filtering into the middle class whenever possible.

More than a decade after Washington's death, white opposition slackened a little and the black masses pushed forward more rapidly. Ironically, black anger began to increase—or perhaps it simply began to show itself more openly. More radical leaders such as Marcus Garvey and the elderly W. E. B. DuBois and later Stokely Carmichael, Elijah Muhammad, and others attracted recruits to more radical movements; nonetheless, quietly, undramatically the majority of blacks, as typical Americans, followed traditional paths and continued to try to work their way up into the sprawling middle class. They instinctively and with hope closed ranks behind a middle-class preacher from Atlanta who rose to prominence amidst severe racial tensions in Montgomery, Alabama, during the 1950s. Imbued with the ancient, fiery optimism of the Southland, Martin Luther King, Jr. marched to the nation's capitol in 1963 and presented his own special vision to the American people from the steps of the Lincoln Memorial:

> Five score years ago a great American in whose symbolic shadow we stand today signed the Emancipation Proclamation. . . . But 100 years later the Negro still is not free. One hundred years later the life of the Negro is still badly crippled by the manacles of segregation and the chains of discrimination. . . . There will be neither rest nor tranquility in America until the Negro is granted his citizenship rights. . . .
>
> We must forever conduct our struggle on the high plane of dignity and discipline. We must not allow our creative protests to degenerate into physical violence. Again and again we must rise to the majestic heights of meeting physical force with soul force. The marvelous new militancy which has engulfed the Negro community must not lead us to distrust all white people, for many of our white brothers, as evidenced by their presence here today, have come to realize that their destiny is tied up with our destiny.
>
> They have come to realize that their freedom is inextricably bound to our freedom. We cannot walk alone. And as we walk we must make the pledge that we shall always march ahead. We cannot turn back. . . .
>
> Continue to work with the faith that unearned suffering is redemptive. Go back to Mississippi, go back to Alabama, go back to South Carolina, go back to Georgia, go back to Louisiana, go back to the slums and ghettos of our Northern cities, knowing that somehow this situation can and will be changed. Let us not wallow in the valley of despair.
>
> I say to you today, my friends, though, even though we face the difficulties of today and tomorrow, I still have a dream. It is a dream deeply

rooted in the American dream. I have a dream that one day this nation will rise up, live out the true meaning of its creed: "We hold these truths to be self-evident, that all men are created equal."

I have a dream that one day on the red hills of Georgia sons of former slaves and the sons of former slave-holders will be able to sit down together at the table of brotherhood. I have a dream that one day even the state of Mississippi, a state sweltering with the heat of injustice, sweltering with the heat of oppression, will be transformed into an oasis of freedom and justice.

I have a dream that my four little children will one day live in a nation where they will not be judged by the color of their skin but by the content of their character. . . . I have a dream that one day in Alabama, with its vicious racists, with its governor having his lips dripping with the words of interposition and nullification, one day right there in Alabama little black boys and black girls will be able to join hands with little white boys and white girls as sisters and brothers. . . .

And if America is to be a great nation, this must become true. So let freedom ring from the prodigious hilltops of New Hampshire. Let freedom ring from the mighty mountains of New York. Let freedom ring from the heightening Alleghenies of Pennsylvania. Let freedom ring from the snow-capped Rockies of Colorado. Let freedom ring from the curvaceous slopes of California.

But not only that. Let freedom ring from Stone Mountain of Georgia. Let freedom ring from Lookout Mountain of Tennessee. Let freedom ring from every hill and molehill of Mississippi, from every mountain side. Let freedom ring. . . .

When we allow freedom to ring—when we let it ring from every city and every hamlet, from every state and every city, we will be able to speed up that day when all God's children, black men and white men, Jews and Gentiles, Protestants and Catholics, will be able to join hands and sing in the words of the old Negro spiritual, "Free at last, Free at last, Great God A-mighty, We are free at last."

As eager as Frederick Douglass to bring real freedom to his people, but like Douglass and Booker T. Washington still "inextricably bound" to the rest of the American people and their system, King spoke to the South and the whole nation and sounded once again the old Southern cry to move forward confidently and grapple with awesome problems. Basically a reformer rather than a revolutionary, he rallied whites as well as blacks. It was no accident that his followers had all along marched to the tune of an old folk hymn now entitled "We Shall Overcome," optimism set to music.

The struggle continues. No single leader has fully replaced the saintly King, for blacks are as diverse and individualistic as other Southerners and Americans. Charismatic Jesse Jackson and a host of similar regional and local leaders still dream the American dream and preach the gospel Washington and others carried out of slavery and King and others shaped and refined in freedom. A preacher like his mentor King as well as a skillful politician, Jackson exhorts his "rainbow coalition" folk to strive and to succeed through education and hard work. More radical voices sound too, often loudly; the black masses listen but they do not really respond. They honor fallen black revolutionaries such as Nat Turner just as white Southerners still hail the rebel heroes of their own special lost cause; yet both groups are too thoroughly, irredeemably American to swing away from the old mainstream paths that run straight back into the South's and the nation's past.

All around, so quietly that it almost goes unnoticed, the black bourgeoisie continues to grow, though it is still only the extension of an old trend that began way back in slavery. The Simon Grays and William Johnsons of the old days live on today, but now they are everywhere, so numerous that they escape the attention of experts who specialize in overlooking the obvious. The tailor with the small shop just off Main Street has worked hard all his life. He has always considered himself a "Negro," and now he worries about his children and their generation. They know a whole new vocabulary of race, but they seem to lack his drive and dedication. He also grumbles a lot about growing government taxes and regulation crippling the small businessman, "the backbone of the nation."

The younger generation of blacks is not really all that bad: they are mainly just young, and they are learning a few good old-fashioned lessons over at the big, consolidated high school. There one of the black coaches moonlights to support his family—a wife who works part-time herself and three children who will soon go to college. He is also totally committed to his young athletes; he treats white and black alike, working them very hard and drumming into them the message that they must practice and train, sweat and suffer before they can win. "When the going gets tough, the tough get going," "pay the price," and on and on he preaches (and believes in) the familiar litany, which is really just old bourgeois attitudes translated into the language of modern sports. His players groan and gripe and occasionally even snicker a little at the enthusiastic old fellow (age forty), but at heart they believe too, especially after whipping their traditional rivals. And over in the main academic building they face an experienced teacher, a no-nonsense black lady, who pounds the same basic message into them and all the other students: study hard and get ahead. She has had all of the required education courses and attended all of the proper workshops and panel discussions, but in her heart she still believes that her students, black and white, need more discipline and less innovation in their studies (and a little more spanking back down the line wouldn't have hurt either).

Later in the day at a nearby department store the night janitor with thirty-one years of faithful service begins his shift. A lean, sinewy brown man, he is already a little tired from an earlier shift at another store. Despite this he is grimly determined to cling to the lower fringes of the middle class and to give all four of his children the kind of advanced education he never had a chance to acquire for himself. All over the town and all over the nation, North and South, blacks go through the same basic American ritual. Hosts of unskilled and semiskilled laborers and growing numbers of skilled workers put in time and, if possible, overtime in factories and mills. More and more officers and noncommissioned officers emerge in the armed forces. The cadre of doctors, lawyers, professors, and other professionals expands steadily. All manner of businessmen and fast-growing numbers of bureaucrats at the local and state as well as the federal level become more and more visible too. Everywhere blacks push into a sprawling American middle class more open to them than ever before.

Not every black has accepted the American bourgeois system any more than every white. Old terms such as "no-count nigger" and "poor white trash" have always had some validity within the huge Southern and American population, and in recent years such harsh terminology may have gained a little more validity as the traditional work ethic temporarily weakened a little all over the nation. But the big picture, viewed accurately within its historical context, shows blacks moving into the American mainstream at an accelerating rate. What is equally important, many blacks not yet securely established in the middle class continue to strive to make it, still seeking the old goal, still playing by the old rules.

At a time when some traditional elite and bourgeois Americans waver and lose some of their old hope and confidence, the fast-growing black bourgeoisie, along with poor whites on the make and others relatively new to the traditional good life, may provide the optimism and vigor necessary to hold society together through trying times of change. Those deprived the longest of the full fruits of their labor may become some of the staunchest defenders of "the system." America's future is uncertain, but blacks are clearly a part of it. Americans to the core, inextricably bound to the Southern and American system all the way back to slave times, they—like their white fellow citizens—are predestined to rise or fall with the nation they built. Here they stand, indelibly American; they can do no other.

EPILOGUE

In the new atomic age the future seems more uncertain than ever, but conservatism and continuity have always been powerful forces in history, including American history; so the South and the nation, inextricably bound together, may well continue to travel many familiar paths. But the prophets of future shock never cease to warn of impending catastrophes and debacles, and at least some drastic change is probably inevitable. Perhaps the American dream will suddenly be shattered by a series of nuclear explosions seeded among giant urban complexes such as New York, Chicago, Detroit, and Los Angeles—and Atlanta, New Orleans, and Dallas. Or perhaps the nation will wither away, slowly smothered by the kind of psychological and spiritual malaises described by Andrew Hacker in *The End of the American Era* and Christopher Lasch in *The Culture of Narcissism: American Life in an Age of Diminishing Expectations*. As Kenneth Clark warned in his *Civilization*, more than anything else a lack of confidence destroys great nations. Certainly the seeds of doubt and despair have been scattered widely over the United States, and some have begun to sprout. Most of this cancerous growth, however, has taken place in a few isolated areas of the North, in the great universities and prestigious think tanks and among segments of the social and economic elite, the "establishment."

Down South the sun still shines brightly, and darker periods are still dawns, not twilights. The mass of the Southern people still retain their ancient birthright of optimism as do many ordinary Americans; many citizens still think that they "carry the world in a private sling." These Southerners and other Americans still see a promising future for their nation. Quietly they wait for the next great leader to sound the call for action. Fundamentally American, indeed the first America and the real American heartland, the South waits, still hearing the old calls from the past: "Life, Liberty, and the pursuit of Happiness," "Virginians, with me!," "that government of the people, by the people, for the people, shall not perish from the earth," "Up! Up! You mighty race. You can accomplish what you will," "make the world safe for democracy," "nothing to fear but fear itself," "ask not what your country can do for you—ask what you can do for your country," "I have a dream." The voices come from far and wide, ranging over decades and centuries, but they all call forth like a stirring bugle, and most Southerners and most Americans still retain the old can-do spirit of a people with a future as well as a past.

Down at the Southern grassroots level, the modern scholar thrashes around in a continuous time flow. Looking back, he records bits and pieces of the past. No matter how hard he tries, he can see only flashes and hear only snatches from the "good old days": Nat Turner and his little band striking out for freedom; thousands of Confederate soldiers massing for a headlong assault up Cemetery Ridge; or, much more likely, hardy bands of blacks and whites moving out to continue their endless struggle to wrest a living from the good earth. The scholar can see the present much more clearly, but even that often becomes a blur of action: a crowd roars and a band blares as young gladiators in bright uniforms struggle for victory; machinery whines as millions of people labor through an eight-hour shift while their children pour in and out of all manner of schools and training centers. Too many people move too rapidly, and the present sweeps into the future. Temporary jolts and detours do not long divert the forward rush, which began centuries ago at Jamestown and still continues, energized by a people still infected with optimism.

The future clouds up quickly, but the scholar, squinting and listening, still perceives (or thinks he perceives) a few shreds of things to come. Inevitably, somewhere ahead, the guns roar again. The chaos of battle stimulates the scholar's latent imagination, and figures begin to form amidst the smoke and thunder. American soldiers move into action again. The landscape is obscure, perhaps a sandy wasteland floating on a sea of oil, maybe a strategic island, or possibly (like Gettysburg) just a chance bit of territory where great armies happen to collide. The American troops emerge more clearly, a long line of infantry, laced with black and white Southerners. The killing begins; the long line ripples and wavers. Then a handful of surviving "Yanks" close for the final, decisive action as a whole nation teeters on the brink of victory or disaster. The scholar's mind races wildly, and he perceives that by chance or destiny these surviving soldiers are mostly Southerners, black and white. My God! The nation's future depending on the actions of a handful of "rednecks 'n niggers"! Well, why not? What could really be more appropriate? Their ancestors came before the Mayflower, the first of the new immigrants who eventually peopled a continent. What better men to fight the last battle? But here the scholar's imagination, so seldom used, fades away. In his heart he hears a high-pitched battle cry and sees a final assault that shatters the alien hosts, but he knows that his vision has faded before the last scene, that he will never know who really won.

A little ruffled, slightly embarrassed by his brief flirtation with feeling and emotion, the scholar returns to his notes and charts and data and statistics—his precious facts. Logically he knows that the American struggle for survival and power will be predetermined long before the final combat by what happens and does not happen in the nation's centers of finance, commerce, education, and industry. But Southern people will play a major, perhaps decisive role in this prosaic world of work and labor too. The farmers, laborers, businessmen, and professionals of the South—the bulk of the contemporary "Sun Belt"—will constitute a large percentage of the total American population and work force just as they always have. From the beginning when they arrived "fustest with the mostest," Southerners of every hue have played a major role in the American pageant. From the beginning they were inextricably bound to the American destiny; they have never been able to separate themselves from the American mainstream, not even in the 1860s when they literally tried to fight their way out. Permanently, hopelessly American for generations and centuries, the Southern people will continue to march along in step with other Americans. Where the long march ends nobody knows, but surely Southerners—aristocrats, rednecks, bourgeoisie, and blacks—will go the distance. Past, present, and future, from the beginning to the end, they stand in the American mainstream.

BIBLIOGRAPHICAL ESSAY

The South and Southerners have been written and rewritten about extensively for generations, and the emergence of Jimmy Carter generated another new round of analysis. This study has cited numerous sources in the text, so only the most essential items are mentioned again in this brief essay. The most reliable contemporary authority on the late antebellum and Civil War periods was probably Clement Eaton, professor emeritus of history at the University of Kentucky until his death in 1980. His *History of the Old South: The Emergence of a Reluctant Nation*, revised in 1975, and his *Mind of the Old South*, revised in 1967, along with his *History of the Southern Confederacy* (1954), provide a sound basis for further study, while his *Growth of Southern Civilization: 1790-1860* concentrated on the culture of the period emphasized in this book. Despite a mild infatuation with the elite and a recent mediocre biography of Jefferson Davis, Eaton's works remain essential.

Many other writers have been fascinated by the vaunted antebellum aristocracy; it did not begin or end in 1936 with Margaret Mitchell's famous novel, *Gone With the Wind*. In recent years various sorts of Marxian scholars have shown a similar interest in and indeed fondness for the elite. Eugene D. Genovese in *The Political Economy of Slavery: Studies in the Economy and Society of the Slave South* (1961) and other works described the "hegemony" that this elite supposedly established, and the Italian scholar Raimondo Luraghi gave this view a more romantic tinge in *The Rise and Fall of the Plantation South* (1978). The new school of women's history almost unwittingly joined the study of the elite in 1970 when Anne Firor Scott's *The Southern Lady: From Pedestal to Politics, 1830-1930* appeared. All the while traditional sympathetic studies by native Southern whites continued and even peaked in 1974 with the publication of Robert Manson Myers's *The Children of Pride: A True Story of Georgia and the Civil War*, a massive collection of the correspondence of the Charles Colcock Jones family.

The antebellum elite has fared very well, but the rednecks and the bourgeoisie, the great mass of antebellum whites, have attracted far fewer admirers over the years. The common people seldom get the spotlight, but a few distinguished scholars have examined the antebellum white masses with sensitivity and sympathy. Frank L. Owsley's *Plain Folk of the Old South* (1949) went straight back to basic sources like county records and federal censuses to reveal the life of the white masses, the real center of power in the democratic Old South. Bell Irvin Wiley followed with several grass-roots studies of the Confederate masses. His short *The Plain People of the Confederacy* (1943) remains one of the very best glimpses of the ordinary rebels, soldiers and civilians, who fought and lost America's bloodiest war. Unfortunately, it is one of the books mentioned here that is unavailable in a paperback edition. Wiley's *The Life of Johnny Reb: The Common Soldier of the Confederacy* (1943) exploited soldiers' letters stored in private homes as well as public libraries to draw a much more detailed picture, and his *Life of Billy Yank: The Common Soldier of the Union* (1952) used the same research technique to reveal the striking similarity between the contending troops, which was the real tragedy of the Civil War. Wilbur J. Cash's intuitive *The Mind of the South* (1941) drew vivid pen portraits of rednecks on the make and other ordinary Southerners that help flesh out the studies of more traditional scholars.

In recent decades the average Southern white has remained on the receiving end of much harsh criticism, but a few writers in the Owsley-Wiley tradition continue to view him (and her) sympathetically. Psychiatrist Robert Coles's works such as *The Middle Americans* (1971) treated ordinary Americans in general in this manner. A specific defense of ordinary Southern whites can be found in the author's own article, "The Redneck," first published in the *Georgia Review* in the fall of 1971 and republished in February of the following year in *Intellectual Digest* (not long before its demise, coincidental or otherwise). This brief work warned the modern reader to beware of cheap shots at the common folk of Dixie, long a favorite target of American intellectuals, Southerners as well as Northerners.

Southern blacks have been the victims of even more cheap shots over the long haul of American history. Finally in recent decades the tide has turned, and a flood of sympathetic material has rolled off the presses. Fortunately a good number of these articles and books have been sound and scholarly as well. The best single volume remains John Hope Franklin's *From Slavery to Freedom: A History of American Negroes,* revised in 1980. Lerone Bennett, Jr.'s more popular *Before the Mayflower: A History of the Negro in America,* revised in 1982, is also useful. In 1971 James McPherson and others compiled *Blacks in America: Bibliographical Essays,* providing a firm foundation for further research and reading, but this volume has not been revised to include the numerous valuable works written in the last decades.

Studies of the slave masses have proliferated as rapidly as any specialty within the burgeoning field of black history. U. B. Phillips's *American Negro Slavery: A Survey of the Supply, Employment and Control of Negro Labor as Determined by the Plantation Regime* (1918) dominated for a long time with its bland assumption of black racial inferiority. When scholarly and then popular opinion moved toward the concept of racial equality, Kenneth M. Stampp's *The Peculiar Institution: Slavery in the Antebellum South* appeared in 1956, and it remains the best single-volume treatment of that complex, controversial subject.

In 1959 Stanley M. Elkins's *Slavery: A Problem in American Institutional and Intellectual Life* proposed the theory that the mass of slaves were Samboized, psychologically broken down into childlike creatures who accepted, even embraced their degradation much as the inmates of Nazi concentration camps did a century later. Since Elkins's theory was presented, some of the best works in black history have been written at least partially to counteract his unflattering image of the slave masses (and, incidentally, of their white masters).

Five recent books stand out, two written by blacks with traditional, Southern, Anglo-Saxon names, and three written by whites with more "furrin" names. John W. Blassingame's *The Slave Community: Plantation Life in the Antebellum South* (1972) relied heavily on published accounts of runaway slaves, and in 1979 he revised the book, significantly expanding the sources as well as the content. Leslie Howard Owens's *This Species of Property: Slave Life and Culture in the Old South* (1976) similarly stressed an independent black culture after work hours with some African retentions. George P. Rawick's *From Sundown to Sunup: The Making of the Black Community* (1972) similarly described a "syncretic" black culture, not just African and not just white but something new and different in between. Even more important, he followed this up with forty additional volumes that included all of the interviews with elderly ex-slaves that were conducted by Fisk and Southern Universities in the 1920s and more extensively by the Federal Writers' Project of the Works Progress Administration in the 1930s, making these valuable grassroots reminiscences readily available for the first time. Eugene D. Genovese's bulky *Roll, Jordan, Roll: The World the Slaves Made* (1974) pushed the same general themes farther, and two years later Herbert G. Gutman, a pioneer in the use of computers in historical research, produced his equally bulky *The Black Family in Slavery and Freedom: 1750-1925*. Using detailed plantation records, he documented the surprising strength of black families—even some nuclear families—during the long night of slavery.

A host of other recent works on slavery, many by promising young scholars, have shed additional light on that still-shadowy subject. Clarence L. Mohr's *On the Threshold of Freedom: Masters and Slaves in Civil War Georgia* (1986) is only one example of these imaginative new studies that are continually proving that black history is not just a trendy, "with-it" phenomenon left over from the turbulent 1960s, but rather a legitimate component of the broader fields of Southern and American and even world history. Ordinary black Americans are themselves beginning to take a more active part in the movement. Initially stirred by popular and romanticized books and films such as Alex Haley's *Roots*—in some ways the black answer to *Gone With the Wind*—many blacks are becoming as curious about riddles of blood and genealogy and history as their white neighbors. Inevitably that curiosity must lead them back to the antebellum South, the land of their American ancestors.

Books and articles describing this mysterious old Southland continue to pour off the presses. Bertram Wyatt-Brown's *Southern Honor: Ethics and*

Behavior in the Old South (1982) and Grady McWhiney's *Cracker Culture: Celtic Ways in the Old South* (1988) join the growing trend of books that picture the antebellum South as profoundly different from the rest of the nation, but James Oakes's *The Ruling Race: A History of American Slaveholders* (1982) offers fresh hope that the concept of a mainstream South will not be lost in this generation.

The general reader cannot help but be confused by the babel of different concepts and conclusions offered by contending scholars. Anyone truly serious about searching for the reality of Southern history has ready access to a great treasure lode of raw, original materials. Every old county courthouse in the South that has escaped the ravages of fire and mildew and neglect contains the basic records of the South's past: annual county tax reports, deed books, wills and estate inventories, local court records, and sometimes other related materials. Some counties such as Southampton in Virginia have retained virtually everything. A few others such as DeKalb in Georgia have lost almost everything from the antebellum era (by fire a half century after Sherman's visit). Many have some gaps but retain most old records. Most Southern state governments have carefully preserved these old records on microfilm in state archives—thanks in part to the determination of the Mormon Church to trace back the ancestry of all its followers and its willingness to share the fruits of this great labor. Many state archives also house microfilm copies of the antebellum federal censuses going all the way back to the first one in 1790, with only a few early gaps caused by the British army's pillaging of Washington in 1814. These are the basic, official records of the South's past, and they are public property, not the private preserve of bureaucrats, scholars, and genealogists. Even a casual examination of some of these antebellum documents will introduce the average citizen to the people of the first American heartland, the sturdy folk of the Old South.

INDEX

Litwack, Leon F., *Been in the Storm So Long: The Aftermath of Slavery*, 200; *North of Slavery: The Negro in the Free States, 1790-1860*, 105
Liverpool, England, 18, 173
Lloyd, Edward, 183
Local records, 3, 4, 19, 22, 56, 105, 111-14, 117-21, 146-47, 150-51, 162-63, 164, 167-68, 181-82, 188-89
Locke, John, 102
London, England, 18, 180-82
Long, Huey, 137
Longstreet, Augustus Baldwin, *Georgia Scenes*, 53
Louisiana, 27, 67-68, 137, 152, 159, 162, 180, 187-89, 197
Louisville, Kentucky, 102
Lovejoy, Elijah, 108
Lucy (slave), 190-02
Lumber industry, 161-62
Luraghi, Raimondo, *The Rise and Fall of the Plantation South*, 17
Lynchburg, Virginia, 103
Lynchings, 188, 204

McCary, Robert, 168
McCormick, Cyrus Hall, 127-28
McCormick, Robert, 127
McDuffie, George, 18
McWhiney, Grady, *Attack and Die: Civil War Military Tactics and the Southern Heritage* (with Perry D. Jamison), 48;*Cracker Culture: Celtic Ways in the Old South*, 44
Macon, Georgia, 103, 186
Magoffin, Beriah, 62
Malone, Dumas, interview in *Newsweek*, 133
Mandingo, 8
"Manifest Destiny," 133
Married life, 65, 202
Marshall, Michigan, 180
Maryland, 102, 183-84, 186
Massachusetts Institute of Technology, 129
Mathews, Donald G., *Religion in the Old South*, 131, 155
Matthews, Jacob, 101
Matthews, Jim, 162
Maury, Matthew Fontaine, 130
Medical experiments, 189-94

Memphis, Tennessee, 103
Merrick, Caroline, *Old Times in Dixie Land*, 27
Merrill, Boynton, Jr., *Jefferson's Nephews: A Frontier Tragedy*, 105
Mexico, 17
Middle class. *See* Bourgeoisie
Middle-class mentality. *See* this heading under Aristocrats, Blacks, Bourgeoisie, and Rednecks
Militia, 45, 66-68
Milledgeville, Georgia, 177
Miller, Caroline, *Lamb in His Bosom*, 34
Miller, James, 166
Miller, William, 168
Mines, 130
Miscegenation, 11, 12, 37, 43-44, 106, 148-49, 159-60, 170, 182, 183, 186, 204
Mississippi, 21, 29, 53, 62, 161-62, 166-68, 180, 198, 203
Mississippi Railroad Company, 167
Mitchell, Broaddus, *William Gregg: Factory Master of the Old South*, 120
Mitchell, John, 193
Mobile, Alabama, 102
Mobility (geographic), 18-20, 58-59, 123, 126, 127, 177-78, 183-84, 198-99, 202
Mobility (socioeconomic), 3, 12-15, 23, 41, 55, 58, 59, 72, 101-02,, 108, 111-12, 117-21, 122-23, 126-28, 141, 151-52, 164-65, 185-86, 207-09
"Model Clerk," 141-42
Mohr, Clarence L., *On the Threshold of Freedom: Masters and Slaves in Civil War Georgia*, 194, 198, 218
Monitor, 129
Moore, Betty, 177
Moore, John Hebron, "Simon Gray, A Slave Who Was Almost Free," *Mississippi Valley Historical Review*, 161-62
Morgan, Edmund S., *American Freedom-American Slavery: The Ordeal of Colonial Virginia*, 106
Morgan County, Georgia, 20
Moseley, William R., 172
Moss, Henry, 193
Moss, William H., 172-73
Muhammad, Elijah, 205